Praise for *BRICS and Beyond*

"In *BRICS and Beyond* Stephanie Jones advises Western businesses on doing business in emerging economies in a refreshingly straightforward manner, integrating in a novel way her three decades of global, practical experience with the daily barrage of reporting on the BRICS – distilling from these many lessons and principles. *BRICS and Beyond* is very clear about the prospects offered, but it is also sober and, as can be expected from an author who deals with the topic on a daily basis, it is grounded in reality. For attractive as the BRICS are for Western firms, they are also fraught with risks, shortcomings and frustrations."

**Extracted from the Foreword, by Professor Wim Naudé,
Director of Research, Maastricht School
of Management, The Netherlands**

"Dr Stephanie Jones' new book will be an essential addition for MBA delivery. The world is emerging and transforming at increasingly rapid rates and MBA programs are struggling to keep students apace of change. This is particularly true in relation to the market emergence of first and second wave developing countries. This book is timely and will be well situated to meet significant needs in business education. Written from the perspective of a highly recognized MBA educator, with practical orientation and use of case studies I can see Dr Jones' book becoming a dynamically useful resource for MBA educators around the world."

**Dr Ian Sutherland, Assistant Professor and Director
of PhD Program, IEDC – Bled, Slovenia**

". . . it is very timely to write a textbook for international business students given the recent changes in the international business environment. These changes have, as yet, not been adequately covered in the current literature. Most of what is currently on offer is directed at the conventional (American) multinational company (MNC) model and really does not cater adequately to international collaboration (the American MNC model has been generally weak on this front). Transnational emerging market corporations have become an important source of international business growth and they need a new pedagogical approach. Exploring them along with the institutional environments which shaped them through cases strikes me as a sound way to proceed. In the coming decades many students will work for or with these companies . . . MBA programs that specifically cater to executives from emerging markets would also find this textbook extremely valuable."

**Edward Buckingham, Former Director of INSEAD
EMBA programmes (2008-10), France**

". . . it is very good to have cases and perspectives from all over the world . . . especially because it's no longer 'business as usual' . . . now, we are looking at a world facing radical changes to the economic and political dispensations of the past, primarily characterized by climate change, the squeeze on commodities, the collapse of ecosystems on which we all depend, and a growing world population. So this book is needed not only because it looks at business from the BRICS points of view; it also looks at business from the point of view of tomorrow's business leaders, and the challenges that they will have to cope with."

Professor Jonathan Gosling, Centre for Leadership Studies,
and co-founder, The One-Planet MBA,
University of Exeter, UK

"I just read Dr Jones' new book and must say that this is very useful, especially for those interested in international business beyond the traditional markets. In addition to the members of our World Trade Center's International Business Club and clients, our international clients of NASH Consulting are now reading it. Until now, I have not seen a business textbook that is covering so many emerging markets and so many relevant topics at once. For companies wanting to make a strategic choice about where they want their new markets to be, this book is of great value."

Joost Dijkstra, Director, World Trade Centre,
Heerlen, Aachen, Germany

". . . in today's business realities, ethics and issues concerning responsibilities are increasingly linked to matters of identity, both as national and especially as business culture. The sequence of chapters in the design of Dr Jones reflects this new reality, and for that reason it helps prepare students much better than most comparable books do."

Joop Remmé, Managing Director,
KnowDialogue, The Netherlands

"The Case Study Method is one of the best ways for today's management students to learn how to approach real life business issues. However, the greatest weakness of this method has been lack of case studies which draw on the issues faced by managers in markets outside of North America and Europe. With this publication, we are looking forward to offering contextually relevant business case studies to our students."

Oliver Olson, Program Director, Maastricht School
of Management, Romania

"Somewhat paradoxically the ultimate aim of teaching MBA students of developing countries isn't to teach the theory of business but the practice. Stephanie Jones is doing an excellent job providing in this book an abundance of practical cases based on real emerging market practice – and by doing so she is filling the gap. Approaching business from this perspective has been long neglected. Well done! Students from newly developing countries can no longer escape. They will be provoked to think about starting businesses in their home countries."

Leo Kerklaan, Director, Franeker Management
Academy, The Netherlands

BRICS and Beyond

Executive Lessons on Emerging Markets

Stephanie Jones

John Wiley & Sons, Ltd., Publication

Registered office
John Wiley & Sons Ltd, The Atrium, Southern Gate, Chichester, West Sussex, PO19 8SQ,
United Kingdom

For details of our global editorial offices, for customer services and for information about
how to apply for permission to reuse the copyright material in this book please see our
website at www.wiley.com

Library of Congress Cataloging-in-Publication Data

Jones, Stephanie, 1957-
    BRICS and beyond : executive lessons on emerging markets / Stephanie Karen Jones.
        p.   cm.
    Includes bibliographical references and index.
    ISBN 978-1-119-96269-4 (cloth)
        1. International business enterprises—Developing countries.   2. Social responsibility
of business—Developing countries.   3. Diversity in the workplace—Developing countries.
4. Industrial management—Developing countries.   5. BRIC countries—Foreign economic
relations.   I. Title.
    HD2755.5.J6676   2012
    658'.049—dc23

                                                                          2012016641

A catalogue record for this book is available from the British Library.

ISBN 978-1-119-96269-4 (hardback) ISBN 978-1-118-35156-7 (ebk)
ISBN 978-1-118-35151-2 (ebk)   ISBN 978-1-118-35157-4 (ebk)

Typeset in 11/15pt Palatino by MPS Limited, Chennai, India.
Printed in Great Britain by TJ International Ltd, Padstow, Cornwall, UK

To Clive, with love

Contents

Foreword

One can hardly do business anymore without an understanding and knowledge of the global impact of a handful of emerging economies, labelled the 'BRICS' – an acronym denoting Brazil, Russia, India, China and South Africa. Whereas half a century ago these were all developing countries and, with perhaps the exception of Russia, marginal in world affairs, today they are aspiring to be fully modern economies. They possess nuclear capabilities and space programmes; they include the world's most populous democracy (India), largest country (Russia) and second biggest economy (China); contain 60% of the Amazon rainforest and boast the record-holding champion of the FIFA Soccer World Cup (Brazil); and can lay claim to the world's largest diamond and longest wine route (South Africa). The list of achievements and contribution to the world's 'best and largest' is a remarkable and growing one.

While many Western economies – most notably the Eurozone and the United States – face high debt burdens and sluggish growth, the BRICS have been the 'southern engines of global growth'. Through the global outsourcing of production they have become integrated into the very fabric of traditional Western multinational firms. As a result there are now very few national or domestic-based industries in the world. Countries and firms do not compete anymore in physical products but in capabilities and in the 'intangibles' that give them a claim to sharing in the global value chain.

While the BRICS have been central in the emergence of a truly global production system they are not the only emerging economies of which to take note. Their influence, their growing geo-political and strategic posturing in global affairs and their investments abroad have had significant ripple effects across the emerging world. From Africa to Indonesia and Malaysia to the island economies of the Philippines and Pacific, business and entrepreneurship have been given a vibrant boost. The BRICS' rise has spilled over to benefit economies beyond their borders and their traditional sphere of influence.

In *BRICS and Beyond* Stephanie Jones advises Western businesses on doing business in the BRICS and other emerging economies. She does so in a refreshingly straightforward manner and integrates in a novel way her practical experience (gained over more than three decades as teacher, explorer, entrepreneur and traveller) with the daily barrage of reporting on the BRICS – distilling from this many lessons and principles for sustainable business. *BRICS and Beyond* is very clear about the prospects offered by these southern engines of global growth. But it is also sober and, as can be expected from an author who deals with the topic on a daily basis, it is grounded in reality. For, attractive as the BRICS are for Western firms, they are also fraught with risks, shortcomings and frustrations.

Some of these downsides are reflected in the fact that China and India remain, in per capita GDP terms, poor countries. China is concerned that it would not be able to complete its rural–urban transition before its aging population erodes its low-cost labour advantage. India is amassing troops on its northern border and is in a naval arms race with China in the Indian Ocean. With more than two million soldiers China has the largest army in the world (India has the third largest with almost two million soldiers). Its military expenditure is growing in excess of 10% annually. Today, China and India alone account for around 15% of all military imports in the world – more than 80% of that supplied by Russia (and a sizeable portion by South Africa). In Russia and South Africa the transition towards democracy has been anything but perfect, and great social and economic inequalities remain alongside corruption, crime and violence. Doing successful business in these countries requires a sound understanding of the country risks involved.

It also requires the important realization that Western businesses can and should make a positive societal impact and not only see these countries as places for easy profits. Ultimately, the improved welfare and wellbeing of all the people in the BRICS are what matters most. For this a high standard of ethical behaviour, sensitivity to cultural differences and the environment, and appropriate corporate social responsibility initiatives are minimum requirements. *BRICS and Beyond* offers useful hints on these, and more.

Professor Wim Naudé
Director of Research, Maastricht School of Management

About the Author

Dr Stephanie Jones is Associate Professor of Organizational Behaviour at Maastricht School of Management (MSM), having graduated with a PhD from University College London, and a Bachelor's degree from the London School of Economics. Dr Jones has authored over twenty-five full-length internationally-published books on business and management. Her most recent books include *Nelson's Way: Leadership Lessons from the Great Commander* (2005), textbooks for MSM on thesis writing, leadership and culture (2007–9), *Psychological Testing* (2010) and *Leadership: Key Concepts* (2012). Previously a journalist and consultant, she has lived and worked in Hong Kong, China, India, Australia, Dubai, Kuwait and Egypt. She teaches MBA students based across the world, in Asia, Africa, the Middle East, Eastern Europe and South America, especially courses on leadership, culture and change management. She has recently published articles on entrepreneurship and innovation in business, business in emerging markets, business ethics and Corporate Social Responsibility (CSR), leadership, knowledge management, human resources, business culture and project management.

1 Introduction

Doing Business in Emerging Markets – Risks, Opportunities and Practice

The acronym BRICs – Brazil, Russia, India and China – was one of the most well-known buzz words of the first decade of the twenty-first century, and seems all set to continue into the next. Now, in 2012, the concept has gained add-ons – first of all the 's' has grown from a mere plural into inclusion of another country – South Africa – and the use of 'beyond' suggests that there are even more countries on the threshold of becoming BRICS. The **N-11** – a raft of countries waiting in the wings – is also widely discussed as offering economic growth prospects worthy of consideration by investors and business people worldwide (glossary items are shown in bold – see Glossary for definitions).

Yet, this observation alone is not necessarily enough to justify another book on one of the hottest topics of the decade. There is a vast literature and wealth of internet-based sources on the financial and economic development and future prospects of these countries and the **emerging market multinationals** becoming established there. There is a multitude of academic analyses of the evolution of these markets, with detailed enquiries into trends, including how the **Emerging Market Index** often outstrips the performance of companies in developed countries, including the **G7** itself. Many consulting firms produce booklets with useful regulatory information, facts and figures and tips and hints about operating in specific locations. But relatively few texts profess to provide the kind of up-to-the-minute blow-by-blow insights available from such on-the-ball media as *The Economist* and the *Financial Times*. These sources provide daily and weekly updates but tend to be thrown way and almost forgotten in the rapid pace of business life, and, as newspapers, sometimes get overtaken by events.

BRICS and Beyond: Risks and Opportunities for Western Business in Emerging Markets aims to distil many months of reading all the latest news from daily and weekly **emerging markets** reports, alongside a wealth of hitherto mostly tacit knowledge gained from living and working in the **BRICS and beyond** for nearly thirty years. After being a journalist, consultant, trainer and teacher in India, many Asian countries including China, the Middle East, Africa, the former Soviet Union countries and South America, I felt that many books and guides to doing business in emerging markets included material that seemed rather obvious or was fairly superficial – or they were so academic that practitioner-oriented readers would find them interesting but not immediately useful.

Now, as an MBA teacher, my students, who are mostly learning part-time whilst working, want real insights into the issues involved in dealing with these countries – from the point of view of **developed countries** doing business with the BRICS and beyond, and these countries doing deals with each other. They are also looking for material that relates to specific courses within their MBA studies – such as Country Risk in International Business, Corporate Governance and CSR, Cross-Cultural Management, Marketing, Entrepreneurship, Strategy and so on. This book has been written with them in mind, as practical business leaders looking to be savvy about risks as well as well-informed about opportunities, and to gain insights from fellow practitioners who have been there before.

This might be another differentiator – I have tried to steer a middle course between doom-saying cynicism about business prospects in the BRICS and beyond and overly-naive optimism about making millions overnight. Most practitioners have no illusions that they could lose their shirts – and many have already – yet they press on. Meanwhile the optimism and excitement about the 'two billion armpits' represented by the opening-up of the China market has given way to more rational calculations of prospects and more sober risk analysis.

Thus, the chapters in this book are grouped into three parts – Risks, Opportunities and Practice. Chapter 2, Country Risk, focuses on one of the greatest challenges for external investors and foreign business people, that of the powerful involvement of governments in most of the BRICS and beyond. This can be particularly arbitrary and unpredictable – or at least it often seems that way to outsiders. Chapter 3, Corporate Social Responsibility, looks at ethics, **transparency** and **governance** in emerging markets – which can present a completely new and worrying experience for those with limited experience of the developing world. Business Culture, Chapter 4, considers the challenges of cross-cultural management and of managing people in emerging markets. Culturally-oriented behaviours are hard to generalize, but there are some useful guidelines to follow and assumptions to avoid. The **globalization** of products and services are making the world a smaller place, but perhaps it's an appreciation of the differences rather than the similarities that counts.

In case these chapters tend to suggest that doing business in the BRICS and beyond is more trouble than it's worth – the opportunities are unavoidably attractive for those willing to think in quite a different way. Chapter 5, Marketing, looks at the possibility of implementing new marketing ideas both inbound and outbound from emerging markets – both sides can learn from each other, especially as developing economies now account for more than half of global consumption, and many developed countries are deep in financial recession. Chapter 6, Entrepreneurship and Innovation, reviews technology and new business ventures in emerging markets and suggests that the developed world no longer monopolizes the source of new business ideas – if it ever did. Again, this is another learning opportunity for those willing to put aside old prejudices.

Finally, the third part of the book focuses on the experiences in practice of companies from the BRICS and beyond – and the businesses seeking to work with them. These are discussed in terms of Strategy and Operations (Chapter 7) and Strategic Alliances (Chapter 8). Many of the decisions made on both sides defy explanation, but they all contribute to the conclusions, overall insights and pointers to the future in the last chapter, Lessons for Global Business.

Each chapter is divided into different sections, each of which provides practical material for the international business person that can also be used as separate case studies for MBA students. Lessons at the end of each chapter are followed by Workshop Activities and Worked Examples, corresponding to each of the sections. Business people in the field will be able to add their own 'war stories', many of which smack of *Lonely Planet*-type experiences.

Working in the BRICS and beyond has given the world a new vocabulary, much of which is introduced in the Glossary section. What if you hear that the world's new **anchor economy's chameleon**-like and **anonymous** companies are leading the world in **disruptive innovation** despite **institutional voids**, whilst its biggest rival **creatively adapts reverse innovation** to **springboard** into **multipolar vertical integration**? And what if you are accused of **corporate imperialism**, yet warned against **cannibalizing your cash cow** whilst you are **reconnoitring for adversaries**? This terminology needs to be cracked, if only to keep up with boardroom and AGM conversations, if not on the golf course and in the club bar – to say nothing of during the long-haul flight and on the ground in the BRICS and beyond.

Finally, many books on this subject of developing economies and emerging markets spend numerous pages struggling with a definition of which countries they are talking about, and which countries should or should not be included. This book prefers to keep it simple, taking from *The Economist* an inclusive rather than exclusive definition, based on what the BRICS and beyond are not. *The Economist*'s definition of developed economies based on 1990 data includes Australia, Austria, Belgium, Canada, Denmark, Finland, France, Germany, Greece, Iceland, Ireland, Italy, Japan, Luxembourg, Netherlands, New Zealand, Norway, Portugal, Spain, Sweden, Switzerland, the United Kingdom and the United States. The BRICS and beyond are, basically, every other country – it may be just a matter of time before their business prospects emerge.

PART I

RISKS

2   Country Risk

Politics and Business in Emerging Markets

Introduction

'Country risk' can be seen as a catch-all concept, which is a primary consideration for all Western executives expanding their businesses into emerging markets. Political risk, financial risk, commodity risk and risks associated with violence and conflict – as well as risks of kidnapping and piracy – must be weighed in the balance against potential profits. Demographic pressures on society, censorship and other ways of controlling information may present risks unanticipated by Western business people, and there are many more risks to be discovered as business opportunities are investigated in more detail and go further down the track.

One of the greatest country risks faced by Western business executives trying to penetrate emerging markets is the tendency towards a much closer relationship between government and business. There may be no Western-style separation between 'church and state' in the country they are targeting. The high level of state involvement in companies can produce what Western business might see as unwelcome regulation and government intervention. The first section, 'Church and state - the impact of politics on business', considers these issues, and the second section, 'The jittery political environment in China – political risk, continued', focuses on the manifestations of Chinese attitudes to political risk and how these make things more difficult for Western businesses operating in China's challenging political situation. China, the greatest and largest of the BRICS, is already seen as an **anchor** economy in the world. As discussed in the third section, in Communist and post-Communist countries, there can be a special form of political risk impacting business, hence the subheading 'Once a Communist . . . another form of political risk', which can be particularly relevant for Westerners doing business in this environment, especially due to the lack of Western-style organizations facilitating business, or institutional voids.

The fourth section looks at the ways in which 'Some countries are (financially) riskier than others'. Financial risks can include high levels of inflation, weak financial management and poor governance practices (another institutional void), banking failure, local government insolvency, a great disparity between rich and poor (including the accumulation of wealth by authoritarian leaders), arbitrary taxation demands and low purchasing power, especially at the **bottom of the pyramid**. These issues are not just impacting emerging markets. They are often present in low-income countries but can – of course – affect developed countries too, especially in periods of economic downturn.

'The haves and the have-nots – commodity risk' is the subject of the fifth section. Some countries can be seen as riskier than others when they lack essential commodities and must have these at all costs. The sixth section, 'War and peace', looks at the risks associated with countries that are currently at war, have recently experienced war and its resulting dislocation, and may be suffering from the rapaciousness of dictators – or are in the throes of continuous conflict most of the time. The section on 'Kidnapping and piracy' considers an age-old risk now on the increase, and the impact on operating costs – especially for Western shipping in shipping lanes in the Middle East and off Africa.

The eighth section, 'Demographic risk', considers population changes, which are making their mark in adding to business risk, especially in terms of the aging society in the more established and high-population BRICS, such as China. The emphasis on the preference for male babies and the continuation of the one-child family policy produces more and different demographic risks, as does the internal passport system. The ninth section, 'Discretion can be the better part of valour – censorship risk', is of increasing concern, in Africa, Turkey and especially in China, and is described in more detail in section ten, 'Information and transparency in China'. Many businesses in China operate almost anonymously in terms of rarely publishing operational details and the low market profile of their brand.

India has particular country risks associated with its politics, economy, society and way of doing business, well-known to locals and potentially causing calamity for foreign investors, who face high **barriers to entry**. So some Indian businesses look overseas, for such reasons as described in the penultimate section, 'The grass is always greener – Indian business avoids its risky home market'. Finally, the last section considers slightly less common and more specific risks associated with certain countries and businesses. 'More country risks. . .' includes the issues of the pariah status of countries under sanctions; tit-for-tat risks of politics interfering with business in terms of inter-country relations; 'tarred with the same brush' risks; the fact that some countries are not as 'independent' as they seem; protectionism, also discussed in our CSR and Business Ethics chapter; and high unemployment and a tendency towards dumping – which all add to the picture of the extremely risky nature of doing business in emerging markets.

1. 'Church and state' – the impact of politics on business

In emerging market countries generally there tends to be a rather conservative approach to economic development and a perceived need for stability in business – and also a tendency to look to governments to intervene and (hopefully) create more stability. Many companies in these countries are familiar with controlling and hands-on governments, so this must be taken into account by Western executives in their negotiations. The populations in many of these countries tend to be more high power distant (see Chapter 4) and tolerant of authoritarian rule. Overall, many emerging markets still tend to be immature in coping with the free movement of market forces as they are unused to the concept of 'the separation of church and state'. When the government looks weak, this can make consumers and businesses nervous.

China has one of the most powerful governments in the world, and when the government fails to offer leadership and direction, strange things can happen, in terms of public and business reactions. For example, early April 2011 saw a rare case of consumers panic buying commodities in China, possibly reflecting an increasing collapse of trust in officialdom – illustrated by a nationwide stampede to buy and stockpile cooking salt. Apparently, the word was spread among Chinese shoppers that iodine in the salt could help prevent sickness from radiation, at a time when people were worrying that radiation was spreading from the stricken Fukushima nuclear-power plant in Japan to China. The Chinese consumers worried that this leak of radiation might contaminate the seawater off China and taint local salt production. So, on one day alone, 4,000 tonnes of salt were sold in the city of Zhejiang, eight times the normal amount purchased. Salt prices are normally controlled by the government and prices are fixed; however, the salt merchants, noticing the massive consumer interest, marked them up, but consumers kept on buying. An online commentary argued that the reason people were engaging in pack buying was that they did not trust the government.

The level of consumer trust in the government in China is usually high and, therefore, panic erupts when confidence is dented. The well-publicized Wenzhou rail crash of August 2011 has important implications for changes in the perception of political risk in China – and a decline in trust of the once almost-infallible government. The important factor of this rail crash was not just the rushed engineering work and lack of safety standards. Potentially a hurtling train can be seen as a metaphor for runaway development that is generating its share of collapsing buildings, lethal coal mines and bulldozed neighbourhoods. The main issues highlighted by the rail crash might be the growing need for scrutiny, accountability and public debate in a country with little experience of these practices. This rail crash has somehow shown the limits of dictatorship – can China go on killing people and getting away with it, especially now in a society with a much-increased level of media debate and recent outpouring of blogs and other internet-based messages? Some of China's rulers probably know that these limits are being reached but, to judge by the news crackdown now under way, clearly not all of them appreciate the changes now happening in the politics and business relationship – or they do and are reacting in a frightened way.

Another example of a country where politics and business are usually inter-connected, and one of the most conservative countries in the world, is Saudi Arabia. Sometimes not regarded as an emerging market because of its high per capita incomes, Saudi is nevertheless emerging in terms of business independence and maturity – as the country is a clear case of the dominance of business by politics. The element of country risk is clearly on the rise here, especially since the Arab Spring revolts have increased in intensity and against the background of the major succession problem looming in the country. It is well-known that King Abdullah is nearly ninety and inevitably weak with age, whilst Crown Prince Sultan, expected to succeed him, is almost as old and in poor health. The next in line after him, Prince Nayef, the unpopular interior minister, is also elderly and suffers from diabetes. In order to control business and the local society, the government generously supports individual welfare and large local businesses like Saudi Aramco, and the money will not dry up if oil production continues – and can be manipulated by the number of barrels a day allowed by the government. Accounts of Saudi ladies driving cars – seen as a big-time protest – shows that changes are taking place in Saudi society and business. The gap between the elderly princes of the royal family and the increasingly worldly population is growing.

Whilst some countries, such as China and Saudi Arabia, are facing challenges to the dominance of the government in all aspects of daily life and political control may be decreasing, in other countries, we are seeing an active increase in an existing high degree of political intervention in business. In much of South America, companies (local and foreign) often cannot freely follow their commercial inclinations unless this suits the government. For example, in Argentina, a row between the government and a top steelmaker continues to brew. The company took legal action to overturn an emergency decree increasing state influence in the running of private companies, and the government hit back with a lawsuit arguing its prerogative to shape the corporate strategy of the steelmaker. Most Western companies take a high degree of autonomy in business for granted, so it can be challenging for the Western executive faced with this situation. Another example can be seen in government interference in Brazil. Business people are facing archaic and restrictive labour laws especially when companies are bought and sold. Organizations must have kept detailed payroll records, showing that they have completed all outstanding labour court cases and must promise to pay compensation if further cases are brought regarding matters that predate the sale, otherwise the purchaser of a company may experience huge unforeseen costs. In one example, an investor in a chain of pharmacies was taken to court by four former employees who had worked in the company years before. They claimed they were owed 500,000 reais (then $570,000) for overtime and holiday pay. Since the new owners lacked the payroll records, the labour court ruled against them and froze their bank accounts, forcing closure of their newly-acquired pharmacy stores and thirty-five redundancies. Basically, they suffered from Brazil's tough labour laws, described in 900 articles, which are becoming tougher by the day.

What can happen to business when governments change? New regimes may come in, some ruling administrations become more paranoid, some governments can take a dislike to a successful business potentially encroaching on its territory, and even expropriation of private business can occur. The continuous mix of business and politics can experience ups and downs as governments fluctuate.

Regime change has an awkward way of turning useful political contacts into liabilities. A business friend can suddenly be branded as a criminal. Rules can change unexpectedly, making it harder to do business, as Research in Motion, the maker of the BlackBerry, found when some governments demanded access to users' messages. The authorities can enforce the law in the most draconian fashion against firms that displease them, as was the case for Russia's Yukos, where executives found themselves in prison. Governments can also unexpectedly nationalize assets: in recent years, Congo has taken several mines from their private owners. Political risk can be seen as the biggest deterrent for investors in developing countries over the longer term, ranked ahead of economic instability and bad infrastructure.

With politics driving businesses in many BRICS and beyond, business decisions are inevitably impacted by political change. For example, when can prices rise? Only after the elections are over, as unpopular price rises can be bad for the incumbent political party. The impact of inflation can be negative. With the reduced government control of petrol prices in India, for example, prices were allowed to rise after a six-month subsidy in 2011, but only when the government felt secure enough to be unpopular.

Less democratic governments do not feel so much need to time potentially-unpopular changes with elections, and make sure that elections are not opportunities for expressions of discontent. Across emerging market countries, populations look to governments to provide security and point them in the right direction. Thus, the presence of security forces across Uganda during elections in February 2011 – including irregulars armed with cudgels – reduced chances of popular unrest. The new government of Uganda, trying to deflect potential discontent, emphasized new economic opportunities, especially with recent oil finds along the border with Congo and plans for regional economic integration. The oil fields could yield three billion barrels of crude oil and give Uganda energy independence, changing the balance of power with neighbouring strongman Kenya. The new leadership is trying to bring security to a country that remains rather unstable and is still suffering the consequences of the rule of Idi Amin, even though this was decades ago. The new leadership wants to be increasingly hands-on, and in this environment can get away with it.

So, political risk in a particular country and its impact on business need detailed assessment before an investment by an external party can proceed. When political dominance is on the wane, what is the impact on companies and business operators? When it's on the increase, in what ways is this situation another problem? How about when political risk is fluctuating alarmingly and no-one can see the direction of the politics and business relationship? This can depend on levels of democracy and perceived political security on the part of the authorities. But many emerging market governments continue to exhibit levels of paranoia, which can be a new experience for the Western business person looking to make inroads into developing countries.

2. The jittery political environment in China – political risk, continued

China's concern with preventing political upheavals has led to a vast increase in security-related activity, which has inevitably impacted on business and even on ordinary people going about their ordinary daily activities, including foreigners. Such is the paranoia of the authorities that a high degree of nervousness is apparent, and communications difficulties have increased (see also Censorship and information risk, below). There is still significant loyalty to the old order, with many locals clearly worrying about getting into trouble and trying hard to keep to business as usual. Although in China there has been no sign of an Arab Spring-type movement, observers across the country see the government as going to great lengths to make sure everything looks calm. Thus, Western business people developing their operations in China now must be particularly careful not to draw attention to themselves and risk upsetting the over-sensitive authorities.

Business visitors to China have noticed the huge security opera-tions in Beijing, Shanghai and other cities, especially after internet messages encouraging silent walk-pasts on certain days – these are not demonstrations as such, but as much as some Chinese feel they can do to make protests. Very few locals respond to these requests, as they can attract unwelcome police attention – and often it can be difficult to work out who the police are: they are everywhere.

Various observers and media have been documenting the impact of the increase in government surveillance in China, discussing how police have regularly pounced on handfuls of locals who looked inclined to take part in the silent walk-past protests and whisked them away. Dissidents have been detained or are watched even more closely, and an American journalist was beaten and kicked by plain-clothed goons and detained for several hours. The country's annual budget includes eye-catching numbers for security reflecting double-digit growth, with 624 billion yuan ($95 billion) spent on law and order, 13.8% more than in 2010. Central areas of several Chinese cities have been saturated with uniformed and plain-clothed officers. They have staked out shopping streets where the internet messages have urged protestors to 'stroll' (a euphemism often used in China for demonstrating, which the police hardly ever permit). These pro-tests have yet to materialize, but the authorities have decided to rescind their 2007 decision to give foreign correspondents freer rein. Many foreign business people have been suspected of being under-cover journalists and are being warned to keep a low profile.

A new tactic of the Chinese authorities concerns Gmail, now more frustrating to use than ever; but the Chinese have been careful not to cut off access altogether. Google have claimed that China was again interfering with its service in the country, cleverly making it look as if the problem lies with Gmail itself. A foreign businessman reflected that 'it does make you feel much more that there is a cost of being here'.

The background to this crackdown is the feeling that most Chinese are still loyal to the memory of traditional communism and Mao Zedong, shown in a petition with the names of nearly 10,000 people accusing a liberal intellectual of slandering Mao Zedong and attempting to overthrow the Communist Party. Diehard Maoists are continuing to defend the emerging markets themselves and confront their critics, which may be seen as a symptom of an escalation of ideological struggles between China's West-leaning liberals and the patriotic conservative hard-liners. However, the Communist Party continues to be jittery about the possible spread of an Arab-style 'jasmine revolution' to China, and the Party is all the more anxious as it celebrates the ninetieth anniversary of its foundation, although in reality it is probably stronger than ever.

3. Once a Communist . . . another form of political risk

Western businesses entering previously Communist-run countries must be prepared for the presence of strong governmental control in apparently privatized enterprises – just because they have been privatized, it doesn't mean they are private in the Western sense. Anecdotal evidence from the field suggests that nasty surprises can emerge when businesses from the West invest in formerly state-owned utilities, for example, because they are still, to all intents and purposes, state-owned or at least state-directed.

For example, a Western European-owned power utility recently purchased a nationwide power supply operation in a former Communist country and soon realized that the prices paid by the consumers – previously heavily subsidized – made their purchase massively unprofitable. They would have to put the prices up to break even, let alone make a working profit. The Western multinational company was then informed by the vendors – the government – that price rises were simply not allowed, as this would make the government unpopular in the election run-up. Its fingers burned in this ill-fated acquisition, the European power utility is looking to dump this now unattractive acquisition – but it's looking difficult, as other possible purchasers have wised-up to the problem.

Vietnam, especially the buzzing city named after Ho Chi Minh (formerly Saigon), hardly appears to reflect Communist values, but they are there all the same. Visits to a local business partner can sometimes produce surprises – what happened to that pleasant co-operative person we used to work with? Why did he suddenly disappear and reappear in a lowly job in the wilderness, when he was in a trusted senior position and apparently doing a good job? Perhaps his competence was nothing to do with it – maybe he was negatively showing up a colleague who was better-placed in the Party.

The same thing can happen in Kazakhstan, now an independent country and free from the former Soviet yoke – or is it? Will our partner colleague there, freely critical of corruption in his country and trying to find a better way, still be around for long when he continues to delight in exposing the ills of society he sees around him?

China is still, of course, officially Communist, but many new developments suggest that changes of a strictly non-Communist nature are under way – such as the rise of a middle class. This group can be potentially in conflict with the 'alienated' people in the population, especially those from poorer areas seeking their fortunes in the big cities, lacking the city-dweller resident status or *hukou* (see below). Relations between China's rich and poor are likely to create more political risk in the future, especially as the middle class was virtually non-existent until the late 1990s. Up to now, well-off city-dwellers have traded the lack of political choice and activity for a new level of prosperity, but they are bound to want more political representation in the future, and meanwhile the economy is slowing down. The Communist Party is struggling to maintain this prosperity, with inflation at 5.5% – although it was much worse, at 27.7%, in 1994.

For a Communist country, China is facing many contradictions, becoming a middle-income country, and with an ever larger number of elderly people. China's state-owned businesses have an insatiable appetite for capital and need much more money. Curbing state companies means that the government will have to deal with all the well-connected people who ride on their coat-tails, including many members of the middle class. Meanwhile, the system of household registration, or *hukou*, the internal 'passport' system, defines even long-staying urban migrants as rural residents, cutting them out of housing, education and other benefits, leaving a dissatisfied, disenfranchised group of potential dissidents.

Anecdotal evidence suggests that people in China still like to see themselves as good Communists, however elitist, capitalistic and middle class they have become. One expatriate businesswoman was observing her local Chinese manager, who had recently become a father. He was buying disposable diapers and foreign-branded milk powder for his child, and was buying a bigger family car. All his clothes, electronic gadgets and even his cigarettes were imported, heavily branded and the most expensive. But he was most upset at being (humorously) teased as becoming quite a capitalist. So this might be seen as an Emperor's New Clothes problem – these countries propound modernity but are still rooted in the past, and are facing an identity problem as many of the new values of society conflict with the old.

4. Some countries are (financially) riskier than others

Financial risks can take many forms – including out-of-control inflation, poor financial management, banking failure, local government insolvency, high levels of wealth accumulation by authoritarian leaders in contrast with a majority of very poor, difficulties in collecting taxes and a lack of basic purchasing power in countries with many low-income people. These risks are not confined to emerging market countries but can be seen as creating greater problems in emerging markets, especially in terms of holding back economic development and deterring outside investors.

Inflation is one of the biggest country risks faced by nearly all emerging market countries, and the impact of inflation and price rises in China especially will inevitably affect business decisions there and overseas. The Chinese economy may be growing between 7% and 9% still, but price rises of over 5% are higher than most observers expected. This is also impacting the stability of the regime, an issue of bottom-line importance to the Chinese bureaucrats, as this is something they will never compromise. The Chinese government's decision to raise the income tax threshold by a third was designed to reduce the burden on wage earners and counteract price rises to boost domestic demand and stimulate the economy. The level of control exerted over the Chinese economy may be seen as completely at odds with the situation in much of the West, and can be hard for Western executives to envisage, but it does mean that China can be less risky generally and more predictable and stable than many other BRICS and beyond countries.

Inflation in South America, by contrast, is becoming more and more out of control. Rather than trying to nip it in the bud at source – as in the case of China – some South American countries are adopting the policy of trying to offset its worst effects. Hence, in Venezuela, minimum wages and pensions are being hiked to compensate for increased living costs, especially to encourage government popularity with an election looming. Brazil's increasingly tough labour laws seem to be designed to have the same effect – politicians are also concerned with high and rising inflation, even though unemployment is still fairly low. The impact on prices and their tendency to rise is dangerous, despite the fairly strong economic growth of around 4.5% per annum in the early part of the 2010s. Inflation is at the upper limit of the central bank's target range, and the country doesn't have a clear way of dealing with it so far.

Rampant inflation is an almost permanent country risk in countries also associated with recent political upheaval, especially related to supply issues. Hence, Egypt is suffering from the highest-ever inflation in recent years and record food prices. Urban consumer inflation reached over 12% in April 2011, with food prices rising 1.2% per month. Any business setting up in Egypt has to cope with this situation, and the continued instability it will inevitably bring.

Some countries that were apparently financially stable in the past can suddenly start experiencing financial management problems and increased financial risk. An example is Botswana, long seen as one of the most stable, prosperous and least corrupt countries in Africa, previously thriving on its diamond business. Since June 2011, the country has been shaken by its first nationwide public sector strike, in which police – usually unarmed – used tear-gas and rubber bullets to disperse rioting secondary-school pupils, and then went on the rampage, in a reaction against the president, now seen as too authoritarian. Botswana's diamond bonanza, which accounts for nearly half of the government's revenue and over a third of its GDP, will apparently not last much longer, with growth slowing from 13% after independence in 1966 to 7% in 2011. Meanwhile, the government is still spending 40% of GDP, as if it had the same revenues as in the past.

Banking failure, reflecting heightened financial risk, is a very real country risk in Russia, in particular. Nearly one-third of Russian banks are apparently ill-prepared for another global financial crisis. A stress test by the central bank resulted in nearly $40 billion in state support being provided to stop these banks from going bust. At least 300 of Russia's 900 banks could see their capital requirement fall below the 10% minimum required if faced with another economic downturn – and then they would have their licences revoked. Financial recessions – especially in apparently politically and financially unstable countries – tend to be quickly followed by rapid deposit outflows and a paralysis in interbank lending. In Russia, the estimated 321 banks judged to be most at risk are controlling half of the country's financial assets.

If banking failure is a very specific and immediate country risk in Russia, the country has long laboured under the reputation of having an unpredictable investment environment. Foreign investors have piled into China and India instead – so what can Russia do about this? One option is to attract large global private equity groups – but how to do that? The Russian President, in mid-2011, considered the idea of creating a $10 billion Russian state-backed private equity fund – to attract these groups and various sovereign wealth funds – by creating a stronger foundation for their investment climate. But Western players are not yet entirely convinced.

Local government insolvency could be another country risk for several countries in the future, including China. The World Bank has already noted a property value downturn in the provinces of China, which could impact negatively on local government finances in the future. The decline of state-owned industries has already caused significant problems for Western investors. In the late 1990s, these local businesses found themselves in a web of triangular debt, owing money to manufacturers but waiting for consumers to pay. Leaders continue to prop up state businesses to maintain stability among low-income workers, at least keeping them in jobs, but these industries may have no long-term commercial future.

The high power distant outlook of many low-level workers (see Chapter 4) means that they may not actively challenge this situation, including the gap in income between themselves and their leaders – yet. But leader wealth is becoming increasingly exposed. The accumulation of wealth by authoritarian leaders is increasingly publicly criticized, especially as it might otherwise be used to stimulate the economy. The Arab Spring movement has revealed the tendency of many leaders to invest funds overseas in safe havens – and when these leaders fall from grace there is a strong likelihood that their funds will be impounded. This cash has very often come from locally-generated wealth, so the sufferers include the local population, as much of their potential income may have been privately accumulated by their leaders.

Entire districts of London and Paris are inhabited by fabulously wealthy emerging market leaders – a spoof tourist guide, in the style of a tour of celebrity houses in Beverly Hills, was recently published. Switzerland is a particularly favourite haven for emerging market leader savings, but now the Swiss are ready to freeze the assets of Arab Spring dictators who have fallen or who are under threat. The accounts of Mubarak of Egypt, Ben Ali of Tunisia and Gaddafi of Libya – totalling at least $960 million, according to the Swiss foreign ministry – have been frozen and are under investigation. At least half of this sum was part of Egyptian leader Mubarak's personal wealth. Questions remain about how much more wealth is hidden elsewhere, and how much of this could have been used to offset poverty suffered by the local population. Recently, before the fall of Mubarak, local Cairo inhabitants were rioting in the wealthier neighbourhoods in protest about increases in the price of bread. Awareness of the wealth of leaders and the gap between rich and poor is becoming greater.

Nowhere is this more apparent than in Africa, whose leaders have lavish villas in the smartest district of Paris, but where many local inhabitants have the lowest per capita incomes in the world. As a result of the few checks and balances existing to impact the behaviour of these leaders, risks associated with doing business in Africa have always been high. Many observers have respected the contribution of the International Criminal Court in The Hague in investigating extremist leader behaviour and trying to establish justice. It would seem that African leaders who may have ignored the court in the past, could now be viewing it more nervously. The ICC's biggest opponents are in Africa, which provides the court with its biggest group of members (31 out of 114) and is the scene of most cases currently (time of writing, mid-2011) being investigated or prosecuted. The 53-member African Union apparently particularly dislikes the court's increasing willingness to go after sitting presidents. The reason that so many African cases are before the court would seem to be because they have been referred to it either by the UN Security Council or by the countries themselves. So lack of leader behaviour control as a financial risk may be in decline – or at least there is greater awareness of the problem.

Further financial risks to be evaluated by both local and foreign investors can include high levels of taxation of perceived profiteering – and once a company has paid the tax, it can be difficult to get it back. In Venezuela, an oil tax hike to 95% on oil revenues above $100 a barrel has hit the local oil industry. This tax used to be 60%, but it was thought that once oil development companies had recouped their original investment, they could be moved to a much higher tax bracket. The impact on future investment is problematic, and this may also impact foreign investors in the future, possibly described as 'biting the hand that feeds you'.

Similarly, Tullow – the London-listed upstream oil company – has had to take extensive legal action to recover tax the company paid to the government of Uganda. The $313 million in capital gains tax was not justified, Tullow feels – and although the company paid it at the time, now it thinks that was a mistake. Trying to get the money back is proving an uphill struggle. This can be seen as a salutary lesson to other investors in Uganda and other African countries.

Finally, perhaps the greatest financial risk facing a potential foreign investor is the lack of customers with money to spend. The lack of purchasing power in many countries, with no sizeable consumer class to purchase products and services, has long been seen as a problem in Africa in particular. But things seem to be changing, with some observers noting the emergence of a broad middle class – even comparable in size with that of India and China – especially when they think in terms of the entire continent (see Chapter 5). The African Development Bank sees this segment as around 313 million in number – but ranged across a very diverse continent. There is money here, but it's a question of accessing it, and here small-unit packaging, widespread distribution and locally-appealing advertising can do the trick and offset this perceived fundamental financial risk.

Many products and services have failed in several countries because of the poverty of the inhabitants – and this is often accompanied by ignorance and a lack of education. For example, a cheap computer – really more of a palmtop – despite being retailed at only $150, failed to take off in rural India in 2002–5. Not only was it still too expensive, but most people didn't know how to use a calculator, let alone a computer. It was too much ahead of its time, and failed. But the world is changing all the time and this risk may decline in due course.

5. The haves and the have-nots – commodity risk

Many emerging market countries are not oil-producing, and rising oil prices have inevitably put a strain on their economic growth. For example, the Philippines must inevitably import oil, and prices above $120 a barrel have a deleterious knock-on effect on the whole economy. The government therefore found itself under pressure to subsidize the popular public transport service run by 'jeepneys' or small buses, to prevent the undue suffering of migrant workers and other frequent travellers. As a result of this decision and a similar situation in many emerging markets, the IMF's bill for fuel subsidies reached $250 billion in 2010; it was a fraction of this amount – $60 billion – in 2003. New products being designed for emerging market consumption must, therefore, take into account the shortage of traditional fuels and how this ongoing dependence acts as a drag on economic growth in these resource-poor emerging market countries.

With these petrol shortage-related problems, many countries are restricting exports of petrol to conserve supplies for local use. So prices are surging and governments are feeling the need to protect consumers – especially with national elections coming up – and central banks are trying to tighten monetary policies to cool their overheating economies. Russia has placed a 44% export duty on petrol and will tighten fuel supplies to the Baltic States and Central Asia. China in particular fears political reprisals with high fuel prices, as was experienced with the short-lived protest by the Shanghai truckers in early 2011, where fuel shortages threatened to lead to the much-feared political instability that China worries about so much.

Therefore, not surprisingly, dominance in specific commodities can give certain countries undue leverage over those around them. These dependent countries can suffer the risk that they can be beholden to these commodity-supplying giant neighbours. Russia's dominance of liquid natural gas has given it great power over needy neighbours. In mid-2011, Russian gas pipelines were carrying 80% of all gas traded in the area, so the firms at the upstream end of those pipelines, such as Russia's Gazprom, which supplies a quarter of all Western Europe's gas, had a strong hand in negotiations with other countries. Control of the pipelines meant that when Gazprom turned off the gas (as it did in 2009 in a dispute over trans-shipments through Ukraine) would-be gas buyers had nowhere to turn for alternatives. However, various factors are reducing the dominance of Gazprom, including energy market deregulation and a drop in overall demand, with power sector reforms allowing different European utilities to compete against each other, at a price sometimes as low as half that of long-term contracts from Russia. As a result, Gazprom was forced to renegotiate contracts with many of its European customers for a three year 'crisis period' to allow up to 15% of gas to be priced on cheaper spot terms.

Although sources of energy can be seen as among the most important commodities impacting country risk, the availability of all basic raw materials makes a difference to economic development for countries. Rising input costs – the price of raw materials and commodities – together with high interest rates – combine to create challenging country risks experienced in many emerging markets. In particular, Indian corporate entities – especially in cement, real estate, textiles and shipping – have suffered margin pressure and hence profit reduction. Many of these products must be imported, and prices and availability are outside of their control. Hence the focus of many emerging market countries on ensuring raw material supplies, like China's activities in buying up mines in Africa, for example (see Chapter 8) – which can be seen as a political as well as economic issue.

6. War and peace

One of the most potentially damaging country risks is war, and the total dislocation caused by war. For example, upheaval in the Ivory Coast in early 2011 resulted in cocoa beans piling up in the warehouses and a dramatic fall in their market price with over-supply and no-one buying. No-one *could* buy – the banks were closed, fuel in cars was in short supply and many were afraid to venture into the interior for fear of being caught in the cross-fire.

Countries undergoing major political and economic dislocation find it challenging to respond to even the most urgent demands for their raw materials. Iraq would like to increase its oil exports to cash in on the big rise in demand worldwide – but is unlikely to make the target of 12 million barrels a day it has been trying to reach. Problems in pipelines and terminals are operating as major constraints to supply. Libya has been in complete turmoil for several months, and the final defeat of government forces and death of the dictator has not assuaged fears of an oil-grab by the West. For many months, oil terminals were being taken by rebels, then loyalists, then back again, and normality is still far away, shown by the fact that in late 2011, business in Egypt has still not returned to normal.

Other countries – even if not at war – have a reputation for political instability and the resultant nervousness of both domestic and international businesses. Nigeria is an example, especially through having a mixed Muslim and Christian population, which occasionally erupts in conflict. When a Christian political candidate gained the upper hand against Muslim opposition, some local authorities felt empowered to evict non-indigenous populations representing religious minorities to other areas of settlement, causing extensive economic dislocation. This scenario might not happen in most developed economies, but in Nigeria it is a regular occurrence.

Also in Africa, Angola and Congo are not officially at war but are fighting over local oil supplies, with much wealthier Angola taking advantage of the poorer Congolese, evicting tens of thousands of Congolese from within its borders over the last half decade. Angola's GDP per person is now twenty-four times bigger than that of the Congo, so Congolese nationals keep migrating to seek a better standard of living, and the government of the Congo has laid claim to chunks of Angola's most profitable offshore oil blocks. If the Congo were to win in its claims, Angola's position as Africa's second biggest exporter of crude oil after Nigeria would be threatened, so the hapless Congolese migrants have become a pawn in the game. Despite the Congo's huge mineral wealth, its government is so short of cash that it may welcome a quick deal with its neighbour, in the interest of short-term gain. Either way, the political instability here represents a serious and ongoing country risk.

'Are countries poor because they are violent or violent because they are poor?' is an especially valid question here and, as argued by the World Bank, the main constraint on development for many countries may not be a poverty trap but a violence trap. Peaceful countries seem to be much better at escaping poverty. Poverty can be seen as endemic in countries riven by civil war, ethnic conflict and organized crime. Violence and bad government prevent them from escaping the trap. If we compare two small African countries, we can see that the former argument seems to be most convincing. Until 1990, Burundi and Burkina Faso had similar rates of economic growth and improvements in national income, but, in 1993, civil war erupted in Burundi. More than 300,000 died – most of them civilians. Placid Burkina Faso, without undergoing conflict, is now two-and-a-half times richer.

Even countries apparently fast-growing and becoming increasingly attractive to investors – such as Georgia, a former Soviet Union satellite now opening its doors to the West and achieving improvements in transparency, and with unique and popular exports – have suffered from war, especially after its open conflict with Russia in 2008–9. Even though Georgia apparently recovered quickly and refused to cancel international events, the rest of the world remained nervous.

So, the impact of war on country risk – and situations of near-war, such as in Africa – can be seen as posing extremely high levels of risk to would-be emerging market investors. But post-war recovery can offer many opportunities, such as the piling into Libya almost hours after Gaddafi's demise.

7. Kidnapping and piracy

The chances of a merchant ship being attacked by pirates, the crew kidnapped and the owners or charterers put under pressure to pay multi-million dollar ransoms have increased dramatically in recent years. Many commodities and consumer products are carried by sea – including dry cargoes, fuel, domestic appliances such as white goods, cars, clothing and food. The threat of **maritime piracy** means longer and, therefore, more costly voyages, higher freight rates and insurance and greater security expenses for ship-owners (such as counter-piracy equipment, training and paying ransoms). This can impact the cost of living of consumers far away, in effect decreasing the value of their salaries, and contributing to rising inflation. Although around seven-eighths of pirate attacks are successfully fended off, the numbers captured and detained are enough to pose a very high risk to shipping.

The total cost of global piracy has been estimated to probably reach $15 billion per year by 2015. In the first quarter of 2011, pirates attacked 142 vessels, seizing eighteen, including three tankers of over 100,000 tons. Pirates killed seven crew members, and injured thirty-four, especially in the 'war zone' officially designated as 2.5 million square miles off Somalia – and the zone is increasing rather than diminishing.

Definitions of piracy vary – the International Marine Board sees it as 'an act of boarding any vessel with the intent to commit theft or any other crime and with the intent or capability to use force in the furtherance thereof'. The International Maritime Organization describes it as 'armed robbery against ships – any unlawful act of violence or detention or any act of depredation or threat thereof. . . directed against a ship or persons or property on board such a ship'.

Recent research findings point to the irony of pirates attacking ships that are carrying food aid from developed countries to alleviate poverty and starvation in their own countries. This is inevitably deterring future aid deliveries, due to increased insurance costs and the high personal risk faced by the crew. As the pirates – and especially the pirate warlords – are getting rich, their compatriots are becoming poorer than ever. Meanwhile, the governments of countries needing international aid are corruptly laundering pirate ransom income, especially through no-questions-asked real estate deals.

There is no sign of piracy losing its popularity as a way of making money in a kind of 'destructive entrepreneurship' in countries at the bottom of the Transparency International Corruption Perceptions Index (Somalia ranks the lowest out of 183). As one half-joking 'job advertisement' for a pirate put it: 'Low risk, high reward opportunity. Fresh air. Sunshine. Work part-time from your own boat. Earn fifty times your expected lifetime income in one day. Little experience needed. Be the envy of your friends and neighbours!'

8. Demographic risk

Another country risk is presented by changing demographic factors, which is especially apparent in the largest of the BRICS. There are several issues here – the ageing population; a flight to the cities and reduction in rural labour; a decline of marriage rates; the continuation of the one child policy and the preference for males; and the matter of the *hukou*.

In China, the population is now becoming older and more urban. City-dwellers of retirement age represent around 1.3 billion of China's population, up 5.9% from 2000 – making for a big change in China's labour market. The pool of potential workers from the countryside is now shrinking, which is impacting on where China decides to do business, and in what way, because if many workers are needed for a project then where to source labour may become an issue. Meanwhile, marriage rates are in decline in China, as young, upwardly-mobile city-dwellers – particularly females – are more interested in pursuing their careers. The increasing presence of this segment is especially impacting marketing decisions (see Chapter 5).

With the decline of marriage rates, the one child family policy is rapidly moving into the no child result, exacerbating the imbalance in the population towards males and shortage of female marriage partners. Although tightly controlled and heavily monitored by the authorities, it is still a risk to political and economic stability, especially as time goes on.

Population control in the cities is a long-term perceived problem in China, especially in terms of the preservation of the *hukou* system. There is concern among the authorities that the number of what they see as 'low-income, low-quality and ill-educated outsiders' should not be allowed to increase in megacities like Beijing. From the 1990s, migrants from the countryside have flocked to Beijing and Shanghai in particular, where they accept low-paid jobs and even work illegally. Looked down upon by snooty city-dwellers, they are heavily discriminated against, with little access to the lifestyles enjoyed by official inhabitants. This can come as a surprise to Westerners, who accept population movement inside countries as quite normal. Western businesses recruiting staff members in China, therefore, must be especially careful – does everyone have a local *hukou*? If not they might find life difficult, in terms of finding accommodation to start with.

These 'outsiders' cannot live in apartment blocks reserved for local city-dwellers (let alone the blocks with a licence for housing foreigners, which is another story) and so often live in underground housing, which, if closed down by the authorities as is threatened, will force them to return to the villages they moved from a few years or more ago. This is substantial – for example, Beijing's population (those living in the city for six months or longer) had topped 19.7 million by the end of 2009, representing 2 million more than official figures had suggested. So, officials are talking about making the *hukou* – a proof of domicile that is hard to obtain when not inherited and that confers all sorts of health and welfare rights – even more difficult to get in future.

To a certain extent, the internal passport system also exists in Russia, with Moscow more-or-less reserved for Muscovites. In the Gulf, the situation of passport issuance is similar – with some locals having official status and being able to travel freely, while others have no personal papers for travel and almost no prospect of citizenship (the Gulf countries do not offer naturalization, even for persons born within their borders and living there for generations). Again, this can be an issue for Western businesses working in these countries and making the mistake of thinking that it might be like home.

9. Discretion can be the better part of valour – censorship risk

The British High Commissioner in Malawi, Africa, found himself deported after a leaked email in which he explained the lack of tolerance of criticism of the government. Not only does the government not accept criticism, it does not accept an observation that it does not accept criticism, so the lesson about careful email writing is well-taken here. This story might sound like a quaint example of a rare phenomenon, but an almost paranoid attitude to censorship is common among many authorities in developing countries.

In another example, in India, there are problems associated with showing a map of the country. The political and economic rivalry between India and Pakistan is such that many maps showing borders are contentious. A map included in the UK edition of a popular international magazine was not allowed by the Indian censors, which tend to censor maps that show the current effective border, insisting instead that only its full territorial claims be shown. It is more intolerant on this issue than Pakistan, and the same issue can be seen with China (to show Taiwan or not?), Vietnam (how about the disputed possessions in the South China Seas?) and, of course, Israel and the Palestinian territories. This might not be seen as a major problem for the Western business person, except when he or she has printed hundreds of brochures with the 'wrong' map.

Censorship of the press and a lack of press freedom can also be a cause for alarm for foreign businessmen seeking transparency and wanting to know the real picture of what is happening. Freedom for journalists to write whatever they want is probably becoming rarer than ever. Even without active censorship, some journalists are becoming lazy and greedy and self-censoring activities that look too much like hard work or are not sufficiently remunerative. Some countries are keen to look increasingly democratic, but their attitude towards journalists contradicts this.

For example, despite Turkey's leadership claims of transforming the country into a 'forward democracy', the detention and imprisonment of two investigative journalists in mid-2011 adding to the numbers already in jail, including many Kurds, has led to concern from politicians in the European Union and USA. This is especially because it is now four years since a series of investigations began, and there have still been no convictions. Some suspects have yet to be charged. The investigation may have become a pretext to round up the government's critics, especially as both of these arrested investigative journalists had produced works that may have brought them enemies. However, the use of secret evidence in the cases so far means that defendants cannot challenge their detention.

The need for sensitivity on the part of foreign businesses cannot be over-emphasized. There can be a huge political backlash against nationals of countries offending the sensitivities of other countries. For example, both Denmark and The Netherlands managed to upset Arab countries with anti-Muslim messages, causing great problems for Danish and Dutch nationals trying to visit and work in these countries. The popular KDD brand – the Kuwaiti Danish Dairies – suffered boycotting, even though the Danish partners had long sold out their business to Kuwaitis. As these were all highly perishable products, the losses sustained were immense.

10. Information and transparency in China

A major risk of investing for many Westerners who are more and more involved in many BRICS and beyond businesses is the matter of knowing what is going on and feeling confident about a more tenuous level of control and knowledge than that which they might be used to.

Hence, there were great concerns voiced by Yahoo! about their investment in Chinese ecommerce group Alibaba. When Alibaba sold its online payment subsidiary to another company – owned by Alibaba's CEO – Yahoo! was worried that its own assets might be diluted, to say nothing of its lack of involvement in this 'hush hush' internal transaction, of which it had no idea. Jack Ma – the CEO in question – was basically involved in buying and selling within the group, without consulting his multinational investors or partners – and this lack of transparency and control is an increasing fear for all multinationals who can find themselves in such a situation.

In many emerging markets, few people know what is going on, and the government tightly controls information flows. To a certain extent, living in ignorance is such a normal state for middle-ranking and low-level employees that it is widely tolerated. China has been famous for (and highly competent at) censorship for years, controlling internet sites, mobile telephone coverage and newspapers – especially during big events. Party milestones are celebrated with millions attending without a single mobile telephone going off. Hotmail and Gmail accounts have become a blank screen. But things are changing, in so far that the Wenzhou rail crash in 2011, for example, spawned a massive outcry, even producing concerns about government corruption and hypocrisy. Microblogging sites, notably Sina Weibo, China's homespun version of the banned Twitter, ran unusually free comment, and it would seem that the authorities decided that trying to reduce this criticism would have been difficult or counterproductive. Microblogs also provided an avenue for Chinese journalists to publish details on the accident in the crucial early hours, before slower-footed propaganda authorities could issue 'guidance' to the populace as a whole.

China does not like criticism – especially from overseas – and has been particularly focused on silencing critics in South East Asia. Although China tends to promote a policy of non-interference in the internal affairs of other countries, it pursues its perceived enemies among its neighbours, such as the Dalai Lama, the apparently rebellious Uighurs and Falun Gong, the quasi-Buddhist sect that China banned in 1999 but it would seem to keep going from overseas. Apparently encouraged by China, both Vietnam and Indonesia have shut down Falun Gong-affiliated radio stations. People in China looking for 'the real story' would appear to have fewer sources of information than ever with the BBC ending its Mandarin language World Service, broadcast for over 70 years, at a time when the US equivalent, the Voice of America, is due to do the same. So, in some ways, China is becoming more closed than open.

One of the ways in which China has been trying to offset unrest and discontent has a Huxleyesque *Brave New World* flavour: the increasing of happiness. Officials in China now insist that happiness is more important than increasing GDP, without mentioning that political freedom doesn't have much to do with happiness. Meanwhile, as the Chinese authorities are encouraging people not to worry but be happy, their statements about the importance of political reform are followed by the repression of dissidents, especially to prevent them from responding to anonymous internet-circulated calls for an Arab-style 'jasmine revolution'. With a strengthening of

China's internet firewall to make it more difficult to use software to evade blocks on sensitive foreign websites, the Chinese are having an uphill struggle encouraging people not to think and to just be happy. Some websites in China recently carried a report that 11% of respondents to an opinion poll believed national happiness is boosted when they express themselves freely on the internet – actually the reverse of what the authorities are intending.

The changes taking place in China in this area should be of increasing concern to Western businesses, as a study of Chinese history shows that periods of national suspicion and paranoia are often accompanied by waves of anti-foreign reaction, as seen in the Cultural Revolution and other more distant episodes. It still may be the case that we need the Chinese more than they need us.

11. The grass is always greener – Indian business avoids its risky home market

Country risk is well-understood by those investors who have developed their businesses at home but have then chosen to take their investment dollars overseas, having perceived that the country risk at home (which they know only too well) makes many investments unattractive. For example, Indian conglomerate Tata has largely chosen to invest elsewhere than in India, as a response to negative experiences of bureaucracy, inefficiency and corruption. In an about-turn to offset criticism of their lack of support of their own country, Tata made the decision to invest $26 billion in India in 2012–17, as part of an overall plan to double group revenues to around $150 billion. Many emerging market companies feel no patriotic obligations, and often feel much safer investing in more mature markets known for greater reliability, and which can have more prestige and status. This opportunity to provide sought-after investing can be a useful bargaining stance for Western executives dealing with emerging market businesses. Investing in emerging markets for a Western business is one approach; these businesses investing in your country can be another option (see Chapter 8).

India is well-known for extensive bureaucracy, inter-corporate disputes, official corruption and heavy pressure on paying taxes – and this has resulted in Western multinationals being put off India completely, or at least taking their time to enter the subcontinent. Vodafone is one of the UK's most ambitious multinationals – but is planning an IPO in India only after disputes with rivals Essar have been resolved and the demands of India's tax authorities have been met to the satisfaction of both parties. India is an attractive possibility for Vodafone because of the development of a large domestic market and a booming middle class – but there are still many barriers to be overcome, and these are largely causing domestic business interested in expansion to look elsewhere.

'What happens in India is not because of the government, but in spite of the government', said an Indian CEO. The private sector, seen as the main engine of growth to turn India from the world's tenth-largest economy into the world's third largest by around 2030, has become fed up, feeling that corruption has 'paralysed the government' and there is the general consensus that many foreigners are fed up too. There have been long delays over the approval of investments by foreign firms, and when decisions are made they often backfire. For example, settling the terms on which mining companies can acquire and exploit land ended up sending share prices lower rather than higher – so the grass must be greener somewhere else.

Yet, perceptions of country risks should not be applied in a blanket style to an entire country, as there may be low-risk pockets where doing business is surprisingly easy.

12. More country risks. . .

There are many more 'niche' risks not covered in some of the topics above, and it is impossible for any text to cover all of them. For instance, some countries are too risky for business dealings as they are under sanctions; there is also the issue of tit-for-tat risks, when politicians and other non-business leaders upset other countries, with whom their nationals are doing business; 'tarred with the same brush' risks can cause problems when honest companies seem to be too closely related to dishonest ones; some countries are not as 'independent' as they seem, and another country might be directing its policies from behind the scenes; protectionism, or preferential treatment for domestic business in competition with foreign entrants; high unemployment in a country and the dangers that brings; and a tendency towards dumping of cheap products, also in unfair competition – all these risks add to the picture of the extremely risky nature of doing business in still-evolving BRICS and beyond and emerging markets generally.

Risky to touch the untouchables

A major country risk is faced when a Western business tries to work with an emerging markets country that is regarded as a pariah by others. An example is Iran, still labouring under sanctions from the USA. So Western businesses – from the USA and the EU – are careful not to deal with the Islamic Republic in order to maintain the sanctions and stick to the rules; but these hands-off policies don't necessarily apply to Emerging Markets (EM) businesses, such as in India. India is anxious to buy Iranian oil and Iran is keen to sell it. But who will lend India the money to pay for it? Strictly speaking, if they are to be consistent, this should not be the US or the EU, who would face their own risks at home if caught 'sleeping with the enemy'. India has got to the point of needing to pay $12 billion to Iran without upsetting the Americans. Meanwhile, a long-standing clearing system run by a group of Asian central banks is no longer being used for this purpose. However, India is still importing 400,000 barrels a day from Iran, mostly on credit, but without an acceptable means of paying for them.

Tit-for-tat

This is another country risk with which Western executives might not be completely familiar. The US Ambassador expressed sympathy for the jasmine revolution in China, inspired by the Arab Spring of early 2011 – so the Chinese elite cut down on applying for US visas and cancelled several bilateral academic and cultural programmes to be hosted by the US. Diplomatic snubs can go both ways. It might sound rather immature, but it happens all the time.

Tarred with the same brush

One danger of investing in a country where local companies can be accused of fraud and suspended from trading is that the Western company can be tainted by the suspect behaviour of the local emerging market unit with whom it has had dealings. This is not necessarily fair, but all part of country risk. The well-known US private equity group Carlyle, for example, invested in two Chinese companies that were then in big trouble and is now no longer allowed to trade on the stock exchanges of New York and Hong Kong as a result. The unwelcome scrutiny that Carlyle attracted through association with these companies came at a bad time, when Carlyle was going for an IPO. Managing $106 billion in funds, it may not be surprising that a few of the businesses in the portfolio might be suspect, but it still undermines the image of the umbrella organization. So, companies should watch out for their investments, they can damage their image.

Leaving the apron-strings

Some emerging market countries might seem to be independent, and investing in their bonds might seem like a safe bet – but how independent is a country like Mongolia, on the border with China? The Development Bank of Mongolia has set up a $700 million sovereign bond issue to attract funds for local lending programmes – but will would-be investors upset China in the process? And what is the involvement of China in this fund? How about Kazakhstan – how independent is that from Russia?

Protectionism

This can be a major country risk facing the efforts of Western multinationals trying to establish businesses – even if the protectionist tendencies are backfiring on the country concerned. For example, Argentina and Brazil have insisted that foreign companies should be restricted from reinsuring risks. Brazil wants at least 40% of local reinsurance business with its own local companies, which would severely restrict insurance companies based in Brazil with overseas parents from carrying out effective reinsurance business. Foreign insurers are protesting and raising formal objections, as this could be an infringement of WTO agreements.

A similar situation can be seen happening in Ghana, with a recent discovery of oil resulting in significant interest from Western oil companies. To ensure the involvement of Ghanaian people in this bonanza, the government insisted that a significant proportion of employees in foreign-invested organizations should be Ghana nationals. However, the experience of Ghanaians in the oil business is limited, so this requirement could be seen as another tax on doing business in the country, as the time taken to get Ghanaian employees up to speed may mean the hiring of yet more expatriates in the meantime, an added burden to the multinational enterprises concerned.

High unemployment

Despite economic growth, high unemployment can be another country risk – such as that happening in South Africa. Joblessness has increased by 25%, the highest of the 61 countries in Africa. South Africa might have the largest economy in the continent, with 4.4%

economic growth in 2011, but this is not enough to absorb new school leavers hoping to enter the workforce, and very few new jobs are being created.

Dumping is going up in the world

The size and power of China is a risk to the rest of the world in this aspect, so inflation on the increase in China could potentially lead to another global recession. Meanwhile China has often been accused of dumping and unfairly undercutting competitions – and European countries have started to complain that government subsidies are being used to boost sales of Chinese products. For example, China's magazines and catalogues are often printed on especially high quality and expensive paper – which, the EU complains, is supported by the Chinese government in unfair competition against European products. In the past, the EU complained about the Chinese dumping shoes and bicycles. But now, there would seem to be a move up the **value chain**, threatening high-end manufacturing in Europe. This may be seen as increasing the 'China threat' – which was seen as less of a concern when confined to the low-end sector.

Executive lessons on emerging markets

- Businesses in most emerging markets experience a much higher degree of political intervention than in the West, which can include unwelcome regulations – governments must be placated and strong relationships built with politicians (and you have to get it right here) before business can be carried out.
- Western business people must be especially sensitive to governments who feel under attack, even if their paranoia is not

totally justified – keeping your head down as a foreigner may be the best policy.

- The need to understand a country's regulatory environment cannot be over-emphasized, and advice on how to prevent expensive fines and court cases needs to be obtained from official and unofficial sources.
- Many emerging markets expect to be able to buy complicity from their populations, and foreigners must be complicit to be tolerated – as a foreigner you are high profile and under scrutiny, so don't do anything that might put your complicity into doubt.
- It may be that post-Communist societies proclaim a new era of capitalist freedom – but this is not always the case, and you may find that a high level of state control still persists, and may be locally tolerated – under a veneer of apparent capitalist 'progress' or at least heightened consumer activity and consciousness.
- Financial risks are much greater in most of the BRICS outside China, they have worse inflation, which is taking its toll across the world – so you must plan how to cope with the impact on your business of a much higher level of inflation than you may have experienced in the West.
- Banks can be notoriously unreliable in many emerging markets – so you will need to check minimum capital requirements, government guarantees and other measures – although bear in mind who is conducting the stress tests, and their levels of objectivity. Your own banks in the West may not offer role models, either.
- The leaders in some emerging markets are far more wealthy than in many Western countries, and their citizens are much poorer, but this imbalance may be changing, or at least there

(continued)

- is greater awareness on both sides – so there may be a need for greater sensitivity here.
- Your ability to grow a business has a lot to do with the absence or presence of commodities these days – especially petrol – and the weakest countries suffer the most, having to make the difficult choice between exporting for survival or looking after the locals.
- War continues to be a massive country risk, but the liberating influence of the 'Arab Spring' movement shows just how much nations were being ripped off by dictators and the potential of each country for improvement in wealth in the future – even if they are not quite ready yet. Most people are impoverished by war, although some get rich in the process.
- You may think you have set up a successful emerging markets business with a well-connected local partner – but then the regime changes and he or she is now in bad company. Be prepared to go with the flow to distance yourself from would-be dictators who might be unseated in future – flexibility is the name of the game.
- Particular countries pose particular risks to Western businesses – excess profit tax in Venezuela, a lack of purchasing power and high unemployment across much of Africa, the ageing population in China, potential banking failure in Russia, too much bureaucracy in India, the pariah status of Iran, protectionism in much of South America and South Africa, dumping by the Chinese, nationalization by a new leader, and so on.
- If you think you are paying too much tax but might be able to complain and get a refund – you may find you have been rather naive, and this is much more difficult than it would seem.
- Timing can be critical – when an election is being held, it might be a good idea to keep a low profile, or your business

might become ammunition used by one interest group against another.

- Don't assume that a country or region doing well economically will keep going that way and not run out of steam – it happens, and prosperity and stability can be short-lived.

- Don't assume that a country or region that is a basket-case represents the whole country or region – some parts might be OK to do business in.

- Don't put anything negative in writing in cyberspace – as mentioned in Chapter 4, save it for a discreet bar – of course, you might not have the opportunity, as your internet account might be blocked and your BlackBerry hijacked.

- Especially in China, don't loiter around the streets – you might attract attention as being a foreign journalist or some kind of unwanted, subversive activist – and don't think most Chinese are ready to junk Chairman Mao, as they probably aren't.

- China may have a growing middle class and lots of capitalist trappings, but don't publicly doubt the status of any Chinese as no longer being a good Communist.

- China is changing so much that your strategy must keep changing with it – what the Chinese wanted last year may no longer be in fashion, things have moved on.

- Don't spread rumours as they might be believed. In some countries people feel vulnerable and need guidance on how to feel and think – they are looking to people in authority, and if this is weak they are at a loss.

- Don't assume that local businesses want to do business in their own country – getting out and going international might be their top priority, for reasons you may not know about.

(continued)

- Is the country where you are investing free to make up its own mind or is it dominated by another behind the scenes – such as Mongolia by China or Kazakhstan by Russia?
- Advice for Western executives is easy to dole out but difficult to follow in practice – watch out for 'tit-for-tat' activities if your country has criticized another.
- Don't deal with dodgy local companies or you'll be tarred by the same brush and won't be able to deal with respectable local companies – do extensive due diligence enquiries, across a range of sources.
- And this is very scary – do you know what is happening to your investment in a BRIC company? Will anyone tell you before you read it in the newspapers?
- Finally, risk assessment is a number one priority for Westerners doing business across most emerging markets – but they are all risky in different ways.

Country Risk: Workshop Activities

1. Political risk I – Your business

Consider a particular BRICS and beyond country where you are interested in doing business. Compare the level of political intervention with your own home country. In particular, which relationships need to be built with politicians and various government officials before business can be carried out? Which aspects of the country's regulatory environment (especially related to your sector of business) need to be taken into account? Where will you go for advice on how to operate within the law and prevent expensive fines and court cases?

Brief worked example

I'm interested in setting up a recruitment and training business in Shanghai, primarily servicing the expatriate sector but with the possibility of working with local Chinese businesses. I've discovered that the level of political intervention is high in China, in terms of all foreign employees needing a work permit including a medical check. Local employees must have a Shanghai *hukou* or local residence certificate and may not come from other provinces, unless there are special exceptions. It might be easier for us to create this business as a subsidiary of an existing foreign-registered business, rather than starting from scratch. We will have to meet with the foreign ministry, and the ministries for education and employment, and discuss how we can hire local staff, as they must be recruited through a government agency, although this situation may be changing. Through internet sources we can evaluate our competitive environment and make contact with industry groups, such as the British and American Chambers of Commerce, a private group of HR managers, and a trainers' network. They would be a good source of informal advice before going to the expense of hiring consultants and lawyers to set up the business formally.

2. Political risk II – You as an expatriate or on a business trip

Reflect on the differences you have experienced whilst visiting a particular country, especially one traditionally nervous about opening up to foreigners, in terms of the levels of security and local attention given to you as a foreigner. Do you see the locals as basically friendly or hostile? In which situations did you feel comfortable, or insecure? To what extent were the people you met open about telling you about the local business situation, and willing and able to help you?

(continued)

Brief worked example

I was recently on a business trip to Vietnam. The security in Saigon (Ho Chi Minh City) was not very obvious – it is more so in Hanoi, where they are much more concerned about knowing who you are and what you are doing. For example, in Hanoi they didn't allow the hotel guests to use the swimming pool except at narrowly-designated times, but in Saigon they didn't care (maybe the hotel staff members don't want to get into trouble in Hanoi, where it's much stricter). The locals in Saigon were very friendly and are hard-working and entrepreneurial. Their businesses are all very small scale, but because they want you to buy, they're quite friendly. When the locals don't know you, they are a bit wary but when you get to know them, it's easy to chat and they are willing to help. They are much more friendly and helpful to foreigners than the Chinese. The scary part is the hundreds of motorbikes in the streets and the danger of having your bag or case snatched from your hand, or beads or a chain grabbed from your neck (this has happened to me twice). Only close local friends and other foreigners will tell you what is really going on, in terms of the government's level of paranoia and wanting to control everything, and most locals want to tell you what they think you want to hear, or what they think they should tell you, so they tend to be reticent and vague. The locals in Vietnam will never openly criticize their country, covering their embarrassment with nervous laughter. Other expatriates, including other Asians such as Koreans, will give you far more insights.

3. For participants interested in Communist countries, and the post-Communist world such as the former Soviet Union area

Reflect on the balance between so-called 'capitalist' activities and the presence of the state as a means of control in your country of interest. Considering the history of your chosen country – what would appear to be the new direction of the government? Which signs may be apparent to a foreign observer? Is it really 'capitalist' or still Communist?

Brief worked example

I was on a business trip to Romania and noticed that even though it appears very 'Soviet-style' outwardly, the people are anxious for change, and are critical and outspoken – mostly against the government. They suggest that an absence of strong and progressive leadership is one of the main problems, and that Romania has lacked an independent vision and has often chosen the wrong side to align itself with – time and again. Although many of the local people appear to be go-getting and entrepreneurial, and indeed are setting up businesses and looking for opportunities, they are anxious to leave the country and find a new life for themselves – anywhere except Romania. As foreign business people, it might be better for us to use Romania as a source of talent for exporting than to do business in the country itself. The people themselves are potentially able in many areas of business, but they perceive their country negatively, which may be due to a feeling that there is still a hangover from the Communist period.

4. Financial risk

In terms of your chosen country and area of business, look at the possible impact of national inflation levels and currency stability issues, the extent of financial reporting required by the authorities, the ups and downs of different sectors, the possibility of banking failure, the levels of taxation and the local purchasing power and implications of this.

Brief worked example

In looking at doing business in India, the inflation levels are not too bad and much more under control than in South America. For example, the currency in India has not devalued over recent

(continued)

years, but financial reporting there is very onerous and bureaucratic. Retail and consumer-goods companies in India, as in other emerging markets, would seem to be doing better than in the developed world, but energy and industrial businesses are not so good. The trade balance is negative, but nothing like as bad as in developed countries, and the banks are fairly stable and well-supported by the central bank, much better than in Russia, for instance. There is a high level of tax avoidance in India, so the communal facilities are poor, and everyone is trying to look after themself and their family. Purchasing power varies enormously between the cities and the countryside. So, in targeting India for doing business, many Western companies inevitably look at the middle class consumers, more like their segments. The bottom-of-the-pyramid segment, with low margins but big numbers, offers specific business opportunities for telecoms, banking and so on – it depends what business you are in.

5. Commodity risk

In terms of your chosen country and area of business, look at the possible impact of a lack of essential commodities on the way you can manage your business.

Brief worked example
Across Africa, and especially in the poorer countries such as Rwanda, there is an ongoing problem with the shortage of power. We are managing a training business and very often the classroom activities are disrupted by power failures. We have had to make contingency plans to deal with this, basically storing electricity in batteries and power packs when we have power, so that we can run computers and projectors off the batteries when needs be. Everything required for training must be prepared ahead of time or brought in from overseas, as we can never guarantee

availability of power, the internet or photocopy machines and so on. So, the lack of power is a big issue here, which affects many parts of Africa and definitely causes problems in managing your business.

The bandwidth of internet connections can be seen as another commodity – also lacking in Rwanda. Large documents cannot be quickly downloaded, if at all. Using interactive websites is almost impossible. So everything must be prepared in advance and screen-captures made when conducting training courses. This would also impact any business person trying to make a presentation to a potential client, for example.

A lack of commodities in many countries can be a great opportunity for those countries that have them – and especially if they can manage the process of admitting foreign investment and not being politically or economically ruled by them. So, our business supplying mining equipment to Peru is helping the Peruvian economy to expand, whereas in some African countries the Chinese have invested heavily in mines in a dominant way and are becoming increasingly powerful in the local communities.

6. War and peace

Consider the impact of war or uprisings or a high level of continuous conflict on your business in an emerging market.

Brief worked example
We have partners of our consulting businesses in Yemen and Egypt – and both of these countries have been affected by the 'Arab Spring' movement. First of all, the businesses closed down completely – they were both located close to scenes of mass demonstration – we even recognized our office buildings on TV! Then things picked up slowly, and are still way behind previous levels, as the clients are suffering their own uncertainties. The local bosses we worked with in Yemen seemed to be getting richer and more influential as a result of the upheaval, but in Egypt I

(continued)

have heard of a friend running a local operation where the local partner is now out of favour. In fact, their partner was a minister in the Mubarak administration and is now literally behind bars. So, this friend is now negotiating with a new partner prospect, which is proving difficult as most locals are now worried about the future. Business has come to a standstill, there are hiring freezes, and decisions are not being made until a new government is appointed. There is excitement about the future since the revolution, but massive short-term damage to the economy. Tourism is down at least 25%, and many other sectors are negatively affected.

7. Kidnapping and piracy

Is this becoming a real problem or is it mostly the stuff of Hollywood blockbusters? Discuss how a Western business shipping products by sea might be affected, and what might be done about it.

Brief worked example
The popular press has covered attacks by pirates in some detail. The *Sirius Star* is the largest ship to be captured by pirates, at 330 metres in length. It happened in November 2008, 450 miles off Kenya, to a ship bound for the USA. The pirates used ropes tied to grapnel hooks to climb up the hull of a ship as high as Big Ben in London. This was a Saudi oil tanker, carrying crude oil worth $110 million in 2 million barrels. This was such a big prize to be captured that the price of oil immediately jumped $1 a barrel. If your business depends on oil it is bound to impact your bottom line, whether or not you are shipping your own products by sea. This ship itself was worth $100 million. It was taken to Somalia and the ship and twenty-five crew members were eventually freed in January 2009. A ransom of $3 million was paid after some negotiation, as the pirates had originally demanded $25 million. This sounds like big business for pirates, and a big disaster for shipping.

It would seem that speed would help a ship avoid pirates, as fast ships are difficult to catch and board – but this comes at a price in increased fuel consumption. Big ships might be safer, but they must be very big. Pirates can be fended off, as they may not be brave, just greedy and aggressive, so owners and crew must make the attacking of ships scary and dangerous. Even loud noise will raise alarm and make their approach unbearable. Water-flooding is also possible, by pumping a curtain of water to sink pirates' skiffs. Putting barbed wire across the decks is another idea. Locked watertight doors and gated ladders preventing access to the crew who control the ship from inside a 'safe room' can work. But naval forces need to know the rules of engagement – internationally-agreed rules between all nations so they know what they can and cannot do – as pirates being fired upon when they approach a merchant ship can claim they are just innocent fishermen.

8. Demographic risk

How do demographic changes impact on your business? Discuss in relation to a specific example.

Brief worked example
In Ghana, we have a partner in the education business. From our point of view as a European education provider, we are usually interested in post-experience education, such as professional qualifications and MBA degrees, for example. But in Ghana, a very substantial proportion of the population is very young. Around 60% are under twenty-five. They don't want MBAs or ACCAs – they want undergraduate programmes, so this is the bread-and-butter business for our partner. Our higher-level work will not attract such numbers, but all these undergraduate courses are creating a pipeline to lead into the more advanced courses in the future. Pre-MBA courses are popular with the newly-graduated, for example.

(continued)

9. Censorship and information risk and 10. Information and transparency in China

From your experience, ideally from China, provide examples of how this kind of risk can cause problems for a Western business.

Brief worked example
In China, our staff members suffered from a lack of access to their private email accounts, shutting them off from family and friends, and making them feel quite uncomfortable, especially as they were being 'spied on' by domestic staff and landlords when at their homes in the evenings. There was also a feeling that one of the local staff in the office was a 'party stooge', appointed to keep an eye on us. He was always looking through our books and papers, and was in the office late at night and early in the morning, easily able to hack into our computers. He didn't seem to do any work, but we couldn't get rid of him, he came from the government agency that provides all our workers. I suppose it was more of an annoyance than a major problem, but we could have done without it. All these issues certainly made Western staff members unhappy about staying in China for a long time.

11. The grass is greener for Indian companies

From your experience or reading, are Indian companies justified in wanting to leave their own country so often?

Brief worked example
Not all of India is like the picture painted in most of the popular media – there are exceptions, such as in the province of Gujarat, which has recently received press attention. Many observers say that so many things work properly in Gujarat that it hardly feels like India, and many believe this. In factories equipped from Germany and China, high-quality manufactured goods are turned out, having been set up from scratch in only two years, including the normally fraught process of buying land in India. There is constant electricity, gas and abundant water. The state government of

Gujarat is able to keep red tape to a minimum, and does not ask for bribes – which must be quite unusual. A nearby village has satellite dishes on the roofs and power metres on the walls of every house. Gujarat accounts for 5% of India's population but 16% of industrial output and 22% of exports. This sounds very impressive, and a good reason to invest here.

12. More country risks

Include a short discussion of any other country risks experienced in managing your business in an emerging market, and how you coped.

Brief worked examples
I – In our operations in Iran, we had to deal with the issue of the country having the pariah status of being under sanctions, but this worked in our favour, as ours was an Australian business, and they could welcome us with no problems. But we did have the issue of tit-for-tat risks of politics interfering with business, as during the time we were operating in Iran, ships from the British Royal Navy went 'the wrong side' of the Shatt-al-Arab and were impounded. It was, therefore, difficult for our British colleagues to get visas to enter Teheran, and when they got there they may have been under threat. But they still went and were OK, because the local colleagues in Iran did not support their government in this matter and were happy that their British and Australian colleagues were still glad to come.

II – A form of protectionism, which was in effect another country risk and had a negative impact on our business, was in the Arabian Gulf, where all the countries are keen on localizing their workforces. As a result, we had many staff members who were local Gulf Arabs, but many were not especially competent. Yet, we had to hire them and pay them to satisfy government requirements, even if they did very little to help advance the objectives of the organization.

3 Corporate Social Responsibility

Transparency, Ethics and Governance in Emerging Markets

Introduction

Corporate Social Responsibility (CSR) is an issue of growing worldwide concern and adds to risks faced in all business transactions – although it may not be seen in this precise terminology. The damage caused by the many corporate scandals in the West – Watergate, Enron, WorldCom in the USA, Rupert Murdoch and News International, parliamentary expenses in the UK – has been well-publicized, and in many cases perpetrators are brought to justice. Corporate governance and transparency issues have increasingly moved to centre-stage.

CSR abuses and business ethics transgressions in the BRICS and beyond may be more widespread and more tolerated, less obvious and more part of the 'normal' business scene – although the situation is impossible to quantify, especially within local regulatory frameworks and where there are few active and independent journalists. This situation may be changing, with globalization and greater scrutiny of governance matters by investors, yet CSR issues remain one of the greatest concerns and major risks for the Western business person involved in globalizing their operations. Businesses from some Western countries such as the US are particularly anxious to avoid prosecution at home when tempted to be more flexible in the BRICS and beyond, due to the **Foreign Corrupt Practices Act** and other legislation.

Which particular CSR issues are of most interest and importance to Western executives trying to avoid compromise and possible business loss? Corruption, the abuse of human rights, a lack of data protection, financial fraud, **copyright piracy**, low levels of transparency and high levels of **anonymity**, workplace discrimination, oppressive economic colonization, an absence of fair competition, poor levels of corporate governance, no respect for intellectual property, the perpetration of monopolies and the tolerance of leaders of dubious accountability and respectability. The list is endless, and can include local practices unknown to the Western executive – although he or she will have their own personal experiences after first-hand exposure. Many relate to **institutional voids** – a lack of the kind of business infrastructure that Westerners are usually familiar with and expect.

As discussed in the first section of this chapter, corruption is the greatest issue, and may be a way of life in countries with low salaries but powerful officials – and greedy business people – such as in India, in China (the second section), and in many other emerging markets (the third section). The fourth section looks at human rights abuse. This is an ongoing issue, and is seen as especially negative by individualistic and freedom-enjoying Westerners, with their insistence on privacy and data protection issues – especially in China (fifth section). The sixth section considers financial scandals and fraud in Russia. The seventh section takes it further by looking at China and elsewhere – who have been rocking the BRICS and beyond, with billions of dollars simply going missing. The eighth section, 'Copyright piracy', shows that, although this is not unknown in the West, the scale in some BRICS and beyond can be alarming – together with the issue of **transparency** and ease of doing business in entering several emerging economies, often related to governance. The example of Brazil is considered in the ninth section to expand on this.

Prospects of equal opportunities for members of different races are an important issue for countries with a mixed population, such as South Africa – but it would seem, as described in the tenth section, that discrimination is still the norm. The eleventh section explores how economic dominance by China, in many emerging countries, is seen as an example of the economic colonization of one country by another, especially by such a strong anchor economy, raising several CSR issues, including (in the twelfth section) protection or the matter of unfairly excluding competition. The thirteenth section, 'Corporate governance', discusses how the concept used to be a preserve of the West, but is gradually impacting developing countries, especially those trying to attract foreign investment, and is particularly concerned with ensuring independent management control. Intellectual property or IP is another concern (fourteenth section), as are state-endorsed monopolies (fifteenth section). In the final section, how a country, company and individual can become respectable is addressed – especially if they just want to look away, to carry on as before and get away with it. Sometimes the most apparently unreliable leader can gain accolades of respectability and a high level of acceptance in high levels of society, which would seem to endorse his or her behaviour, even if irresponsible and unaccountable.

1. Corruption in India

Corruption in India is arguably out of control, and a main source of risk for Western business seeking to set up there. India is imposing tougher and tougher jail sentences on offenders – the five executives jailed in early 2011 for selling telecoms licences below market prices, for example, were refused bail. These businessmen – from Reliance, Unitech and DB Realty – have already caused damage that cannot be undone.

An estimated $40 billion in revenues was lost from the crooked sale of 2G telecoms licences; and at the same time over $40 billion was stolen in Uttar Pradesh alone from schemes subsidizing food and fuel for the poor. Foreign businessmen are less interested in investment as a result, and rank the problem of graft as their biggest headache behind the poor infrastructure in India. Corruption raises costs not just to Indians, but also to the foreigners whose capital India badly needs, given that India's stock market was the worst performing outside the Muslim world during 2010. But as India is becoming more prosperous, and the faster the economy grows, the more chances arise for theft, bribes and other forms of corruption, so wealth is tending to increase rather than reduce the problem.

Observers of the Indian business scene point to the impact of corruption in the undermining of government and regulatory authority, and the threat to business sentiment – not just among Indian executives but by Western business leaders looking (with reduced enthusiasm) at investment opportunities in the subcontinent. One of these is Telenor, one of the largest telecoms companies in the Nordic region, having just concluded a joint venture with Unitech. Telenor is understandably worried about the outcome, given Unitech's involvement in the problematic sale of telecoms licences.

A second major area of corruption in India is in sport and games, with the chief of the controversial Commonwealth Games of 2010 arrested in a graft probe for allegedly fixing equipment contracts. The games were seen as an opportunity to showcase India as an up-and-coming emerging economic powerhouse – but shoddy and scandal-plagued preparations, cost overruns, delays and constant accusations of corruption instead led to a focus on the country's deficiencies, and put off even more investors.

A large Western firm involved in the Games described a High Court decision, which if upheld would cost his company billions – and the court decision could only be explained by judicial graft. A British media firm, SIS Live, which broadcast the Commonwealth Games from Delhi, was millions of pounds out of pocket because payments due to them were frozen by investigators digging up evidence of corruption at the event. This is all contributing to a lack of business confidence in India. In 2010 the country drew just

$24 billion in FDI, down by nearly a third on the year before, and barely a quarter of China's total. Some observers note that bribes in China at least get a return, unlike in India where crooked officials demand cash but mostly fail to deliver, which makes it worse.

The government of India is seen as not much better in terms of corruption levels, with India's Prime Minister calling for a change of culture of civil servants to prepare India to face the modern era. This is seen as all being part of the reason why India is not expected to achieve double-digit economic growth in its five year plan up to 2017.

Examples of corrupt practices by the authorities include the illegal theft of minerals in the state of Karnataka by the chief minister, who collected corrupt payments of at least $7 million. His connections with mining barons extended to making some of them state ministers. For years, Karnataka's iron ore has been plundered, much of it going to China. Owners of many of these mineral firms made fortunes, not bothering with paying royalties, applying for permits or abiding by safety standards. Some $3.6 billion were lost in potential tax revenues in this district in 2006–10 alone. It was an open secret among locals that illegal miners enjoyed political cover bought with illicit donations, whilst the chief minister claimed ignorance or powerlessness to stop it.

Meanwhile a WikiLeaks revelation described American diplomatic cables including an envoy's account of meeting officials of the ruling Congress party, in which the diplomat said they showed him two chests full of cash to bribe opposition MPs, based on a going rate, not containing but at a going rate of $2.2 million each. Congress members even bragged about how they could even offer opposition MPs jet planes for their votes.

This followed an earlier revelation describing the grilling in parliament of P.J. Thomas, the official appointed to lead India's fight against corruption. The Supreme Court forced him out after allegations of Thomas' own corrupt activities. The government claimed that a vigilance chief need not have an impeccable character, that 'it takes one to know one' – but there was disquiet over Thomas' long-standing charge over an import scam. Thomas pointed out that

28% of sitting lower-house members of parliament were also facing criminal charges or inquiries!

The extent of corruption in India is such that it has become a target for popular discontent, especially with the arrest of Anna Hazare, an elderly activist, at the start of a rally against corruption in Delhi on the grounds that he was violating police orders. Mr Hazare's detention in late 2011 transformed the protest into one about freedom of expression, with thousands taking to the streets in Delhi and elsewhere. When the authorities back-tracked and released Hazare, he went on hunger strike, and has subsequently been joined by others.

Finally, corruption in India is a particular concern in the challenge of doing business there because it is all-pervasive and taken for granted in daily life. India's form of corruption is often on a mundane level, as officials demand bribes even to deliver routine public services. This small-scale graft is seen as especially damaging, as this official extortion erodes the trust of the people in the authorities. A well-known Indian website, ipaidabribe.com, set up last summer by anti-corruption activists, revealed just how grasping officials can be, documenting over 8,500 instances of bribery adding up to nearly 375 million rupees ($8.4 million) in backhanders. These include 100 rupees ($2) to get a policeman to register a complaint about a stolen mobile phone and 500 rupees ($10) for a clerk to hand over a marriage certificate. The site also recorded the payment of 200 rupees ($4) to pass a driving test, 1,000 rupees ($20) to register a baby, and the list goes on. Bangalore's transport commissioner likes this website, as it lets him see how corrupt his junior ministers have become!

2. Corruption in China

Corruption is also widespread in China – and much of it is on the level of individual business dealings. Anecdotal evidence suggests that in agreeing contracts you should watch out for the small print. The Chinese are good at making sure it's in their favour. Western executives with several years of experience on the ground in China attest to an inability to get the upper hand in a negotiation. There are many examples of business deals that turn out to be not quite what the Westerner involved expected – and this often reflects a degree of opportunism bordering on dishonesty. For example, an expatriate contracted Chinese labourers to pave his yard, having bought expensive marble paving slabs. While he was away at his job, the workmen swapped the paving slabs for cheaper ones and laid them quickly so he wouldn't notice.

In another example, a head hunter recruiting Chinese candidates discovered that it often happened that, when a Chinese executive joined a new company, he or she didn't quit their previous job, but took leave from work and then would decide if they liked the new job or not. The company doing the recruiting (often a Western business) thought they had finally got a new person on board, at great cost of time and expense, and having turned away other candidates, just to discover that this 'new hire' was not committed and might leave again after a few weeks to rejoin their old job after their 'vacation'.

A Western purchasing business in China discovered that hiring Chinese to deal with other Chinese did not guarantee a good price, reliability and a way around the intricacies of negotiating with Chinese businesses. Instead, anecdotal evidence in this case suggests that the Chinese employee of the Western firm would side with his fellow countryman to make the best deal for the Chinese side – regardless of the interests of his or her employer. There is a need for Western companies to be cautious when hiring nationals from countries eager to cash in on the benefits of Western technology – without payment and without their knowledge. Where do an employee's loyalties lie? Is it with their country or with their employer? As discussed in Chapter 4, how should a Westerner try to cope with the situation whereby a Chinese employee in an American high-technology defence company is leaking the information of his employer's latest projects to the government of his country? Many Western companies simply don't realize that employees might do this.

3. Corruption worldwide

Corruption is not just confined to the major BRICS – it is a way of life across the emerging markets. Due to their high per capita incomes, many Gulf countries are excluded from the definition of being developing countries, but in many ways business practices here are more similar to those of India or China – especially in terms of 'who you know'. The concept of *wasta* – or nepotism and the use of connections through family and friends – is all-pervasive. A study of recruitment in the banking sector discovered that the vast majority of employees in this prestigious sector knew little about this business but had highly-connected relatives who steered their CVs in the right direction. Applicants were shamelessly asked 'who is your *wasta* person?' The CVs of those without contacts were rapidly binned. A foreign resident of one Gulf country, offering to help first-time visitors, explained how to navigate the visa system as the plane from Europe was landing. 'It's OK', they responded, 'we have an official meeting us', and quickly jumped the queue on arrival. Another foreign resident was working illegally without a work permit for over a year, as his foreign joint-venture employer lacked the *wasta* to fix it. A concerned customer, discovering the problem, put his cousin in the Foreign Affairs Ministry on the case, and the expatriate had his work permit in ten days.

Corruption is a worldwide problem – here we consider further examples from Nigeria, Sierra Leone and Cuba.

In Nigeria, corrupt practices by the political class are widely identified as the main reason for the lack of prosperity. The economy may be growing by 7% a year, but much of this wealth would appear to be enjoyed by government officials. The speaker of the lower house of the government was accused of misappropriating $140 million, whilst about 70% of Nigerians live on less than $2 a day. Meanwhile many apparently senseless restrictions and arcane procedures abound, making it more and more difficult for foreign investors. Procter & Gamble had to shelve a $120 million investment in a factory to make bathroom products because it could not import certain types of specialist paper. An American airline waited a year for officials to sign off on an already agreed route from Atlanta to Lagos.

Sierra Leone, meanwhile, has established the 'Attitudinal and Behavioural Change Secretariat', but embarrassingly the country's Anti-Corruption Commission has indicted several of the secretariat's senior people, accusing them of siphoning off donated funds. WikiLeaks suggested that senior military men here had squandered an aid grant worth $1.9 million from Britain on plasma-screen televisions and hunting rifles. Sierra Leone's budget is a tiny $500 million a year, but its leaders still enjoy rich pickings. An observer remarked that 'if you have been here for some time, you will know that anybody and everybody is stealing everything'.

In Cuba, the management team of Habanos, the state cigar monopoly of the country, are facing trial accused of masterminding graft on a grand scale. The cigar baron in charge of Habanos and his colleagues apparently sold genuine cigars at a fraction of their normal price to black-market distributors in the Caribbean in return for bribes. Up to 45 million cigars may have been sold in this way, in addition to the small-scale peddling of black-market cigars on the streets of Havana itself. A bigger threat is from online cigar retailers, from Switzerland as well as from the Caribbean. This is threatening the lucrative monopoly in Cuba's most famous product on which the prosperity of the country depends – it is well-known that handmade Habanos cigars fetch up to $65 in the St James's district of London. It may be good for customers in the short term, but the income is not being ploughed back into the economy and to pay the workers.

4. Human rights in China – and elsewhere

If India faces the stigma of corruption, for China it is often the issue of human rights that puts off foreign investors and possible business partners – but not necessarily forever, as trying to 'punish' China is sometimes more a case of the 'punisher' becoming more 'punished'. Australia – which was widely seen as benefiting in terms of its bid to gain the 2000 Olympics, when China was in the doghouse over Tiananmen – still plays the human rights card in criticizing China. But China has become Australia's top export market for resources and energy, and China has developed a strong foothold in Australia in the Pilbara mining region. It doesn't pay to be too critical of China, and Australia is not the only country changing tack.

Overall, the USA claims it is still 'disappointed' about China's apparent backsliding on human rights, with the Chinese authorities implementing a severe crackdown on any signs of political dissent accompanying the Arab Spring movement of early 2011. In particular, many Western companies are aggrieved at the treatment of renowned artist Ai Wei Wei – the designer of the famous 'Bird's Nest' Olympic stadium – who was detained at Beijing airport on his way to Hong Kong. But despite this crackdown on dissidents and ongoing criticism from China, the two countries continue to work together to try to maintain mutual economic growth, as the two largest economies in the world.

Human rights violations are one of the most commonly seen CSR issues across many emerging market countries – and not just in China. The diamond trade in Zimbabwe is frequently cited as an example, especially in terms of the 'blood diamonds' trade, supposedly managed by the Kimberly Process, but again up for grabs as diamond sales are opened up. Two Zimbabwean–South African joint ventures, Mbada Diamonds and Marange Resources, resuming their diamond mining and sales, have provoked criticism from NGOs, who have continued to monitor the disputed fields. The NGOs say that human rights abuses are continuing in this profitable business, estimated to be worth $1–2 billion a year. Some previously evicted civilians have been forced back by soldiers to mine the diamonds for low pay, whilst observers claim that most of the proceeds are going into the pockets of army leaders and President Robert Mugabe's ruling Zanu-PF supporters, whilst the Zimbabwean Treasury has seen barely a cent of the income.

Many workers around the world suffer human rights abuses, but have little power – such as domestic workers or 'maids', many of whom come from the Philippines, Sri Lanka, Indonesia and other Asian emerging market countries. Around 50–100 million domestic workers, mostly women, make a big contribution to their local economies. Working mainly in the Middle East and Asia, their wages often go unpaid, they are rarely granted any time off, and many face physical and sexual abuse. One of the most encouraging local changes is the emergence of many Facebook groups and blogs, such as Migrant Rights, that talk about abuse openly. These websites show that younger people in the Middle East and Asia are increasingly embarrassed about the exploitation of expatriate workers in their countries.

However, human rights workers – and others who are trying to right wrongs – must themselves be seen to be above board in every way. In Argentina, a once-revered human rights group has run into a controversy. The group – of women – was set up in order to learn what had happened to their disappeared children during the country's 1976–83 military dictatorship. But the group's social work arm, aiming to build houses for the poor, is now being investigated after allegations of fraud, money-laundering and illegal enrichment, having allegedly misused an estimated $45 million of public funds.

5. Privacy – another human right

Meanwhile, in India – like in China – the government is also interested in what's going on within the population, and does not want big surprises. The Indian subcontinent has joined the ranks of countries able to intercept the emails and cyber-chats of its citizens, and has created a centralized monitoring system in thirty locations – but why does it need to do this? What are the ethical implications for Western businesses setting up here? This issue is also discussed in the first chapter as a country risk matter.

Expatriates in China, especially in the early days of the 1990s, became used to being spied on by domestic helpers (it was mandatory to hire one) and hearing a knock on the door late at night or early in the morning. Chinese officials spying on a European Union embassy worker would freely let themselves into her apartment, and in the course of their 'duties' would watch her TV and smoke, leaving the TV tuned to a Chinese channel and cigarette butts in her flower vases. When having friends to visit, she would switch languages during conversations to annoy the Chinese officials bugging her apartment, who would struggle with English and be unprepared for German, Italian and French.

A lack of trust of politicians is endemic among BRICS and beyond, which undermines the economy and business, especially with the West – and as a result their privacy is being exposed. Turkish sex scandals have significantly compromised local politicians. A series of revealing rather than compromised videos posted online has forced the resignation of ten senior members of the far-right Nationalist Action Party. This has pushed this party under the threshold of 10% of the votes needed to win seats in parliament, and has allowed Prime Minister Recep Tayyip Erdogan to write a new constitution tailored to enhance his presidential ambitions. The invasion of their privacy has, thus, been used by the ruling party. Sexual politics is nothing new in Turkish politics. In the process, at least 3,000 senior people in Turkey were wiretapped, and the government has apparently done nothing to stop it.

So, privacy may be seen as another human rights issue. Wiretapping is much criticized in the West, but is seen as a legitimate way of exposing wrongdoing in many countries – but what is the definition of 'wrongdoing'?

6. Financial scandals in Russia

If India = corruption, China = human rights abuses, then Russia = inefficiency, lack of justice, fraud and especially financial wheeler-dealing and scandals. This is seen particularly in the sale of a

Moscow bank by the municipal government, when more than $3.7 billion in revenues from the proceeds went missing. No-one noticed for over two months, and the amount did not appear in the city's budget records. The former CEO of the bank – it was the fifth largest in Moscow – blew the whistle on the loss of the funds, but they were not recovered.

The non-existence of justice in Russia, with a negative effect on business, is seen as evidence that the political system is held together by corruption and the rule of politics over law. Observers feel that political leaders have to decide what they care about more – the rule of law or the opportunity for extrajudicial reprisals, as seen in the case of Mikhail Khodorkovsky, the jailed business tycoon. His oil company Yukos was dismantled, and he has already spent eight years in jail for underpaying tax on sales of oil – and now another five years for apparently stealing the same oil.

7. Financial scandals in China – and elsewhere

China's financial scandals can negatively affect business – but are almost taken for granted in the country's private sector, and have not received much attention until recent times. They would seem to have a limited impact on the markets unless the government is involved. In 2011, their exposure by self-appointed foreign watchdog Muddy Waters is bringing these issues to the fore, much to the interest and value of Western observers.

Many Chinese companies, whose shares have collapsed on foreign markets amid allegations of deceptive accounting, have been exposed by this watchdog. For example, Sino-Forest, a forestry firm listed in Canada, saw their shares slump to only 10% of their original value after the watchdog questioned its accounts. The study found that companies caught up in accounting scandals saw their shares drop by an average of around 10%. Those involving the bribery of government officials or theft of state assets suffered bigger problems, where their stock fell by almost a third. Sino-Forest was particularly hard hit. Clearly, the value of a company in developing markets is tied more tightly to its relationship with the government than with its investors.

The watchdog concerned, Muddy Waters, apparently released a report accusing Sino-Forest of overstating its timber holdings. Spooked investors sold their stock, which plunged 78% in a matter of days. It was commented of the Muddy Waters' founder by close observers that 'it's not that people concluded he's right about these companies. It's that they realized they don't know whether he's right or not'. Muddy Waters' work has sounded an alarm-bell for investors in Chinese companies. Including Sino-Forest, Muddy Waters has released reports on five firms. In each case the company's stock sank, and in some cases, like China Media Express Holdings, which sells advertising on Chinese buses, the companies were delisted after the revelations.

Sino-Forest is not the only firm under the spotlight. Similar charges like those of Muddy Waters have been laid in the past against Chinese firms listed in America and Singapore. If concerns are rife in places where there is lots of scrutiny, how bad might things be in Hong Kong, the largest market for overseas Chinese listings? Many Chinese firms have used 'reverse mergers', in which a private company goes public by combining with a listed shell company, to float in America. That allows firms to avoid some of the scrutiny that comes with an initial public offering. But in the meantime, doubts over how to separate bad from good hurt everyone, the blameless and the scammers.

Meanwhile, the Western press is avidly warning readers of what they see as more proven scams across business sectors in China, especially in the flourishing ecommerce sector. For example, Alibaba's chief executive and chief operating officer both resigned after taking responsibility for a scandal at this Chinese ecommerce website, in which some 2,300 online dealers conned their customers. The sellers had used fake documents to set up their businesses on the site, allegedly with the help of a small number of Alibaba staff. At least

56 million people use its business-to-business website, and 370 million use Taobao, its online mall. Alibaba admitted that it had granted 'gold' status (a mark of supposed integrity) to 2,236 dealers who subsequently defrauded buyers. Apparently, about 100 sales staff and several supervisors and sales managers were directly responsible for either intentionally or negligently allowing the supposed fraudsters to evade various controls. To deal with this, Alibaba has set up a compensation fund, which has so far paid out $1.7 million to 2,249 buyers. More claims are expected. The damage to Alibaba's reputation as a place to find reliable Chinese suppliers and buyers has inevitably been compromised – shares dropped nearly 15% on the news.

Meanwhile, Russia – mentioned above – is not the only country unable to account for massive bank losses. Cover-ups are rife in many emerging markets. For instance, a bank scandal in Afghanistan left two enormous holes in the ground in Dubai, which were to have been the foundations for a pair of twenty-floor towers of luxury flats. They were being funded by $40 million belonging to depositors with accounts at Kabul Bank; Afghanistan's central bank spent $820 million of its reserves bailing out Kabul Bank. In total, close to $1 billion is missing, due to a binge of interest-free and mostly illegal insider lending to shareholders, in the context of an official GDP of just $12 billion a year.

The IMF is now taking a tough line in many of these countries, which has dramatically slowed the flow of donor funds on which the Afghan government depends. Most foreign experts agree that retrieving even half of the lost money would be an achievement. Just $61 million has been recovered so far, a relatively tiny amount.

Money often goes missing in emerging markets. Payments are received in aid donations and are expected to be utilized for a prescribed purpose, such as training and capacity-building – but this doesn't always happen according to plan. As in the case of the World Bank putting funds into relatively poor African countries, often to deliver skill-building courses, cash often goes astray. In one case, funds intended to train managers in procurement, and financial

and human resource management, were 'spent' on hiring a business school – but the training provider never received the payment.
Meanwhile, the director of the local training institute is languishing
in jail for misappropriation of funds.

8. Copyright piracy

Another example of the CSR-related challenges particularly affecting
Russia – one of the most controversial of the BRICS and beyond – has
impacted mail.ru, the country's largest internet company. Investing in
Groupon and Zynga in the US, mail.ru holds a 2.3% Facebook stake,
valued at $1.5 billion. When mail.ru listed on the London Stock
Exchange it raised $1 billion, and overall is valued at $5.7 billion.
Meanwhile, the group recently declared that media companies in
Russia will have a hard time charging for online content because of ram-
pant piracy. So this kind of business might be a bubble about to burst,
and it can be difficult to discern a sustainable business model here.

India, Russia and China all came up on the list of the world's worst
copyright pirates, according to a copyright theft list researched and
maintained by the US. It has been suggested that in some countries,
copyright piracy is almost institutionalized – the authorities take
it for granted. In China, the film industry is booming – with box
office revenues of over 10 billion yuan on over 500 films a year, as
many as in the USA. But observers note that such films are profitable partly because their stars do not expect to be paid much, if anything. Compensation for some films amounted to less than the cost
of lunch boxes for the crew. The easy money is in patriotic movies,
widely distributed in China. To the Chinese, copyright piracy is not
necessarily the CSR issue that the West sees it as, but it should certainly be seen as a country risk issue. Tickets to Chinese cinemas are
expensive – about 80 yuan at weekends. The lack of copyright
protection means that almost all revenue must come from the box
office rather than DVDs or television. Audiences are paying for

the experience of an afternoon away from their cramped apartments rather than simply to see the film (illegal versions of which are widely available). Cinemas are clean and air-conditioned. Many have state-of the-art screens, sound systems and snacks.

9. Brazil – not poor anymore? How do we know?

The EU has voted to rescind trade benefits to several developing countries, such as Brazil, on the grounds that they have become too wealthy and no longer need preferential treatment to one of the world's largest markets. But how do we know? Brazil might like to see itself as still poor when it comes to gaining preferential treatment. How can we define which countries still deserve this special arrangement when the official reports and accounts of many companies are suspect or simply unpublished? The lack of transparency in Brazil's corporate sector casts some doubts.

Brazil might be one of the most progressive and dynamic of the BRICS and is trying to be more transparent to attract more foreign trade, but political leaders are finding that the price of trying to clean up politics involves foregoing reforms the country needs. New leaders soon find themselves sucked into the capital's political swamp. Attempts to deal with corruption and fill senior government jobs on merit rather than through political connections are not always successful. The president's chief of staff faced allegations of influence peddling; a magazine published evidence of systematic overbilling on contracts at the transport ministry; and police arrested more than thirty officials in the tourism ministry on suspicion of stealing public money intended for training hotel staff ahead of the 2014 football World Cup. Meanwhile, the difficulty of managing Congress seems to have persuaded the president to try to do without any big legislative reforms for the immediate future. Similar scenarios are happening across South America, such as in Chile, Argentina and Peru – the ongoing battle between politics and economic growth.

10. Attempts to create equal opportunities in South Africa

Positive discrimination may also be seen as a CSR and ethics issue. The Black Empowerment scheme and the promotion of affirmative action in South Africa can have the reverse effect. South Africa is still widely seen as one of the most unequal countries in the world. Affirmative action programmes seem to have largely failed. Instead of redistributing wealth and job positions to the black majority, it would seem that a few individuals have benefited more than others. The leadership of most large companies is still dominated by whites. The black masses, the intended beneficiaries of Black Empowerment, have hardly gained, despite the scheme. The richest 4% of South Africans – a quarter of whom are black – now earn more than $80,000, a hundred times what most of their compatriots live on. Whites still hold three-quarters of the senior jobs in private business. Of 295 companies on the Johannesburg stock exchange, only 4% of the CEOs are black. Meanwhile, many whites complain that incompetent blacks are being promoted beyond their ability. This apparent failure of equal opportunities is seen as harming blacks by discouraging self-reliance and an entrepreneurial spirit; instead, it is seen as fostering a sense of entitlement. The government of South Africa has tried to give preference to companies employing blacks as part of the criteria for the award of contracts, but it would seem this has only happened in times of economic strength, and has not survived the economic downturn.

11. The economic dominance of China – the new colonialism

In many Western economies, the economic development of China and its ability to flex its economic muscles overseas is widely resented and criticized – especially in the US. Similar feelings are being expressed – often in more violent ways – in several emerging market countries, especially those who value their precious independence. This has often been more scary for many observers than old-style Western imperialism.

For example, Kazakhstan has fairly recently freed itself from the constraints of the former Soviet Union and is feeling its way to becoming increasingly independent, although still with a substantial presence of its former overlord. This may be one of the reasons for complaints against growing business ties with China. Azat All National Democratic Party, a leading opposition group, called for street demonstrations in response to the growing influence of Chinese companies, especially in the oil and metals sectors. Public protests are not normally allowed in Kazakhstan, but this issue would seem to be of major concern, with ethical implications of the dominance of one country over another in a quasi-colonial way.

As a further example, China's oil trade with Africa is dominated by a Chinese business syndicate of which little is known. Ordinary Africans appear to do badly out of its deals. Angola – along with Saudi Arabia – is China's largest oil supplier, and China's top deal-maker here is a partner in a syndicate founded by well-connected Cantonese entrepreneurs. These Chinese business people, with their African partners, have taken control of one of China's most important trade channels, having signed contracts worth billions of dollars for oil, minerals and diamonds from Africa. These deals are mostly secret, but seem to be depriving some of the world's poorest people of desperately needed wealth, in a negative neo-colonial way.

Economic colonization of developing countries by Western multinationals was much criticized in the nineteenth century, but in some ways it still continues. Ghana is one of the world's largest producers of cocoa, but it would seem that most of this output is bought up by Swiss multinational Nestlé. Anecdotal evidence suggests that attempts to purchase prepared cocoa – to make a hot drink, for example – without buying a Nestlé product, can be in vain, even in Ghana itself. Foreign visitors trying to take home 'Made in Ghana' souvenir products may find plenty of Ghana-produced items – but all with Nestlé branding. So why can't Ghana make the increased revenues associated with producing branded goods? To what extent will this situation be tolerated for the foreseeable future? And would an alternative be in international interests?

The investments of many China-based interests in Laos are another case in point. At home and abroad, China is a byword for fast-track development, where yesterday's paddy field is tomorrow's factory, highway or hotel. Less noticed is that such development can just as quickly go into reverse. A thirty-year renewable lease between China and the Lao government in 2003 to set up a 1,640 hectare special economic zone resulted in thousands of Chinese tourists and entrepreneurs pouring into the enclave, drawn largely by the forbidden pleasures and profits of gambling. But the main casino in Laos lies abandoned, mainly because Chinese gamblers found that the operators refused to let them leave until they had paid their betting losses. There are even cases of gamblers being murdered and their corpses dumped in a local river.

12. Protection or unfairly excluding competition?

Can protection by governments of their domestic production be seen as a CSR issue? As we have seen in our discussion of strategy and operations, telecoms operators in India *must* buy 80% of their network equipment from manufacturers in India. The ethical dilemma here might be seen as a trade-off between the benefits of providing a steady stream of business for local factories, employing local people and encouraging local economic growth – and forcing the customers to buy overpriced, poor quality products when they could buy better and cheaper in the global market. Will it really help India in the long term? And Western executives looking to penetrate this market can only penetrate 20% of it, which may not be such an interesting or profitable proposition.

A similar issue might be Ghana's insistence that foreign oil and gas companies entering Ghana's newly-explored fields must employ a substantial proportion of Ghanaians – but what if they are not competent and unskilled? It may be seen as an extra cost of doing business, and will just be offset by hiring more expatriates.

Meanwhile, many observers are expecting a continuing backlash against Chinese investors in under-developed countries. Africa now supplies 35% of China's oil. Two-way trade grew by 39% in 2010, when many African leaders were willing to make deals with Chinese business interests, especially when offered vast loans for infrastructure projects. But it would seem that the honeymoon is coming to an end, with Africans complaining that Chinese companies destroy much of the local environment – including national parks – in their hunt for resources, and that they routinely disobey even rudimentary safety rules. Workers are killed in almost daily accidents and roads and hospitals built by the Chinese are often faulty, not least because they bribe local officials and inspectors.

Although China has boosted employment in Africa and made basic goods like shoes and radios more affordable – and despite the fact that without the Chinese, unemployment in parts of South Africa would be even higher than the current 60% – there is widespread criticism of China in Africa. Much of this criticism is probably disguised protectionism. Established businesses are trying to maintain their privileged positions – at the expense of the consumers. For example, Chinese traders in Soweto market in Lusaka halved the cost of chicken; cabbage prices dropped by 65%; but, 'how dare the Chinese disturb our market?' complained an African market seller. As a result, the government of Tanzania has banned Chinese from selling in its local markets, saying that they were welcome as investors but not as market vendors or shoe-shines.

13. Corporate governance

As a matter of increasing importance in many Western companies, many businesses are feeling under pressure to appear to be more transparent and accountable to their shareholders, and more co-operative with governments, anxious to avoid Enron-type debacles in the future. Succession planning, the appointment of independent board members, transparent and accountable control functions, fair compensation and promotion policies, meritocratic-based recruitment, a focus on corporate values and a long-term view of the organization's role in the community – these issues are under the spotlight for most Western businesses.

The concept of governance is new for many emerging market companies, but not unknown. For example, the pressure is on Mehmet Emin Karamehmet, the founder of Turkcell and one of Turkey's most powerful businessmen, to allow a wider influence in the operations of the business and, therefore, more independent control functions. Mehmet's company owns only 13% of the shares, but dominates the daily running of the company through a complex ownership structure that no-one seems to clearly understand. Altimo telecoms of Russia – who are outside investors in the business – are trying to elbow Mehmet aside, in order to find out what is going on. Any other investors in this kind of scenario, especially from more mature economies, would be most uncomfortable if the control of daily operations seemed to be too centralized and not reflecting the actual ownership of the business. Corporate governance in emerging markets can be entirely different from that taken for granted in the West.

Many countries facing high fuel prices are trying to cut inflation to appease consumers. For this reason, Petrobras of Brazil is under pressure to cut fuel prices by 10% – and is also being investigated by anti-trust authorities accusing the company of abusing its dominant market position. Fair competition is often seen as a governance issue, especially in terms of having a long-term orientation and transparent risk assessment for all stakeholders.

Another corporate governance concern is the 'say on pay', banker-bashing and the extra-generous rewarding of chief executives for long-term performance without considering the business context. The variance between the chief executive's pay and that of other executives has grown dramatically. The dilution of other shareholders' holdings by awards of shares to executives has increased. And retirement benefits have become even more excessive in some cases. Many poor governance practices are being highlighted in the West, and the same is happening among several corporate entities in many BRICS and beyond – except in most cases we as Western business executives don't know about it yet, and find such insights hard to come by.

14. IP – especially in China

Within the context of IP, what about the issue of suing another company in a commercial intellectual property dispute? The decision of Chinese telecoms giant Huawei to call a truce with American counterpart Motorola – both companies tried to bring lawsuits against each other – seems to have been a pragmatic and opportunistic way to avoid future damage and trouble. Although Huawei might have really believed that the Nokia Siemens Networks' acquisition of Motorola wireless assets was out of order, it suited them *not* to stir up trouble unnecessarily. Huawei knows that the US is uncomfortable with the fact that the founder of Huawei was formerly a People's Liberation Army officer. After much counter productive criticism on both sides, Huawei and Motorola temporarily called off their on going battle, realizing that although they dislike each other, they perhaps need each other.

This can be seen as another reason why Huawei decided to publish a list of its board of directors in an effort to appear more transparent, featuring names, pictures and biographies. For the Western executive negotiating in China, bearing in mind that Chinese businesses are now becoming conscious of how they appear to the West, this could create effective bargaining tools. Many companies are considering the need to improve their corporate governance practices – even if mostly they are just paying lip-service to the idea.

The relationship between China and the US constantly raises CSR-related issues, especially as a result of the opportunistic nature of their relationship – politicians talk about sovereignty and transparency, business people discuss pragmatic company dealings. Despite their reservations about each other, China and the US maintain talks about economic co-operation. The Chinese are interested in sensitive US technology, and meanwhile have pledged to fulfil contracts for the Americans without using the knowledge they gain in the process to improve their domestic technology base. Basically, the Chinese are promising the Americans that they will not take advantage of their technology for their own benefits, and that China will show more respect for IP. There might still be some suspicion of the ultimate Chinese agenda but it can be hard for the Americans to ignore the Chinese contribution, given their own economic uncertainty.

15. Monopolies

Does one country have a right to monopolize supplies of rare but vital commodities? How could these be shared equitably? For example, the US wants to access more production of 'rare earth' or vital metals needed for essential manufacturing, but China controls 97% of the supply and has stopped exports in order to fulfil her internal needs. So the US, to hedge bets against a lack of supply from China, is encouraging the Maycorp minerals company in Colorado – with a mine in California – to go into full production, as one of only two such mines outside of China. China's stand on putting itself first might be encouraging other countries to be more self-sufficient, but this may not be an efficient and economic approach to developing raw material supplies.

Monopolies are not just in manufacturing and utilities, and the 'monopolist' label can be used to attack competitors – such as criticism of the country's biggest search engine by China's main state broadcaster CCTV, who alleged that it is easy to commit fraud through its website. It described Baidu, which has around 75% of the market for internet searches in China, as a 'monopolist' that abuses its power. Observers noted that CCTV has just launched its own search engine. In the same context, should BP always gain approval to purchase oilfields wherever it wants, to ensure continuous supplies and perhaps ramp up prices? What is behind the purchase of ten exploratory and production blocks in Brazil? Could the Brazilians not develop these by themselves?

Even if a business seems to favour free competition, the reality may be less transparent than it may appear. For example, in many Gulf countries, services and manufactures in supplies to Iraq are commonly provided and sought after by various military forces. Usually, they have instructions to gather at least three bids – but may not realize that Ahmed, Mohamed and Ali are all friends and take it in turns to win bids by manipulating the offers to make sure that one of them is sure to win each time.

Some governments try to stop monopolies, but sometimes the monopolists still feel it's worth their while just to carry on. Telcel, which has 70% of Mexico's mobile-phone market and is controlled by Carlos Slim, the world's richest man, is accused of abusing its dominant position by charging competing networks sky-high connection fees, 44% higher than the average in the OECD. But this is despite a billion dollar fine from a 2006 law. Telcel is to be charged up to 10% of their assets, but enforcement remains a problem. Mr Slim's lawyers could stall payment of Telcel's fine by a decade or more. To fund these costs, excessive connection fees have cost mobile-phone customers $6 billion a year, most of which has gone into the pockets of the telephone companies. Suddenly Telcel's $1 billion fine doesn't look such a disincentive.

16. Gaining respectability

Western countries are hiring BRICS suppliers – and at the same time giving them opportunities to do business, which are empowering these BRICS businesses more and more. For example, China's Huawei has become extremely successful in telecoms infrastructure supply around the world, enough to dictate terms to the West – such as the row with Motorola discussed above. Huawei's business in the UK – also considered in our view on strategic alliances – has given the controversial Chinese government-backed company added respectability. It is already admired for its cheapness and efficiency – but what long-term price will be paid for overlooking Huawei's many CSR and especially governance issues?

Respectability has always been for sale, and it can also be on an individual – not just company – basis. Imagine a business or political leader from an unpopular country, which could be an oil-rich enclave within the Middle East or a former Communist territory. If this leader would like to shop, invest, socialize and study in the richest and most popular parts of the world (and flee there if necessary) – how will this be done? This leader may not deserve it and has not earned it, and may not stop conducting a variety of ethically questionable practices to obtain this access. These are ways of 'legalizing' money laundering, sponsoring the arts and various charities, educating children at the most expensive smart schools, entertaining royalty, investing in props such as yachts and private jets (ideally captained by distinguished and upper-class ex-Royal Navy and Royal Air Force officers from the UK) and purchasing racehorses, ski chalets and mansions. Further respectability-enhancing moves include sponsoring chairs at prestigious universities, gaining honorary doctorates, making friends in the media and – after much respectability has been gained – developing relationships with politicians, especially when there is a need to defend this status.

Executive lessons on emerging markets

- Ethical standards are very different in the BRICS and beyond – what might be seen as fairly acceptable in these countries may be quite shocking to a Western executive – you may not even imagine what is happening in countries in which you are seeking to do business – so keep an open mind!

- Corruption can take many forms and governments through-out the BRICS (especially in India) are trying to crack down – but the Western executive should still expect the unexpected, and you may encounter a mind-boggling prevalence of corruption everywhere.
- Teamwork and loyalty are areas of concern when hiring employees and working with suppliers and customers from the BRICS (especially in China) – you must always ask: whose side are they on?
- Don't think of taking a stand on perceived human rights abuses in the BRICS and beyond – you may be reflecting a judgement that might be inappropriate in some contexts – 'freedom' is what a Westerner thinks it is, but the definition might be very different in other countries.
- If your privacy is invaded – your emails are read and your phone is tapped as a Western executive when working in emerging markets – and the contents get you into trouble, this is your problem more than theirs. Keep the discussion of contentious issues to smoky bars or walking down the street. Don't name names and don't write anything down. Westerners are often seen as potential trouble in the BRICS and beyond, which often have enough manpower – and the technology – to keep an eye on you.
- 'Show me the money' is a popular phrase from the movies but it could be valuable for the Western executive too – because sometimes the money involved *was* there but is no longer *actually* there, as vast tracts of it have gone missing and services used (such as those provided by you) may not receive payment.
- Colonialism is not dead, it just takes different forms now, and it can have a lot to do with ensuring the supply of vital raw materials for the future – so the newest imperial battles are about vital commodities, and the West may not have the

(continued)

pulling power of China, especially looking to the wealth of Africa. This is what you may be up against.

- Don't take all the complaints against China in Africa (and elsewhere) at face value – the Africans may not be ready for the level of competition this means, and are trying to protect their own inefficient businesses at the expense of the consumers, often seen as being at the bottom of the pile.

- Corporate governance is not necessarily widely understood in the BRICS and beyond – and the pressures for adopting transparency and CSR may be reduced as attracting Western investment is becoming less of a viable option in the worldwide recession – so the efforts of the past may be being suspended.

- Intellectual property is another fairly alien concept, so for the Western executive you are probably only as good as your latest idea – the previous one may have been copied and stolen already and there is nothing you can do about it.

- Compromise is unfortunately – but realistically – the name of the game in CSR and ethics between the West and the BRICS and beyond – or at least flexibility. It depends on how often you can afford to say no.

- Monopolies are not necessarily seen as negative in emerging markets, where business people will happily go on enjoying them as long as they last – all is fair in love and war and business – and may be supported by governments, or the fines are not high enough to really deter active monopolists.

- Monopolies and duopolies may exist under the surface, so beware of the chance that your 'impartial' and 'independent' bidders are all colluding behind the scenes.

- Gaining respectability is often a major ambition for a BRICS and beyond country, company and business person, and this may be an attractive perceived outcome from dealing with a Western executive – so high ethical standards must always be the starting point, even if the resort to flexibility occurs later.

CSR, Transparency and Ethics: Workshop Activities

1., 2. and 3. Corruption

Consider a situation where corruption in an emerging market country caused problems for your business, and how you were able to manage the situation.

Brief worked example
A firm I know well had made an acquisition in the hotel business in Egypt, and had hired a project manager from the head office in Europe to manage the refurbishment process. When he arrived and started asking for bids from suppliers, it became clear that the existing managers in the hotel had 'favourite' suppliers who provided services and who had, over the years, paid substantial bribes to these hotel managers. Then the suppliers felt free to supply shoddy goods and to miss delivery deadlines. The foreign project manager insisted on researching and recruiting his own suppliers, requesting competitive bids in each case, looking at the market with 'no baggage'. Suppliers who suggested that there would be 'something in it for him personally' were told that they were no longer being considered in the bidding process. Word quickly got around that this foreign project manager was not accepting bribes and was now personally reviewing all the suppliers. He was able to complete the refurbishment on time and stick to the budget, as these suppliers had been adding the kickbacks to the bills to the hotel. The situation reverted to the way it had operated before on the project manager's departure, but at least he had shown that it was possible to overcome corruption in this case.

4. Human rights abuses

Explain, with examples, how this issue can have a negative or potentially negative effect on your business in one of the BRICS and beyond countries.

(continued)

Brief worked examples

I – When we were working as journalists in a Hong Kong-based publishing group, we were horrified when one of our fellow journalists was imprisoned in China. We took to the streets of Hong Kong with banners and were shouting slogans about freedom of the press and human rights, and our demonstration was reported in the local press. I was rather shocked to discover my photograph carrying the banner emblazoned on the front page of the *South China Morning News*. Every week or so I was travelling on business to mainland China to launch the Chinese language edition of our magazine, and what if I was refused a visa on the grounds of being a human-rights activist? So I decided the time had come to make a choice here. Although many foreigners feel strongly about these perceived abuses, making a stand can put your organization on a collision course with the authorities, which can jeopardize future business deals.

II – I was consulting to a foreign-owned tea company in India, helping them with PR work, and they had a problem of being accused of human rights abuses towards their thousands of tea pluckers. The company was actually trying to be very kind to them, offering fairly generous wages, quite good living conditions, healthcare and long-term security of employment. However, we had to be very careful in the pictures we published of them, so they didn't look starved, or they weren't carrying baskets of tea leaves that looked too heavy, or that their babies clinging to them didn't look neglected or undernourished. There were plenty of tea companies abusing their pluckers, but we didn't want to be one of them and attract negative publicity. Because of the Western perception of human rights problems on tea gardens in India, and the fairly common incidence of neglect, underpay and excessive working hours among locally-owned tea companies, we had to be especially careful, so all the published materials were very carefully scrutinized, and we encouraged external visitors, and even invited journalists to visit us.

5. Privacy

How can different concepts of privacy impact on Westerners doing business in emerging markets?

Brief worked example
When I was working in Kuwait, the boss asked to see the bank account statements of all the staff members. The practice in Kuwait was that your employer would 'sponsor' you to come to Kuwait, obtain your work permit and pay your salary and expenses, so any kind of 'moonlighting' was regarded as illegal by the Kuwaiti employers, although I'm not sure that this was actually prohibited in the labour law. However, as teachers and researchers we were used to doing extra teaching on the side, carrying out consulting work for companies and writing articles, which may or may not receive payment. The African and Indian staff members were intimidated into showing their bank statements to the boss, but the Westerners completely refused to do so, even though we actually didn't have anything to hide. I was invited to give the keynote speech at a prestigious local conference, which was beneficial to the institution where I worked, and I was certainly not being paid for this, but the boss saw it as 'moonlighting' and totally forbade me to accept the offer. The boss refused to believe I wasn't being paid, so to prevent further problems I didn't go to the conference. We were paid into the Bank of Kuwait, and I guess the boss could have looked at our bank account details anyway, as the owner of the institution was also a shareholder of the bank! The Western staff members felt very uncomfortable.

6. and 7. Financial scandals and fraud

Consider emerging market examples within your experience of financial fraud, where funds went missing, and how this situation was resolved.

(continued)

Brief worked examples

I – When I was managing a training business in China, where the participants paid in cash on the day of the event, we had to hand-carry the cash from the training venue – usually a hotel ballroom, because these were big events – back to our office. The particular staff member entrusted with this job – the first time it wasn't me as the only expatriate – ran off with the money, and we never saw her again. It was equal to about five years' salary for her. That was the last time we ever allowed local staff to handle cash, the only way we were able to resolve the matter was to remove the temptation – and I had to hand-carry the cash every time.

II – At a college in Europe focusing on providing courses for executives from emerging markets – mostly from Africa – the participants hacked into the college phone system, running up the most enormous phone bills. All the college could do was to create further controls and keep changing the passwords.

8. and 14. Copyright piracy and IP abuse

This can be quite commonplace in some BRICS and beyond countries. In what ways can this be a problem for a Western business? What strategies can be used to minimize the losses incurred as a result?

Brief worked example

The textbook publishing industry is prone to the practice of the ripping off of books and training materials – mostly by photocopying. Many of the textbooks are big, glossy, expensive American productions, and can be photocopied for a small fraction of the cover price. The publishers are, thus, being defrauded, and students in countries with soft currencies – most of the emerging market countries – argue that they can't buy textbooks because the websites won't deliver to their countries and won't accept their non-convertible money. However, close investigation suggests that many of these students do have hard-currency credit cards and dollars, although they are careful how they spend them.

The creation of a textbook series at a cheap price – on a par with or below that of photocopying a book – might still attract illegal copying, but is much more affordable. As educational institutions spread into emerging markets to offset reduced student numbers at home, this policy also enables them to provide more targeted materials. However, sometimes this runs into trouble as the textbooks can be holed up at customs – as they were in Peru – pending payment of customs duties seen as unacceptably high by the local purchaser. During this time the course was completed without them, so the students no longer wanted to buy them!

9. Poor or wealthy? How do we know?

This lack of certainty of financial stability and the availability of assets, and the details of who is in charge or not, can occur not only in a country but in the official reporting of a business. It does mean that a Western business does not have a clear view of what is going on, and can naively lose out on a deal. Can you think of examples?

Brief worked examples
I – In Abu Dhabi, we were working on the recruitment of a CEO for a high technology centre. He said it had very little money and, therefore, the salary would be very low, so the person recruited would need to have a sort of philanthropic attitude. The existing CEO was also running another organization, and he said he wanted to find a suitable person who could take over this part of his work, to run the centre so he could focus on the other organization. Really, unknown to us, he was using us to argue that it was impossible to find anyone suitable, and he just had to do both jobs, and terminate the search – getting free research from us in the process. In reality the centre was very profitable and he was getting a huge salary, which he intended to keep! So every candidate we presented (and this was a difficult

(continued)

search) was turned down, and he refused to pay our bills, using the excuse of the centre having no money! A foreign insider in his organization finally explained this to us, so it was a big waste of time and effort. This is not easy to prevent, besides stopping doing business altogether in these countries. It is impossible to find the real information, especially at first.

II – In Kazakhstan, our partner had apparently decided they didn't want to work with us anymore. They said they couldn't get any more customers and told us they were terminating the agency contract. However, in reality they were still advertising our services with our branding, and pretending the deal with us was still on, in order to get customers but keep our share of the deal for themselves. What these customers would have done when they finally found out, we wouldn't know – Kazakhstan is a long way from our head office in Europe, and we don't have a lot of good contacts on the ground. But, in the end, the Kazakh partners came clean and asked us to come back, especially when they realized they couldn't provide all the services without us.

10. Equal opportunities

This requirement is often made in emerging markets to encourage Western investors to train local staff and give them opportunities to do the job of an expatriate, in a technology-transfer or capacity-building deal. What might be some of the challenges here?

Brief worked example
I was posted to the Yemen for a couple of weeks to train a Yemeni in human resource management techniques. When I got there, he was a pleasant gentleman but very elderly – he had gained his PhD in HR at Baghdad University in 1954. He was a very strict Muslim and was not allowed to permit a woman who was not his wife, sister or mother to sit with him in his car. I had insisted on him collecting me from the hotel each morning as I had heard many horror stories of foreigners being kidnapped. Eventually, much to

the surprise of his colleagues, he relented, after I was 'inspected' by his wife and those of his colleagues. He spoke no English but luckily we knew of a South Yemeni from Aden with excellent English who was willing to help in the training. The Adenite was an accountant, so he had to first learn HR! In the end the training was enjoyable and productive, but it was difficult to inspire enough confidence for my 'student' to use the material in teaching and consulting, although I think I succeeded in opening his eyes to a whole new world of modern, Western HR.

11. Economic dominance by China

When this is seen as an example of the economic colonization of one country by another, it can raise several CSR issues. What might these include?

Brief worked examples
I – In Malawi, there are many blue-collar Chinese workers involved in many infrastructure projects – but there is high unemployment amongst the Africans. The Chinese don't speak English and don't train the Africans, so there is no capacity-building opportunity. The Africans can't always maintain these structures built by the Chinese, because they have not been trained. The government officials are glad of the Chinese investment money, but it would seem to be helping the Chinese much more than the Malawians. The local people would seem to be deprived of possible work and are not learning any more skills, but the Chinese insist on using their own labour. The Malawian government is anxious for their investment, and would seem to accept it at any sacrifice in the longer term.

II – In Rwanda, the local souvenir factory in Kigali is owned and managed by Chinese. They employ Rwandan workers to make the cute little baskets and carve the wooden objects, but the Chinese are reaping the rewards of the sales, in a country with a tiny GDP.

(continued)

But the country would seem to lack entrepreneurship and capital, and the Chinese are moving in and offering attractive deals.

12. and 15. Protection and monopolies

The matter of unfairly excluding competition can raise more ethics issues, especially in terms of customer choice. How can this sometimes lead to poor quality?

Brief worked example
Malta, a small Mediterranean country within the EU but widely seen as an emerging market, has a small domestic population so there's not always a lot of choice for consumers, and nearly everything must be imported. A previous national leader experimented with the idea of import substitution to encourage local industries, banning imports of popular luxuries such as chocolates. Local chocolate was regarded as almost inedible, so residents smuggled in their own supplies from overseas, and protection was dropped after distinctly failing to encourage local manufactures.

13. Corporate governance

Can be useful in trying to attract foreign investment – what might be some of the difficulties for emerging market countries?

Brief worked example
In Vietnam, great efforts are being made to raise standards of corporate governance, but it has been difficult to persuade companies to truthfully report their ownership and management structures, remuneration and promotion issues, board composition, etc. Researchers have relied on self-reported information, which might fail to capture the real picture. Although companies like the idea of attracting external investors, they are afraid of tax implications, and don't always know the answers to the questions the investors ask. If I purchase this land, I'm allowed to have it for fifty years, then what happens? We don't know, because we only created this law

a few years ago. The road to understanding corporate governance requirements, let alone meeting them, may have only just begun.

16. Respectable but not

Provide an example of how a business in an emerging market might have been used to make another business or individual look more respectable and above-board, when it may not have been.

Brief worked example
We were running a consulting firm in Dubai, and had a client managing an information technology business. He was newly appointed as the boss, and decided he wanted to get rid of a number of his colleagues – they were also investors, so he had to buy them out. He was concerned that the board might not agree to his plan. So he hired us to 'advise' him to fire these particular people, so he could still appear to be acting appropriately. We thought this was rather unethical but our firm was struggling financially at the time and he paid us big consulting fees, so we were complicit in this arrangement, but against our better judgement.

4 Business Culture

Cross-Cultural Management and People in Emerging Markets

Introduction

Business cultures across the BRICS and beyond are exhibiting much more convergence than ever before, and are especially moving towards Western norms of participative leadership, teamwork, focus on individual results, the need to use personal initiative and so on, but the cultural differences in doing business across the world are still significant – and cause considerable operational risks. The challenges of dealing with cultural differences are arguably greater now, as they are much less obvious and not openly expressed, and can result in miscommunications and misunderstandings with disastrous consequences. These differences can be appreciated through available theoretical constructs, but there is more to cultural understanding than looking at textbook frameworks. Reliable generalization is not easy, so Western business people engaged in emerging markets must work things out for themselves on the ground and discover their own ways of operating effectively and minimizing risk.

Communication is inevitably the most difficult area, as discussed in the first section of this chapter, 'Cross-cultural communications'. This process involves different kinds of thinking, which are not always appreciated by both parties. How could the Spanish government have misread the Chinese so dramatically? And a large and apparently well-informed British company misunderstood the Russians so completely? Was it arrogance and making assumptions or genuine misunderstanding and the misreading of signals?

There are many cultural issues to consider here, which impact on the Western executive trying to manage people in businesses in emerging markets. These people can be local staff members, customers, suppliers or officials, but they will certainly exhibit cultural variations different from the home base. The second section, 'High power distance', looks at one of the most significant of these differences – levels of respect for authority and tolerance of control – followed by the related third section, 'Big brother is watching you'. The tendencies to accept individual responsibility or not, or accept or avoid blame, are then discussed in 'Individualism and collectivism' (fourth section). This is followed by considering the need for clarity over instructions and expectations in the fifth section, 'Avoiding uncertainty'; giving priority to relationships, or obeying the rules, is reviewed in the sixth section, 'Relationships, not rules'. Respecting authority for its status, or being more impressed by achievements, is a further issue explored in the seventh section, 'Achievement or status?' 'Showing emotions – or not' (eighth section) is followed by a look at separating work and leisure or mixing them up in the ninth section, 'The right time to have a business meeting'. Planning and scheduling work, or doing tasks as they come up and according to changing boss demands, is considered in the final section, 'In real time, as it happens'. Because these cultural considerations cannot be generalized, the experiences of other Western executives can be useful for the first-time visitor, together with a good deal of reflection and openness to learn. Otherwise the risks associated with dealing with emerging market countries keep mounting in disturbing and unexpected ways.

1. Cross-cultural communications

Business culture and, therefore, communication differences can lead to massive misunderstandings costing millions of dollars and – amazingly – happen again and again. Executives from the West must ensure that mutual clarity is achieved before decisions are announced. This sounds obvious: but take, for example, the experience of Spain in mid-April 2011. The Spanish proudly announced that they had negotiated a massive investment from China in Spanish domestic savings banks or *caja* of up to $9.3 billion. China already holds over 12% of foreign holdings in Spain, worth around $25 billion. Spain at the time needed at least $50 billion in bail-out money – and this seemed like a good start. So imagine their national embarrassment only a day later when China publicly announced an official denial of the $9.3 billion 'investment'. They had never agreed. It was not their understanding of the discussion. You might think that this will never happen to you as an executive from Europe or the US doing business with emerging markets – but it might do. There were too many assumptions and not enough cross-checking, or it could have been that the Chinese got cold feet after a day's reflection. In either case, the premature official announcement created considerable damage.

Similarly, the long-running scenario of the failed BP and Rosneft joint oil exploration plan also owes much to communications breakdown and a lack of cross-cultural understanding between the British and the Russians in this case. Even the one month extension to the $16 billion share swap, timed to save face for BP ahead of its AGM in London, was not enough to get the joint venture back on track. The origins of the problem seem to have come from BP's misunderstanding of its previously-made agreement with another business in Russia. But how could BP have assumed there would be no problem in going back on a deal it made before? Did they think that everyone would be so grateful to do business with the mighty BP that they would forget about previous arrangements?

Communication is a matter of interpretation – it's what the other party understands, not what you might have thought you said – perception is reality, and this can be one of the most important challenges in doing business in countries with a vastly different way of seeing the world. The only solution is for the Western business person to put himself or herself in the shoes of the emerging market counterpart – which can only be possible after time and experience. The rest of this chapter is an attempt to flag some of the main areas or issues where differences may be apparent.

2. High power distance

National cultural differences have been explored by well-known authors such as Hofstede and Trompenaars, widely referred to in all international business and culture textbooks. Their constructs are used as a framework for much of the discussion in this chapter. These include power distance, individualism and collectivism, ways of coping with uncertainty, observance of rules, perceptions of status, willingness to show emotions, attitudes to one's job and free time, and tendency to plan and organize work or complete tasks as and when. There are many exceptions to these generalizations and cultural norms are changing all the time, but they can be used as a starting-point, and can help ensure more smooth-running business relationships.

Firstly, we can consider the impact of the concept of high or low power distance. The business culture of China – and many other emerging market countries – assumes and expects a higher degree of power distance than tolerated by many Western organizations. Junior staff members are expected to show extreme deference to seniors and to the authorities, who exert far more control than would be tolerated in the West. On a national scale in China, the existence of the one child family policy – although now with some opposition and adjustment – would be unimaginable in many countries, where people expect a high degree of personal freedom.

One of the results of this one child family policy has been a big increase in elderly people – now 48 million of China's 1.339 billion (13.3%) are over sixty. There is also a relative lack of young people and too few women for marriage partners, given a preference for male children. Permission of when to have the allowed one child must also be sought from the boss of the work unit of the mother, as she will be given extensive maternity leave – but only once. As the work unit must plan ahead and cannot allow all the female workers to have their baby at the same time, requests are often turned down. Again, it is not easy to imagine such a scenario in a Western culture.

Thus, in this context, a protest march in China against rising costs – common in many countries and not necessarily unduly feared by most authorities – is subject to harsh suppression in China. A strike by a mere 1,000 Shanghai truckers was put down quickly by the authorities, with some protestors detained. The strike in an inflationary period was obviously seen as even more scary by the Chinese authorities, who made the concession of some reduction in road tolls to get the truckers back to work. Labour unrest is a very disturbing phenomenon for leaders in China, far beyond the imagination of many Western observers, who might accept a degree of labour unrest as not unusual, and try to deal with it in a constructive way for the benefit of all.

Perhaps related to this concept is the strong sense of patriotism and obligation to follow authority of many Chinese, even if they are working for a non-Chinese company – and perhaps especially when they are working for foreigners, when they might feel that they are somehow being less than loyal to the motherland. Hence, a Chinese employee in a US high technology firm was found photocopying sensitive company documents, to be sent to his own government. He would see this as a patriotic duty, whereas the Americans would see it as industrial espionage and disloyalty. Signing a non-disclosure agreement might not seem prohibitive to the Chinese executive, who is probably more relationship-driven than rule-bound (see below). So this might not be the answer for a foreign company in this situation. The first loyalty of the Chinese might be to his or her country – which is now unlikely to be true for many Westerners.

3. Big brother is watching you

Government control is at an even higher level and can be all-pervasive in smaller and less-developed Communist states, where governments can be struggling to keep the economy on track. Anecdotal evidence suggests that, in Vietnam, the government has cracked down on the apparently innocent pastime of drinking beer in restaurants with several friends or colleagues around large tables, where drinkers take it in turns to propose a toast to each other and loudly knock their glasses together.

The government has also expressly forbidden the method of opening vacuum-packed moistened paper towel sachets by squeezing them and loudly popping them – also arguably an innocuous habit.

These phenomena can be of interest culturally, as not only are we looking at a government that feels it necessary to exert so much control at such an everyday level, but at a society willing to accept it. Most of the time, this occurrence would not be explained to foreigners, except those well-known and trusted, and by quite outspoken locals, not the shyest and more typical kind. The local person concerned would usually be most reluctant to appear critical of his or her country.

The Western business executive travelling in Asia for the first time might find such a level of all-pervasive authority – and the acceptance of this as a way of life – almost unimaginable. In the business context, this can be seen as an acceptance of authority far beyond Western norms. The Western manager might not be too comfortable with the way that Asian supervisors treat their staff, but it may not be a good idea to intervene between them.

4. Individualism and collectivism

Many emerging markets are predominantly collectivist societies, where people like to be identified with a group and where family ties are stronger than in many Western environments. Consider this question: would the provision of care homes be popular in an increasingly-prosperous emerging market country? Possibly, in more Westernized emerging market countries, but most have not even heard of such a service. Many executives in Asia are shocked at the way that Westerners might pack off their elderly relatives to such a home and pay others to take care of them. Collectivist societies respect elderly relatives, and family members tend to live in extended family units.

By contrast, Westerners are much more individualistic, living alone or just in couples. In another example, many Indian executives go on business trips with their entire family, whereas a Westerner would fully expect to travel alone. A Westerner assuming individualist work behaviours in his or her staff members – pressing them to finish urgent tasks before going home, for example – might risk unpopularity, a lack of co-operation in future, and higher staff turnover.

In a practical context, in the workplace this tendency towards collectivism in many emerging market countries can mean that many staff members from the BRICS and beyond avoid blame and cover up for each other. The most important thing is being loyal to your workmates and protecting yourself from exposure, not necessarily satisfying your customer or even your boss. A Western person engaging workers for a job on his house in Egypt complained repeatedly that mistakes were being made causing further damage and inconvenience. No worker was ever willing to admit to making a mistake, fearing the consequences, and always blamed a sub-contractor or another worker. The Westerner didn't really care who was responsible but just wanted it fixed. The workers spent so much effort avoiding blame that the job took longer and longer.

Westerners are more interested in gaining individual credit, and in that context are willing to take the blame when things go wrong, freely admitting failure and being ready to apologize. This is much more difficult for most emerging market executives, who might be willing to forego the credit in order to avoid the blame. Showing initiative is also problematic for the worker in a collectivist culture, who risks 'showing up' or exposing the lack of initiative or poorer performance of his or her fellow workers. 'We're not paid to think, so why should we?' was one comment by a worker anxious to show solidarity with his fellow workers and distance himself from the bosses. A sense of job and task ownership might be more common in a Western business context, especially if this behaviour is incentivized and rewarded. The risk is that many Western executives expect behaviours from emerging market staff that are uncommon or non-existent, and for which there is no tradition of encouragement.

5. Avoiding uncertainty

Ambiguity and a lack of the obvious may be popular in a Western workplace context, where the possibility of using creativity and imagination and having a high degree of autonomy are often seen as making a job more interesting and attractive. But in many emerging market countries, a lack of structure and guidance in the workplace can be seen as scary. So, as a result, many employees need more precise instructions and much clearer expectations in order to feel comfortable with their work. For example, an employee in many Asian countries would be very worried by a Western boss giving him or her rather vague instructions, but might be too nervous to ask for more information. When the task is late being delivered, the Western boss will question why the employee needed more clarification, and especially why he or she didn't ask for it at the time. The tendency of the Asian employee to nod and say 'yes' even when not fully understanding a problem is even more perplexing to the Westerner.

A further example may be seen in Dubai, dominated by workers from India and Pakistan, who seem to hesitate to ask for more instructions and give feedback to their Arab bosses. A large sign announced a new office building and invitations to rent and purchase offices, but it had many spelling and grammar mistakes. It is likely that many of the employees – who are highly proficient in English – knew of the mistakes but were unwilling to mention them to the bosses, reflecting high power distance and high uncertainty avoiding behaviours, common characteristics in emerging markets.

Thus, detailed guidelines and instructions, beyond those required in a typical Western workplace, may be needed – and the culturally-sensitive Westerner will be looking for body language suggesting discomfort, continuing to provide more detail until the colleague looks happier. This comes with practice, and does not need to be made too obvious.

6. Relationships, not rules

This attitude – of placing high emphasis on the importance of relationships – might account for an apparent lack of reliability on the part of business associates, who may suddenly disappear to help a sick relative or meet a friend at the airport, rather than sticking to a pre-arranged meeting schedule. Any trouble with the authorities may be met with a closing of ranks, as friends protect friends. This may be part of a collective way of thinking, but is also a very effective way of solving a problem. Obligations to support relatives and friends are much more powerful than in the West, and such relatives and friends can also be relied upon to help out to a much greater extent than in more 'universalistic' cultures where the tendency to follow rules is much greater.

In many emerging markets, a traffic accident can be handled more effectively through 'contacts'; work permits can be obtained more quickly this way; and any task requiring the circumvention of rules needs relationships, which are built up over many years through relatives, schoolmates, former work colleagues and so on. This can be an opportunity as well as a risk of operating in emerging markets, but the Western executive must be wary of perpetuating possibly unethical business practices, and aware that some of these 'short-cuts' might appear in the context of the Foreign Corrupt Practices Act applying to US-based executives.

The importance of relationships is sometimes seen in the reluctance of colleagues and business partners from highly relationship-driven countries to be willing to work and relocate to an overseas posting. Universalistic or rule-bound people – mostly from Western countries, such as the UK and the US – expect to make friends wherever they travel and work, but don't necessarily expect to rely on these friends to 'fix' things. They follow the rules their organization or the country in which they are working lays down.

Relationship-driven people, by contrast, can feel that they are lost in another country. They don't know anyone, so they feel vulnerable if something goes wrong and they don't know who to call. Also, many people in relationship-driven cultures are very status-conscious. In their own society, they may be wealthy, high class, well-connected and looked-up to generally. In another country, they are suddenly a 'nobody', or at least no-one remarkable. By contrast, many Westerners are used to this scenario, and to making their own way when moving from country to country.

7. Achievement or status?

Many societies – including many BRICS and beyond countries – tend to give respect to status, although they are increasingly impressed by high levels of achievement, especially as pressures for heightened individual and corporate performance increase. This phenomenon may account for the respect given, in many countries, to high-position leaders who nevertheless are not producing results. This can create an unsatisfactory situation that is hard to change.

Thus, many BRICS and beyond companies tend to support a culture respecting the status and position of bosses, and admire those from aristocratic families, even if they are not particularly successful. In India, despite the rigid caste system and high respect for those in managerial positions, poor performance over consecutive quarters can lead to shake-up and dismissal for the worst offenders, as in the case of the second-largest technology outsourcing company Infosys in mid-2011. Now, performance management is no longer a preserve of the West, as many other emerging market companies are having clear-outs of non-performers. However, this is culturally at odds with their perceived image of protecting high-status individuals. Democratic India leads the pack here, but this is still the exception rather than the norm, and may explain why some executives still retain important positions whilst doing relatively little to add value to the organization.

Arab countries can be well-known for this attribute, with local Arab executives from well-known families occupying high-status positions as company directors – and expatriates acting as their deputies who are, in effect, doing all the work. In doing business with an organization with such characteristics, it is obviously necessary to direct efforts towards the high-status individual first, but this might be in a more educative role – this director might not know his job at all, but must not be exposed, and must be treated with great deference at all times. The expatriate underling might have no responsibility to spend money, and might think it's his or her job to save money. He or she might also think that his or her status is being undermined by an outsider, so there are many challenges and risks in doing business here.

The manager of a Western training company was trying to sell training courses to a high-status Arab government minister, and made the assumption that this official would definitely like to make big changes, and that he wanted his staff to be more high-achieving. Although this might be a reasonable assumption in the West, and the Arab minister had to agree with it in theory, it was obvious that this training company's proposal was going to end up in the bottom drawer if not the litter bin. It was much more important for the minister to preserve his status and respect, and the wide-ranging changes might undermine this and bring him into conflict with other ministries.

8. Showing emotions – or not

For some Western executives, it's unacceptable to throw tantrums at work and have big public fights with colleagues. Meanwhile, some employees in emerging market organizations are much more reserved than Westerners, to the point of being inscrutable. Global influences are leading to the adoption of a midway point, which would seem to be a level of personal control, but with a willingness to show feelings if this is necessary or appropriate.

It can all add up to a high degree of frustration for the Westerner. In one example, a newly-recruited staff member from a Mediterranean country spent a whole day crying at her desk when her boyfriend dumped her – whilst her Western boss thought she should 'pull herself together'. In another case, two male colleagues who bitterly liked each other made no effort to work together, even though their jobs were closely inter-related.

Many Chinese staff members may seem to be unhappy but it will be hard for their Western manager to know why. They may not reveal any emotions, and kept it all bottled up. There are Vietnamese colleagues who don't understand their jobs but won't ask, who are given benefits at work but their Western manager doesn't know if they really like them or not, and they won't say. A training course presented to Asian colleagues might have seemed to go down well – but the Western presenter actually had no idea if the participants knew it all already or found it interesting and useful – because there was no feedback. The list can go on forever.

9. The right time for a business meeting

In some countries, there is no such thing as business time and leisure time, as business meetings are scheduled at all times of the day and night – after all, business partners must be friends first, right? And, thus, business meetings might focus on relationship-building for several hours first, before any discussion of the business to be transacted, which can be highly time-consuming.

In highly diffuse cultures, where business and private time are all mixed up, doing business seems to take much longer. It is impossible for the business person in a diffuse culture to do business with someone who may be unknown and not trusted. Also, if trust is broken it can rarely be reclaimed. The concept of 'the emotional bank account' (introduced in Stephen Covey's *Seven Habits of Highly Effective People*) arguably doesn't really work in a diffuse culture. Building up credits for when a relationship turns sour – so that it can then recover – may not necessarily work everywhere. But, if the relationship is strong and the friendship is deep, then there is nothing that your partner would not do, and looking after a customer outside of office hours is not a problem.

This may be seen as being in complete contrast with the Western approach of buying on price or quality or specific product attributes. Sometimes, business partners in a diffuse culture might pay too much for poor quality, but it was from a trusted friend, so these problems might be overlooked.

Also, in diffuse cultures, employees may do much more than their job description and work much longer hours, because their concept of personal time might be quite different from that of a Westerner. A person from a more specific culture – recognizing the separation of work life and home life – might feel they need not volunteer for extra duties at work, whereas an employee from a more diffuse culture might feel obliged. But many employees from collectivist cultures may be collectivist – and value family time – and want to go home early on special family occasions. The Western manager should take this into account when asking a diffuse or collectivist employee if he or she minds doing extra duties – and the Westerner is unlikely to receive the directness of reply that would be expected elsewhere. For example, if a boss in a diffuse culture wanted an employee to help him with a private job over the weekend, the diffuse employee might say yes, especially with the thought of currying favour with the boss with a view to future benefits. By contrast, an employee from a more specific culture might feel no such sense of obligation and could well be justified in sticking to the letter of his or her job description.

10. In real time as it happens

Western executives attending business meetings in many emerging market countries – and particularly in the Middle East and the Gulf – may be surprised that the private, individual meeting they thought they would have with a potential business partner turns out to be a fairly public affair. The meeting starts late as the local participants are engaged in an unscheduled meeting with someone else. Other business visitors come and go. The telephone rings and is answered, and calls are made. There is no attention to completing the meeting in a fixed time frame. The Western executive – used to planning and scheduling – may think he or she is not important, and might even feel insulted. Not necessarily. The Arab business partner would be thinking: I'm just doing my usual job of 'being open all hours', available in case anything happens, the way things usually go here. For them it's not being rude at all, just normal.

Any work processes that assume an element of 'queuing' – of customers being attended to one at a time – may not work in a 'synchronic' culture – where things happen as they happen. 'Sequential' managers – as are many from the West – like to plan ahead and become frustrated if to-do lists are not ticked off. A Western executive telling a colleague from a contrasting culture to wait until he finishes his immediate tasks before attending to him may be interpreted as inflexible, rude and unhelpful. Sequential managers working in synchronic cultures may find that they have to suspend their highly-sequential behaviour in order to go with the flow, even if this means that some items on the to-do list are a bit late getting finished.

Executive lessons on emerging markets

- The need for agreed clarity over business contracts and the finalizing of deals may seem obvious, but many executives from the West make unfounded assumptions, which can lead to dramatic miscommunications – check with your partner first!
- There is also a tendency on the part of Westerners to expect business partners to abide by agreements through changing circumstances, which may not often be the case – times have changed, why should we stick with this?
- But, meanwhile, some Western companies expect emerging market partners to fit in with their needs, oblivious of previous arrangements – the sin of arrogance on the part of large Western multinationals is all too easy to commit.
- Many Western executives are shocked by the level of personal and societal control by the authorities in many countries, and fail to appreciate the power of leaders and obligations they require – but it's there, it reflects high power distance, and definitely influences behaviour.
- The executives in many emerging market companies have a more collective and less individualistic outlook than most Westerners, so they must not be expected to accept individual blame – and nor may they be looking for individual recognition, or perhaps the fear of blame offsets that.
- Executives in most emerging market countries need to know the exact requirements and expectations of their bosses in completing a task, so a vague approach to instructions and the assumption on the boss' part that they are understood is not going to work – Westerners need to be more sensitive to this.
- In many emerging markets there's a much stronger sense of obligation to family and friends than in the West, so

(continued)

Westerners should not consider emerging market executives as rude if they change appointments at short notice for family reasons – they really have no choice.

- Many senior managers in emerging market organizations may not have much idea about their jobs and may entrust a lot of work to deputies – but this fact should not be revealed – they gained their position through status and others do their jobs: this is accepted.
- Workplace behaviours in the West can be quite different to those in emerging market countries, especially in terms of levels of emotion shown – which can be much more than in the West, or much less and almost imperceptible.
- The separation of work and non-work activities can be less clear in emerging markets, and there can be a much greater need to build relationships before business can be transacted – many Western bosses do not appreciate this need.
- Attitudes to time management, planning and queuing can be very different in emerging markets. Westerners often see this as showing disorganization and being out of control – but it's not necessarily seen as negative in emerging market countries, just the normal way of working.

Business Culture: Workshop Activities

1. Cross-cultural communications

Explain how a major miscommunication can happen, suggesting ideas about how this might be prevented in future.

Brief worked example
I went to work for an organization in the Middle East that was working in a joint venture with a European business. I suppose I

made the assumption that it would be run in a Western way, but in retrospect I don't think the European partners had any idea about how the executives there were treated – including the expatriates. I was told that it was a good company to work for, because every month the employees were paid their whole salary, usually on time. So, did that mean most companies didn't pay their staff, or paid them only in part, and late? I had asked for leave at a specific time for a specific reason before joining the company, and was then told that no leave was allowed for the first six months, or even a year! The passports of all staff were kept in the company safe. The company requested access to the bank accounts of the staff members, to check that they weren't earning money from freelancing and working on the side, which was not allowed. This was fairly common practice in this Middle East country, but I didn't know. The fact that all this was a big surprise when I joined the company was mainly a communications issue. I didn't ask the right questions, or the people I asked hesitated to tell me for whatever reasons, or they thought I knew. I made assumptions – probably the biggest communications error. The challenging thing is to write everything down, and find people to talk to – preferably other expatriates who are not high 'power distant' (see below) and who will tell you the real story, which they have found out for themselves – the hard way.

2. High power distance

In practice, how can a clash in power-distant attitudes create difficulties in the workplace? How might these be resolved?

Brief worked example

A manager I know – who's British – has Turkish staff members who are very high power distant, and he can't get used to this. One member of staff accidentally broke a piece of equipment and couldn't bear to admit it, so he hid it for months until it was

(continued)

discovered. On a social outing, the Turkish employee wanted to take his colleagues and boss – from varying nationalities but mostly Western – to a Turkish restaurant. They didn't have the particular dish the boss wanted, so the Turkish employee was extremely embarrassed, as everyone else had their food and the boss had nothing. These difficulties happen again and again in this clash of cultures – such as an American boss I had in China who wanted to sit in an open-plan office, but the Chinese forced him to sit in a separate corner room. This British manager tried to handle his Turkish staff by being over-friendly and chatty, and talking to them as if they were fellow Westerners. This was a disaster, as then they lost respect for him, started complaining about the smallest things and abusing his good nature. This would not have occurred to them if he had behaved as they thought a boss should behave. The only way to resolve these issues is to build strong relationships so that matters can be more out in the open – although they won't go away. Discussing the problem with another Western executive with similar experiences can help – it's a matter of developing sensitivity and empathy.

3. Big brother is watching you

Discuss how a Western executive might display some sensitivity towards colleagues and other contacts living in a highly-controlled society, where many issues are not open for debate.

Brief worked examples
I – When I was working in China I used to smuggle in banned books from Hong Kong – mostly about Chairman Mao and the Cultural Revolution. Then I would offer them to my Chinese colleagues to read, thinking it would be a treat for them to have something that was banned, a bit like a kid not allowed chocolate would go to a school friend's house to enjoy this special treat – how wrong can you be? They were horrified. They didn't

want to know about something that could get them in trouble. So that was not very sensitive of me.

II – Similarly, when I was training sales executives in Iran, discussing ideas for a new advertising campaign involving examples of Western ads fell very flat indeed, because the American marketing textbook had pictures of girls wearing bikinis. It was also referring to Iran as 'the axis of evil'. In each classroom there is always a government spy, and on this occasion this participant was really freaking out, although the others didn't have a problem – they were very interested! So in a highly controlled society – like those of China and Iran – a good piece of advice is to use only those materials and refer to only those topics that are compliant to the often-unwritten laws of these societies. And we can't assume that people always want what they are not allowed!

4. Individualism and collectivism

What might be the advantages and disadvantages of a 'collective' attitude (common in many emerging markets, such as in South America and many African countries) and how can a more individualist manager understand and deal with these different behaviours?

Brief worked example
Collectivist staff members can be very supportive team players, and are often good friends amongst themselves. They take care of sick and elderly people in their communities. No-one is lonely or neglected, everyone is included in outings and functions, even when it requires some effort for the rest. However, collectivist employees tend not to be competitive in the workplace, because if one employee is outperforming the others, he or she is showing them up, and they are forced to work harder, which they may not want to do. If anyone makes a mistake, the others will close ranks and support him or her, all blaming someone else outside their

(continued)

team. Also, if one staff member is promoted over the others and has to conduct performance appraisals, they are always going to be positive. They'll be thinking: how can I be critical of my friend, when we have known each other for years, and our wives are friends, and our kids are friends? For an individualistic manager, the disadvantages might be seen to outweigh the advantages. The only way to deal with these behaviours is to understand them, realize they are going to happen, and try not to make colleagues feel uncomfortable by putting them on the spot. For example, as an individualist manager, if you are asking a collectivist supervisor to assess the performance of former colleagues, it might be an idea to take them to one side, asking him or her to frankly assess them, but then somehow to present the assessment outcomes as your own insights, allowing yourself to be blamed for the 'bad' report, rather than their 'friend'. This must be handled very carefully.

5. Avoiding uncertainty

How can a Western executive, doing business in an uncertainty avoiding environment, ensure that customers, suppliers or work colleagues are feeling comfortable about agreed tasks?

Brief worked example
The only way here might be through close observance of body language, but even this is inscrutable in some cultures. If people look happy and quite excited about doing a task, they may have understood and have enough information. If they are still squirming in their seats, they need more guidance and detail. They must be encouraged to ask questions, but one-on-one and in private, as communally they might be embarrassed about asking questions in front of others. They might think their English is poor, or worry that the question they ask might be seen as stupid. Writing things down for them can help. Arranging a second

meeting can be comforting, even though it may be just a repeat of the first. Progress meetings at interim stages of a project are also seen as uncertainty-reducing, because the potentially fearful employee can know how he or she is doing, and if they are on the right track. Practical examples of previous, similar work can be comforting.

Including a local colleague in the briefing meetings can also be helpful, but only if the local colleague really clearly understands the issue, otherwise this can create even more confusion and uncertainty. Sometimes a local colleague can explain requirements in the local language, but if the Western boss doesn't understand what is being explained, misunderstandings can be perpetuated, especially as they are apparently endorsed by the boss – although the boss didn't understand the colleague's interpretation!

6. Relationships, not rules

What can be the upside, and the downside, of operating in a relationship-oriented society? How does this differ from a more rule-bound environment where people follow universal rules rather than being influenced by community practice?

Brief worked example

Relationship-oriented societies are great if you have relationships. If you want to jump queues, get special treatment, solve problems and have an easy life, it can be very comfortable if you always know the right person to phone up or meet with to sort out what's needed. But if you don't know the right people you are just at the back of the queue with everyone else, endlessly delayed and frustrated – especially because people with better connections are being looked after first. This can be the case in many South American and African countries, as well as in Russia and the former Russian satellites. When you are enjoying the power of the relationships, you can also forget that there is an element of corruption

(continued)

here. Some enjoy, others suffer. Rule-bound societies can be more egalitarian, as the rules apply to everyone. But there is no point making a judgement and complaining about the situation, because it is unlikely to change anytime soon. Most relationship-oriented societies – such as China, India and the Middle East – are probably going to remain relationship-oriented for many years to come. Western executives operating in these societies either 'go local' and try to build relationships and operate like the more 'successful' locals, or take a no compromise position, which is strictly ethical and legal but makes life quite difficult for themselves.

7. Achievement or status?

How can a Western executive do business with an organization where status may be quite separate from achievement, and may not relate to capability to do the job?

Brief worked example
In many countries, the person with the most senior job title is not the person actually doing the job, or who even knows anything about it. But they have huge status, and must be treated with great deference. It may be that the person actually doing the work – the implementer – is resentful of consultants and other outsiders, and might think you are coming between him or her and their boss – especially as they may well have a job security concern. Adding to the status of the overall boss is the only viable tactic, as long as directives used by the high-status individual will be accepted by the implementer. Things are changing, though, and high status bosses can also be known for achievement. But 'saving face' is a good concept to bear in mind – everyone in this kind of society wants their status recognized.

8. Showing emotions – or not

How can the Western business person handle 1) an over-display of emotions and 2) inscrutability?

Brief worked example

Although over-emotional people sound like a difficult problem, it could be that the completely blank expressions of others can be a bigger difficulty for the Western manager. If the working environment is one that usually allows for the free display of feelings, it could be that the emotional outburst is more of a problem to the Westerner than it is to anyone else, and can just be ignored. Inscrutability in a colleague or contact is harder. We don't know if the person is happy or not, agreeing or not, giving us the business or not. We need to keep looking for signs, giving them the chance to respond, talking with them individually and listening for hints of any reservations or problems. Faint praise is also indicative of not being comfortable, and so is hesitation. So the Westerner can handle an over-display of emotions by seeing it as typical and nothing unusual, and inscrutability by a high level of sensitivity, which can get easier with experience.

9. The right time for a business meeting

Is it rude or presumptive to have business meetings out of hours? Should all business-related activities be confined to 9–5?

Brief worked example

Westerners working in environments that could be described as 'diffuse' might find that their own time is being encroached upon, but may have to get used to this. In such environments, they might find other Westerners inflexible and rude if they stick to the 9–5 rule. The easiest thing can be to go with the flow, and be open to discussing business at any time, because it is not seen as separate. During Ramadan in the Middle East, business meetings might be held late at night, so that the participants can eat and drink freely, and have more energy and ability to concentrate. It can be frustrating for sequential Westerners (see below) but it can be completely pointless trying to continue 'business as usual'

(continued)

when events like this happen, so the best advice might be to follow local practice, and be as flexible as possible.

10. In real time, as it happens

Is it insulting if your business contact fails to show up for the meeting? When might it not be?

Brief worked example
People who are synchronic – they don't plan much, they don't try to manage time, they just try to respond to every situation as it arises and get through their day – worry about committing themselves to an appointment. What if something more important crops up? I don't want to have to disappoint anyone. I might be too busy doing something else at the time. I might miss an important opportunity if I restrict myself. So I'll just see what turns up and not make any promises. If I, as a sequential person with a diary and a to-do list, turn up demanding a fixed appointment, I might put my business contact in a difficult spot. He might agree to an appointment and I think it's fixed, but he doesn't necessarily think so, and might not remember it. It was just an intention to have a meeting sometime. So your invitation – 'come to dinner at my house at 8pm on this coming Friday' – sounds to him like 'we must have dinner sometime'. So when he doesn't turn up, or has apparently forgotten, it's not necessarily insulting, but just reflects a different mindset.

PART II

OPPORTUNITIES

5 Marketing

Implementing Marketing Ideas into and from Emerging Markets

Introduction

Marketing by many businesses in emerging markets is in total contrast with the Western scene, but most Western executives have not yet caught up with the differences – or are not willing to keep adjusting their marketing approach to get it right and, therefore, don't appreciate the opportunities. Some are suffering from a phenomenon seen as 'the end of **corporate imperialism**' where the old marketing strategies don't work anymore. Thus, some Western products and services don't stay the course in emerging markets, but are here today and gone tomorrow, especially with no **vertical integration**. Demographics impacting marketers can be very different in developing countries (discussed in Chapter 2), the relative importance of different market segments can vary dramatically especially in terms of **purchasing power parity**, and culturally-influenced behaviours (see Chapter 4) can be hard to explain for a Western-experienced executive.

How can the Western firm customize its products for a completely different market? How can such a company avoid '**cannibalizing its own cash cows**' when the same products are more expensive in its home market? What might the previously unconsidered potential customers at the **bottom of the pyramid** be looking for? How can companies **reach the unreachable**? Could there be lessons here for the West, especially from **polycentric innovation** (see Chapter 6) – especially as demand is changing all over the world in line with economic ebbs and flows? Can Western brands learn from their emerging market competitors – in terms of their **chameleon** qualities and ability to **creatively adapt** – maybe not immediately, but for future opportunities? Western brands might be popular now – but for how long? When to move on? And, if the fruits of Western marketing are no longer appealing, where are the final frontiers still to be explored?

Some Western businesses start off with a big fanfare but then become a flash in the pan, as discussed in the first section, 'Need to keep it going'. And although many Western luxury products are popular among wealthy individuals in China and India, for example, the demographics and other characteristics of the customers can be quite different from those in the West – such as younger and female, for example, examined in the second section, 'Hitting the spot'. The thinking and behaviours of the customers may be different too, reflecting a cultural contrast between the predominantly individualistic tendencies of the West and collectivism of Asia, for instance – considered in the third section, 'Following the herd'. The need for high fashion items and the status associated with them is much less elastic in emerging markets – if I'm going to be fashionable, I want to stay that way – I have an image to maintain, and I must not be seen as at all disadvantaged compared with my peers (described in the fourth section, 'Keeping up with the Joneses').

Products specifically tailored for customers in emerging markets – especially designed to attract lower-income consumers in countries with a large but economically-growing population – are ones-to-watch, as explored in the fifth section, 'Customizing for success'. These products could also be popular in the cash-strapped West, given how times are changing, and many families and individuals are managing with fewer resources.

So how can Western products penetrate the BRICS and beyond? Buying foreign franchises and allowing the entry of foreign companies is popular in some emerging markets, but it might only be a means to an end – because the development of their own local brands may be the long-term plan for many of these businesses and the governments that support them. So, the products of Western marketing may only have a limited window of opportunity, before they become a tool to help local businesses to progress, as looked at in the sixth section, 'Leveraging foreign interest'. The seventh section, 'The rise of the locals', analyses how, having reached maturity, local brands can become increasingly dominant in their home markets.

For the adventurous Western marketer, when one door closes another opens, as there are still many fairly under-developed yet large and possibly profitable markets to explore, as seen in the eighth section, 'Areas for future marketing potential'. Internet-based businesses are particular areas of opportunity. The final section, 'Still closed to the outside world', discusses the fact that some possibilities are probably more distant prospects, but still worth considering.

1. Need to keep it going

Western multinationals can be successful in emerging markets if they get their marketing right. But what works well doesn't necessarily last, as the young populations of many of these countries are constantly evolving, and some Western products can end up being one-hit wonders. An example is Virgin in India, which established the Virgin Mobile joint venture with Tata, the giant Indian conglomerate. The Virgin brand was an immediate hit with Indian youth, but the business could not sustain its initial popularity and demand, and soon faced a sliding market share. The youth-directed advertising was popular, but not quite enough to keep the business viable. Western executives doing business in the BRICS and beyond must think through the product marketing process, not just the product launch. They must nurture their products through the whole product life-cycle, not just at the beginning.

Many Western businesses start off successfully in a blaze of publicity, but get the product wrong and have to start again. In India, the beef hamburgers offered by McDonald's went down like a lead balloon – until the reappraisal resulting in Maharajah burgers, made with chicken and mutton (or lamb) and therefore more acceptable to Indian religious beliefs, were introduced.

McDonald's was much more appealing right from the beginning in China – where Chinese are looking for an American experience and its associated high status – than in countries where the locals would seem to prefer their own food, such as in India. In Vietnam, where many branches of KFC have popped up, the locals might buy these products for foreign visitors and eat there occasionally themselves. Generally, they seem to prefer their own dishes, given the choice, so the Western brands may only ever occupy a small segment here, and their attempts at 'localization' are inevitably limited. For instance, KFC meals are so totally different from Vietnamese dishes that minor modifications are hardly possible, although chilli sauce is on the menu as well as the more standard ketchup.

Therefore, the sustainability of newly-introduced foreign brands depends on accurate assessment of the market niche, planning of the entire product life-cycle, localization where possible and an open-minded attitude to the way your brand might be seen in different markets. For example, many American-style fast food eateries are popular in the Arabian Gulf for discreet dating – not possible in Arabic or Muslim restaurants. But in the West, a date at McDonald's or KFC might be seen as the last place on earth for romance!

2. Hitting the spot

Luxury products in the China market are much more of a sure hit, however, and are well-established with a long-term popular following. For example, UK up-market country clothes brand Burberry enjoyed record sales in China, increasing by 30% in 2010–11, which significantly boosted overall profits. Italian jeweller Bulgari and sports car maker Maserati have also achieved an important contribution to their bottom line through sales in the PRC.

Yet, many of these luxury product producers are noticing a distinct shift from the need to appeal to Chinese men looking for ultimate male status symbols, to the need to attract self-made female entrepreneurs. So Maserati has been hosting private cocktail parties with Giorgio Armani cosmetics and La Perla lingerie – having noted that 30% of the 400 cars sold in China in 2010 were bought by women (up from 7% in 2005) and far more than the ratio in Europe. Consulting firm McKinsey observed that women accounted for over half of the estimated annual sales of luxury goods in China – around $15 billion. Burberry's female-oriented products are, thus, also on the rise, and are being sold more actively in China than in many other countries. So, Western executives marketing into emerging markets must rethink the typical demographics usually assumed in the West.

India is more complicated marketing-wise than China, and many companies are now 'scrambling to decode the Indian consumer', as another potentially profitable market. In many ways, Indian consumers want to be like the Chinese, as they would love to amass consumer goods the way China's middle class does but are not yet there. However, in ten to fifteen years' time, India's economy could be as big as China's is today. Its 1.2 billion people are getting richer faster, and may not have the aging problem of China, so could stay young and energetic for years to come.

Several characteristics make India less attractive from the marketing perspective. There are many problems and issues associated with distribution in India – for example, of dairy products, because of India's poor roads and difficulties with the **supply chain** or 'chill chain' (i.e., it is difficult to keep milk chilled from the farm to the consumer). With 1,500 dialects and a multitude of faiths, India is more culturally diverse than China, and this makes for problems with promotion, advertising and packaging. India's regions also vary widely. Although nearly every Indian likes carbohydrates and spices, Indian preferences for soap and shampoo differ much less from place to place than their taste in food.

How can a business in India overcome these problems? One example is a successful food and body care business that has recruited 45,000 poor rural women as sales agents, turning them into micro-entrepreneurs, who teach their neighbours about basic nutrition and hygiene – in turn helping to create demand for healthy food products and soap.

Distribution is clearly challenging in India, and few consumers have credit cards, hence the Indian version of Amazon – Flipkart – operates in quite a different way with an **innovative distribution model**. This business, which has enjoyed 20% per year growth, collects cash on delivery by taking books and other products ordered online direct to homes and offices, by motorbike. The company makes up to $20,000 in sales per day, and is set to expand further thanks to the huge growth in internet users in India – the current 50–100 million is expected to double in the next few years. As an indication, nearly 2 million new Facebook users sign up every month in India. There are no courier services in India as there are in the West, so motorbike delivery in this way is a reliable answer to the problem, and cash on delivery replaces the need for credit cards in this context.

Another significant difference between India and China is that Indians do not have the same preference for foreign brands that Chinese consumers show. This means that, on the shelves, foreign brands such as Coke sit alongside local brands such as Thums Up.

For many years, there were no foreign brands in India. The market was closed, so Indians became completely familiar with their own brands. The situation in China is the other way around, with foreign brands first and local brands being developed later (see below). So, the main issue here is that some countries are hugely impressed with foreign brands and are eager to experience a taste of life in other environments, and other countries are much less influenced by this perceived need. Cultural factors are very important (see Chapter 4).

Religious differences also need to be considered by marketers. What works in one area does not necessarily score a hit in others, for this reason. This is a challenge of advertising in Nigeria, where affiliations vary across the country. Nigeria's north is mostly Muslim, whilst the south is mostly Christian. Young and old, rural and urban, Ibo, Hausa and Yoruba: each group sees the world differently. So, Nigerian advertisers must be sensitive, as it would be dangerous to run the kind of suggestive ads popular in the south in the north of the country. When a Nigerian newspaper printed a light-hearted column speculating that the Prophet Muhammad might have enjoyed the Miss World contest, 200 people died in the ensuing riots.

How do people choose products in emerging markets? The most powerful influence on decision-to-buy can also vary dramatically between East and West, and Western marketers will have to be especially savvy to hit the spot, because some marketing insights don't appear to make sense to the Western marketer. A recent study of the pharmaceutical industry in Vietnam – looking in particular at over-the-counter pain-killing drugs – suggested that in Vietnam (potentially generalizable to other parts of Asia) customers are predominantly influenced by the advice of pharmacists. A man (or woman) in a white coat with a clipboard is listened to much more seriously than family and friends and the pharmacist's opinion even surpasses the drug-taker's previous experience when making a choice. In the West, much advertising is directed at peer satisfaction – I took this drug, it worked, so I would take it again and recommend it to others. Surprisingly, this is discounted as being of least importance in Vietnam, at the bottom of the pile, compared with the voice of authority of the pharmacist. Any advertising that fails to take this into account will clearly be ineffective.

Therefore, in marketing and promotion, it's important to understand shifting demographics, new ways of getting your brand name in front of your audience including possible tie-ups with non-competing other luxury labels, detailed appreciation of cultural and religious variants and practical issues of distribution. Every country is different, and on-the-ground experience is the only effective approach. Even marketing surveys can produce inaccurate results, as consumers may tell data collectors what they think they want to hear, rather than the truth. So, there is no alternative to observation and building up personal relationships in the targeted country.

3. Following the herd – especially in China

Cultural approaches to shopping may be quite different in most emerging markets from those in the West. This is especially due to the tendency towards collectivist modes of behaviour in many of these countries – whereas the developed world is often more individualistic. So, private sneak-preview viewing of fashion items can be more popular in China than London. It is very important for a Chinese male or female to know what the latest fashions are. It would seem that Chinese men and women may feel more pressure to stay up to date with trends and not fall behind their peers than Westerners, who might be more interested in individualism and vary their wardrobe according to individual likes and dislikes. This applies even more to women, although many Chinese men may be much more fashion conscious and consumer aware than most Western men.

To illustrate the point, a Western woman going to a party would *not* want to see another woman wearing the same dress; but a Chinese lady might think her fashion sense and status trappings were spot-on if she looked similar to others in an admired peer group, and would not see this me-too approach as a problem.

Yet, although most Chinese want to appear up-to-the-mark with the latest consumer products and fashion items, sometimes they will cut corners to save money. Chinese consumers above all want to show off among their peers; conspicuous consumption and status is the name of the game. As a result, consumer behaviours can be completely different from those in the West and, due to the pressure to have the latest fashion, sometimes fakes and cheaper versions are popular. Truly wealthy Chinese differentiate themselves from these 'cheapskates' by explaining how they bought their luxury items in Paris or London (see below).

For a start, a typical Chinese middle-class yuppie-type will wear a lanyard with a little plastic card around his or her neck, even at weekends. It is a badge of honour; it shows that he or she has a 'white collar' job, and is not a worker. A company-branded sweatshirt or casual jacket is also good, but not a t-shirt – it doesn't look expensive enough. This indicator of job position shows everyone his or her basic status. He or she uses Apple earphones to go with the cheap Chinese mobile phone in his or her pocket, so it looks as if it's an iPhone. And most Chinese yuppies drive to work, although it takes four times longer than public transport, just to show off that they have a car. After decades of deprivation and conformism, Chinese consumers regard expensive consumer goods as trophies of success. In public, they show off, even if in private, they may try to save money and buy cheaper alternatives.

The collectivist nature of Chinese thinking means that many Chinese are searching for identification with an organization, a job function, a brand, even a location – so marketers looking to appeal to the Chinese consumer must appeal to this need. A new area for marketers is employer branding – building up the brand of an organization to attract and retain staff. As a result of the status associated with a white-collar job and international branding, employers do well to produce copious items of branded merchandise. As mentioned above, Chinese working for well-known and heavily-branded multinationals will wear company shirts and casual jackets all weekend, as well as identification cards around their necks. However, prestigious local Chinese brands are rapidly acquiring prestige, reinforced by patriotism, and are challenging the multinationals (discussed below).

4. Keeping up with the Joneses

A more upscale version of following the herd is 'keeping up with the Joneses' or deliberately shopping for aspirational products to emulate admired peers or neighbours – and these are mostly luxury items. The CEO of fashion and fragrance brand Chloe observed this trend, especially in relation to Chinese women. Seen as increasingly independent, career-oriented and powerful in the market – and with 76% of female graduates aspiring to be managers – they seem to be less interested in work–life balance than in the West. They don't mind working hard as long as they can make more money and spend it on status-related items, and are less interested in settling down and getting married. Having a child – even the one child they are officially allowed – is on 'the back-burner' as a priority for many. Often, men are more interested in being fathers than women are in being mothers – particularly in the fast-paced city of Shanghai. Buying the most expensive luxury items can be a self-reward or way of building status.

These women can shop in a different way to men in China. They have more of a tendency to shop online and are more influenced by blogs – an observation reflected in approaches by more successful Western marketers targeting women. Chinese men would seem to be more influenced by word of mouth recommendations. This particularly applies to the more upscale products and brands.

Chinese women will spend more than a month's salary on a handbag – unlikely to happen in the recession-hit West. Even when the West was more prosperous, few women would drop so much money at one time for a single item to make a one-off fashion statement.

This situation is not only true in China. Anecdotal evidence suggests that well-to-do women in other countries – but not typical Western countries – would do the same. Two Egyptian women – only one married and both with high-powered jobs – took themselves off on a shopping holiday to Paris and came back with 3,000 euro handbags each, having egged each other on to buy something more and more extravagant. Many Western women would not do this, even if they had the money, often looking for outlet store bargains instead. Bargain-hunting is *not* chic in emerging markets – but splashing out is. Western women are probably less influenced by peer pressure in this way, and Western men probably even less.

5. Customizing for success

Products specifically designed for emerging markets, especially given their lower incomes, amount of disposable cash and particular needs, can be more successful and revenue-generating than products aimed at developed countries. In this way, these buying habits can be in considerable contrast to those in the West – although economic factors mean that times are changing and these products might have wider appeal. But customizing doesn't always work, and must relate to cultural differences. Here we look particularly at consumer goods, motor vehicles and mobile telephones.

In many poorer emerging markets, customers cannot afford to buy large quantities of famous branded consumer products. They can't afford a large bottle of Procter & Gamble's Head & Shoulders. But they can buy a sachet a few times a week. This is actually much more expensive in terms of price per quantity for the purchaser and, therefore, potentially more profitable for the vendor and manufacturer.

The automotive sector can also have quite different characteristics than in developed countries. Car sales have experienced decline in many mature markets hit by recession – but not in India or China. The Tata Group has considerable business in the UK, for example, but it's the Tata Nano in India – the world's cheapest and smallest car – that is driving sales for this big international Indian conglomerate. At only $3,000 each and measuring ten foot by three foot, the Tata Nano has wind-down windows, no air conditioning, no air bag and the body is made from sheet metal and plastic. Adhesive is used instead of welding. A 13% increase in total passenger vehicle sales is largely attributable to increased sales of the Nano, having reached the 10,000 mark by late 2011. Who is buying the Tata Nano? Motorbike owners who would like to upgrade to a car? First-time car owners? All of these people are. Tata is also aiming to replace the simple Indian tuk-tuk rickshaws with Nanos – once the drivers have learned how to drive them.

China can also be seen as offering opportunities for customized small vehicles, with the Wuling microvan and the BYD – 'Build Your Dreams'. As discussed in Chapter 8, the former is 44% General Motors-owned, and was created as a cheap and small van for the China market. It could be that these especially economical products, designed for lower-income countryside-based people, could also be a big hit in cash-strapped more developed countries in the future. They will have been prototyped among lower-income groups already and, if successful, distribution could be more widely extended.

The same could apply to BYD, a Shenzhen-based business making mobile phone batteries, cars and solar panels – and now cars for the masses. Warren Buffet bought a 10% stake in the company, whose share price then rose nine-fold. Unit car sales increased from zero in 2003 to more than 500,000 by 2010. The BYD is a small sedan with a 60,000 yuan ($9,150) price tag, making it highly affordable. However, success is not guaranteed as many observers feel that Chinese buyers are more loyal to features than brands. Therefore, when a product with more attractive features is launched, they may buy the new one instead. Sales of the BYD rose 18% in 2011, but this is well below the 800,000 cars the firm expected to sell by this date. So there might be a good reason to look at markets further afield.

Customizing can be widely applied, as in the case of mobile telephones in Africa, where a $90 'smartphone' made by China's Huawei and running Google's Android sold out in several African countries in less than a month. Around 90% of mobile telephone models sold in Africa are fairly basic, especially because of the lack of bandwidth. The laying of three submarine cables to Africa during 2011 has quadrupled data speeds and cut internet usage prices by 90%. Since mobile telephone coverage in most of Africa is usually better than fixed-line availability, the result has been that mobiles are swiftly becoming Africa's computer of choice. With 84 million mobiles in Africa having at least rudimentary internet connectivity, being online is rapidly becoming the norm in Africa, impacting on a range of marketing strategies – including online banking, for instance.

So, Western companies targeting emerging markets must be willing to customize their offering not just for one country, but for different districts, sectors and demographic segments. They also have to realize that this will always keep changing, as these countries are much less culturally static than the West. But useful lessons can be learned here for more mature markets, too, where economic profiles are changing.

6. Leveraging foreign interest

Foreign businesses in emerging markets can help develop more opportunities to fulfil consumer needs – sometimes in connection with local businesses – but there are many barriers in the way, and ultimately many developing countries want to develop their own local brands, as seen in the next section. Here, we look at the restaurant business and electric cars in China, and retailing in India. International businesses have – and could have – a significant impact here in expanding market potential, but this is not necessarily happening, or not for the long term.

An up-and-coming Chinese brand is Yum!, which owns KFC and Pizza Hut outlets in China and has been targeting the Little Sheep chain of hotpot restaurants, trying to buy all their shares as part of an expansion strategy of the brand. The foreign franchise here helped the local organization to become established. Following that they are able to branch out into buying up local businesses and expanding their appeal, which is happening in many cities in China.

Electric cars in China are also benefiting from lessons learned from foreign providers – but only if the government will allow it. China has a large population and a lack of domestic oil supplies, so makers of electric cars worldwide see China as the market of the future. A government plan looks to have 500,000 electric vehicles on Chinese roads by 2015 and 5 million by 2020. They are willing to provide subsidies of nearly $10,000, but foreign producers are being told about

new 'draft' rules that mean they must share more intellectual property and branding rights with their Chinese joint-venture partners.
Nissan launched a range of plug-in models, and is trying to adapt
their strategy to fit the rules, but this is acting as a difficult barrier
for the development of a potentially valuable product.

Many observers feel that the opening-up of India's chaotic, under-
developed retailing industry to foreign supermarket chains would
bring many benefits to the country, but there are so many local rules
operating across the Indian subcontinent. As described in the previous section, Customizing for success, the diversity of India is a great
deterrent to foreign marketing initiatives in the subcontinent. With
more than twenty officially recognized languages, fourteen main
types of cuisine, three main religions and countless religious and ethnic festivals in this most heterogeneous of countries, the idea of chain
stores has not caught on. Chain stores are a style of retailing popular
in the West, but account for only 7% of India's $435 billion retailing
business – a far lower proportion than in other countries, including
most of the other BRICS. The biggest success to date, in terms of
a local Indian supermarket building market share, is a firm with
stores in seventy-three cities, employing around 30,000 people, with
forecast revenues of $4 billion for 2012. Most Indians would wel-
come improved consumer choice according to surveys, so would
be only too glad to welcome a foreign retail business – if only there
was one that was sufficiently committed to make a go of it in India.

7. The rise of the locals

Even though some famous Western brands may have been successful in China for many years, it doesn't mean that this situation will
always continue. Local brands are rapidly increasing in popularity.
However, as we have seen, it's a different story in India, where local
brands have been popular for a long time. The issue in the Indian
subcontinent is more one of too many local brands fighting over a

limited and confined market, and to a certain extent this is true of China – especially the retail business. In both scenarios – China and India – these local brands are making it difficult for foreign brands to really dominate, so there are many lessons for Western marketers here. What are local brands doing that they are not? Or is their success just because they are local?

In China, Coca-Cola has long enjoyed the biggest share of the country's $49 billion soft drinks market, but local products are becoming increasingly popular and fast-growing. These include Wahaha's vitamin-fortified smoothies, Nongfu Springs' exotic fruit blends and Wang Lao Ji's herbal teas, now being marketed as equally appealing as Western products. The Chinese domestic market is certainly big enough for a variety of offerings. It could be that the fascination with anything Western in the 1990s is now waning twenty years later. Perhaps the Chinese are becoming increasingly proud of their own home-grown beverages, especially as this represents a more patriotic approach, already seen in domestic appliances, beer and many other products.

Trying to build a brand is a big challenge for China, but Lenova, now a big name in the computer and telecoms industry, seems to have made huge leaps forward. In particular, Lenova's price and practical style seems to appeal in more rural markets. As an example of a local Chinese brand building an international business, Lenova has been challenging HP, Dell and Acer in rural areas of Indonesia, Brazil, Mexico, India and Turkey in a strategy designed to gather pace in 2011–13.

Lenova is following in the footsteps of many other well-developed Chinese brands. When China's brands are taken seriously – as Haier white goods, Huawei telecoms and Tsingdao beer and wine have been – then Western products face even more of an uphill battle. White goods manufacturers around the world are finding the good quality and low price of Haier fridges a highly competitive threat, for example, and Huawei services are winning tenders all over the globe. Tsingdao is yet to make it big outside of China, but with the size of the domestic market and widespread consumption of beer and wine, this is hardly a problem.

The fragmented nature of the fast-growing Chinese retail market includes both local and foreign brands, but none have an overwhelming market share. This sector in China is seen as potentially one of the biggest worldwide, and not surprisingly Carrefour, Walmart and Tesco are piling in. Yet, none of them, or any of their local rivals, comes close to dominating China in the way that Walmart dominates the supermarket business in the US. The largest Chinese chain, Shanghai Bailian, has only 11% of the market. Wumart, a Beijing-based chain, is cheaper than foreign competitors like Walmart, and when launched it aimed to have 1,000 stores by 2010, but reached only 469 by mid-2011. Wumart stores have achieved annual sales of $2 billion, but total retail sales in China are around $1 trillion a year and growing by around 18% annually, so there is still huge scope for growth here. China's 1.4 billion people are rapidly urbanizing and enthusiastically purchasing goods they could never have a generation ago.

Fragmentation and too many local brands all vying for position can be counter-productive – and this would seem to be happening in India. The local mobile telephone industry is booming, with mostly local providers, and is highly fragmented, with market share split among many firms – it is almost too competitive to be profitable for individual providers. India has almost 600 million active mobile telephone subscribers and among the lowest prices anywhere, including a home-grown, world-class operator, Bharti Airtel. However, with more than ten operators in most of each of its twenty-two geographical licence areas, the consumers are happy but providers are finding it tough to make a living. Most countries have only three to six operators in each licence area, by contrast. Returns on capital have declined for all the major players due to this situation, which has been described as unfair and erratic, detrimental to investment and wasteful.

So, although local brands are rising rapidly, especially in consumer businesses such as retail, home computing and telecoms, they are still often juxtaposed with foreign brands and are yet to work out how to develop transparently competitive marketing environments that can be profitable for several players and serve consumer needs at the same time. The Chinese and Indian markets are big enough for many players, but it would seem that these markets are yet to mature and develop clear niches – and foreigners are piling in with a lack of direction as to how they can be differentiated.

8. Areas for future marketing potential

Much of the emerging market world is yet to be adequately explored by marketers – because of misunderstandings, confusion about maturity, misreading of the signs and fear of what might go wrong. These areas of potential marketing possibilities can be geographic, such as Indonesia and much of Africa, and can concern different sectors or segments, such as consumer businesses and specialist niche areas like gambling and betting. There could well be scope for international businesses here – although there is a substantial element of risk.

Consumer booms can mask other problems in an emerging market – just because shoppers are buying, it doesn't mean the economy is now stable for the long term and, therefore, clearly attractive to investors. This is a problem in Indonesia, for example. Although the country would appear to be in the middle of a consumer boom, which is fuelling economic growth, this doesn't mean that investors should rush in. With a population of 238 million, Indonesia has long had the potential to become one of the world's biggest economies – which is growing by 6% per year – but, unlike China and India, Indonesia owes much of its apparent economic success to a commodities boom. Coal and gas go to India and China, palm oil to the world – but this is not necessarily stimulating manufacturing. There is some consumer activity, but the country's prosperous middle class is still small, probably no more than around 50 million, only 20% of the population. They are buying two-wheeled scooters and smartphones, but not enough to lead to a sustained boom. Indonesia, according to many observers, remains a hard country to do business with – the ethnic and religious diversity in the population, the confusing political system and the tendency for regulations to emerge out of the blue, all make this country challenging for marketers.

The consumer growth in Africa, also based around an increasing middle class (now up to one-third of the population) suggests plenty of potential, but marketers should not get too excited. These 'middle class' Africans may be able to buy a telephone, washing machine or television, but not often – and probably not all three. However, a decade ago, two-thirds of Africans were living on less than a dollar a day – and now one-third may have between $2 and $20 to spend daily. Many of these aspirational Africans started out as subsistence farmers, and are among the first in their families to earn a regular wage. They certainly do not carry credit cards, nor can they be counted as part of a global consumer society, but they do represent a large advance on the previous situation.

A very small proportion of Africans can be described as 'rich' – they can afford to study for an MBA (but their employer might be paying the fees), they drive an off-road vehicle (but again it might belong to their organization) and they certainly have access to consumer electronics and a fancy lifestyle. But this is a small number still because much of the consumer wealth has not been generated by entrepreneurial activity, so it may depend on their job – often a foreign-funded unit. It's not necessarily their money they are spending. However, there are many things they can't buy even if they want to, as they lack hard currency, international payment mechanisms and many goods are simply not distributed in their countries.

Specialist niche areas offer all kinds of possibilities for marketers, some unexpected. For example, China has no onshore casinos, but Chinese people mostly love gambling. The Chinese authorities allow casinos in Macao and betting in Hong Kong, at two race courses. But there are no signs of this potentially highly-lucrative business opening up. One 450-table casino in Macao, Galaxy Entertainment, controlled by a Hong Kong cement magnate, was built at a cost of

$1.9 billion. The Chinese government has capped the number of gambling tables in Macau at 5,500, approximately the current number in late 2011, with only another 3–4% allowed annually. When the three-hour bus ride from Guangzhou to Macau is replaced by a forty-seven-minute trip on a high speed train, this business could mushroom. A broker predicts that gambling revenues could rise by 35% by the end of 2011, and up to 20% thereafter. The Chinese government in the past has limited the number of visas it issues for mainland visitors to Macau. It may be that in the future the mainland market will open up. This would appear to suggest a strong future marketing prospect for casino operators targeting the China market. Yet, this may be politically contentious, so it remains very much an area for marketing potential, not imminent reality.

Chapter 4 discusses the existence of collectivist and relationship-oriented cultures – such as India. Traditionally families arranged marriages for their children, with children from other, suitable families. This was widely accepted in the past and to a certain extent is still widespread, but the gradual breaking down of this system is leading to more unexpected business opportunities, especially with internet-based marriage-broking. Traditionally, the village holy man – who knew everyone – would make introductions – and some money for himself on the side. Then young people started to want to find their own marriage partners, as power distance in the family started to break down. The convenience and wide reach of the internet has created a massive new business in India, now with more than 35 million registered users, paying around $10–15 for three months' membership. With 50% of Indians under twenty-four years old and the popular marriageable age being between twenty-five and thirty-two, this service is set to take off. Unlike the more sleazy dating sites popular in the more promiscuous West, the Indian marriage-broking sites are highly respectable, with sections for professionals and MBA-holders, for example. The future potential of new-style internet-based businesses with completely novel applications is beyond calculation.

9. Still closed to the outside world

Many emerging markets and countries beyond the BRICS show few signs of real marketing potential yet, mainly because they are still not open to foreign investment. However, it may be just a question of time and, therefore, these more distant prospects can still be ones to watch. Many prospects are currently monopolies, which might just be freed up in the near future.

Mexico is an especially interesting example, particularly because of its untapped potential in the existence of a wealthy but undeveloped market. With a large share of the world's billionaires, wealthy entrepreneurs in Mexico are feuding over converging television and telecoms markets. About 80% of landlines in Mexico are connected to Telmex, one of many companies controlled by Carlos Slim, the world's richest man. Another of Slim's firms, Telcel, has 70% of the mobile phone market. Meanwhile, a second-division billionaire maintains almost as tight a grip on the Mexican television business, which, in 2011, claimed 70% of the country's free-to-air TV.

Although this situation has been in existence for many years, these businesses are now being accused of being a negative monopoly, expensive for the people and offering a poor service. The country is now facing a battle between the consumer interests and the billionaire businessmen, who are fighting back. The Mexican government has shelved such proposals for years, anxious not to upset the powerful interests involved, and with a presidential election in 2012.

These monopolies, such as in Mexico, may well be broken down in the months and years to come, depending on political developments. But they are seen as long-term prospects, especially given the entrenched position of some of these wealthy operators, who may well hand down their power to aspiring family members, so that the situation continues for generations.

Executive lessons on emerging markets

- Western businesses need to think through a sustainable long-term marketing strategy for th eir emerging market operations – not just a flashy launch plan – and they should not underestimate the local competition. Not all customers want something foreign everywhere and this feature alone may not be enough anymore.
- The appeal of certain luxury products varies between Western and Asian customers – and, therefore, the marketing approach must be modified accordingly. Advertising must be directed at the customer in the target market, who might be quite different from the customer in the home market – even inexplicably and irrationally so. Marketers may need to be there on the ground to find out.
- The collectivist culture of many emerging markets can mean that customers may want a me-too look, recognizable as a specific brand, whilst the individualist culture of the West may prefer highly individualistic, less obviously consumer-oriented and more minimally-branded products.
- Many emerging market countries have developed a small middle class, who deliberately emulate high-class consumers in admired Western countries – and some Asian countries, like Japan – and are focused on copying a desired lifestyle rather than trying to do anything different or new.
- In another cultural difference – marketers from the West should be mindful of high and low power distance factors (discussed in more detail in Chapter 7). The opinions of an authority figure can count for more than personal experience, even if it conflicts with it – so advertising must be adjusted accordingly.

(continued)

- The concept of disposable income may be different too – so splashing out on hugely extravagant items may bear no relation to incomes, and cut-price discount items are not necessarily appealing – status can be everything, even at the price of a whole month's salary.
- Some products designed specifically for emerging markets can be uniquely successful, and may have potential for transfer to more developed markets, so the possibility of marketers learning from developing consumer environments is there – but of course is not guaranteed.
- Foreign franchises can be popular in emerging markets – but only to a limited extent. They may be used as a stepping-stone and learning experience to gain credibility by emerging market businesses that then go local. Therefore, foreign franchise-owners should not expect their businesses to go on forever.
- Westerners can only add value to a limited extent, as unless we really know the emerging markets we can't understand what works and what doesn't. Western advertising is seen as very sophisticated and superior in many emerging market countries – but it needs a local flavour to be successful.
- Local businesses and brands will triumph in the end everywhere, often because of the energy of local entrepreneurs, their deep market knowledge and the patriotism inherent in many countries. The foreign businesses only have a window of opportunity to pave the way.
- The world is full of areas for potential opportunity waiting to be tapped, but how? This is the challenge.
- Beyond this is a world currently out of reach, but there will come a time when it must open up.

Marketing: Workshop Activities

1. Need to keep it going

Give an example of a case of marketing failure, and of marketing success, experienced by a Western organization trying to penetrate the market of an emerging market country. How can we account for these?

Brief worked example
In the 1990s in China, many Western companies were excited by the '2 billion armpits' idea and thought if they could only sell their products even just *once to everybody* in China, they would be onto a winner. But this rarely happened. For example, Kellogg's came to China thinking that they could jump on the bandwagon. However, the whole idea of Western-style breakfast cereals was a big flop in China, as most Chinese don't eat Western-style breakfasts and many don't like milk, or are intolerant to lactose products. By contrast, yogurt was a different matter, especially as a drink, and flavoured – that was a big hit. The product was tested in supermarkets with push-girls, and many opportunities for sampling were presented. The lessons here are obviously in the need for market research and consumer testing, and it appears strange that this was not adequately done in the first instance, or perhaps the initial research suggested more promising results. The '2 billion armpits' appeal often overcame more carefully considered marketing research when China was first opening up.

2. Hitting the spot

Explain how a product or service can be exactly right for a very particular market, and how this has been achieved.

(continued)

Brief worked examples

I – In India, people like their own food, designs and fashions, but many consumers want them to be upmarket too – so fashionable and sophisticated, but local. There is a fashion store in New Delhi – it is in many other cities too – called FabIndia. The ownership is local, but these entrepreneurs have had a lot of experience over-seas. The fashions (and home furnishings and related products) are local in style, but made of natural fabrics and in homespun colours such as beiges and browns. They appeal to the more wealthy and Westernized Indians, and to the many Western expatriates living in India. This shop was launched at a time when most Indian stores were selling saris and salvar chemises made from nylon and other artificial fibres, in what some customers saw as garish colours and over-fussy designs. FabIndia stores are laid out like a Western shop and with lots of fitting rooms for trying on clothes, without heavy or pushy sales techniques. Prices are fixed and not negotiable. It has been a huge success, but really only appeals to a narrow segment, and there may be a limit to how far the brand can be extended.

II – In many South American countries, such as Brazil, Argentina, Chile and Peru, there is a big demand for management education – mostly in Spanish. However, bilingual Spanish and English pro-grammes with overseas branding can be extremely popular with a very small segment – and they are willing to pay high prices for a prestigious product that can add to their status and enable them to land jobs with sought-after multinationals in retailing and banking.

3. Following the herd

Explain how Western-style individualism and Asian collectivism can produce very different marketing results.

Brief worked example

In Vietnam, many of the houses are identical, especially as they must be very narrow to fit in with house-building regulations, because land is in short supply. Various Western painting and decorating businesses have set up in Vietnam, and are trying to give people a choice – but in reality most people who can afford to buy and decorate their own house are not necessarily looking for something very different. They are aspiring to join the elite group of home-owners, so they want to follow this particular smart crowd. The colours they like are more-or-less the same, and the most popular brands of paint are widely accepted. The clever approach of the Western paint brands has been to cash in on this, especially in contrast with the Western scenario. In more individualist countries, many people would actually want to choose colours and designs that were completely different, and following the crowd would be a strategy to be avoided.

4. Keeping up with the Joneses

Prestige and status is everything in emerging markets – do you agree?

Brief worked example
In many parts of Africa, it is important to arrive for meetings in a smart car and wearing a suit – not walking along the road wearing shorts and sandals, even if this is cheaper, more comfortable and more convenient. Westerners might admire the African practice of making footwear out of used car tyres and think this is very environmentally friendly, but well-to-do Africans would 'not be seen dead' wearing them. Westerners are likely to prefer understated, unbranded consumer products and even think that flaunting wealth is in poor taste – but this is in great contrast with the under-developed world. However, we are probably only talking about a very small segment of the emerging countries. The consumers at the 'bottom of the pyramid' are looking for practical usefulness, affordability and convenience – such as the remote

(continued)

banking services in the villages and use of cheap mobile phones for a variety of applications, as discussed in this chapter.

5. Customizing for success

Exact tailoring of goods and services for different markets and segments can pay off – but it can be in considerable contrast with Western preferences. Explain.

Brief worked example
I was buying gold in Hong Kong, and Hong Kong airport shops are heavily geared towards the mainland China market. If you are buying gold in Europe, such as sovereigns or small gold bars, you get them in a small plastic pouch, which really just keeps them safe. In Hong Kong, your small gold ornament – which if you are Western you are probably only buying for the gold content, as an investment – is set off in a huge display frame. Many Chinese like showy signs of wealth, but Westerners generally prefer to make small, unostentatious purchases and put them away in a safe. Therefore, as these shops in Hong Kong airport are mostly customized for the well-off mainland Chinese, the items are presented in flashy cases to be given as elaborate and showy gifts, appealing to this segment even more strongly as a result.

6. Leveraging foreign interest

How can a local emerging market business use a foreign business – especially a foreign franchise – to develop its own local business?

Brief worked example
In South America, many businesses were initially influenced by the North American model, but now local businesses have developed their own way of operating and presenting themselves, which can be more popular. Although companies such as McDonald's and Starbucks are still attracting thousands of locals in these countries, more indigenous versions of these products with local

variations are now becoming preferred. An early example of foreign interest was the Chinese restaurant, but now so many Chinese have settled in South America that they have become locals, with their own hybrid brand of local Chinese cuisine, known only in South America. Emerging market countries with restrictions on attracting foreign franchises have developed their own businesses using ideas based on foreign businesses as substitutes. In Iran, for example, the sanctions imposed from the US mean they can't attract the famous US fast-food chains, so they have developed local lookalikes, which have taken off significantly in the major cities.

7. The rise of the locals

Discuss how some local brands are more popular than foreign brands in certain markets, and vice-versa.

Brief worked example
In China, local Tsingdao brand beer, and beers brewed in Shanghai and Beijing, are cheap and widely popular, but in Vietnam *everyone* is drinking Heineken, with the distinctive green bottle on every restaurant table. In a typical Indian shopping mall, only one or two food outlets are foreign, although all the rest might be local but different, reflecting the cuisines of the contrasting regions of India. In Malaysia, local products also predominate, with items designed for Muslims being in contrast with those created for Christians.

Advertising is usually targeted at the local consumer, and the choice of foreign products can be limited. But the contrast is not necessarily between Western and emerging market brands – it can be between Chinese or Indian brands, for example, especially in the case of food items and healthcare products. In many emerging markets, pharmaceuticals that would normally be prescription-only in the West are sold over the counter. Together with expensive

(continued)

Western imports, local substitutes – and Indian and Chinese versions – are easily available, at vastly differing prices. Many countries have customized foreign brands and have made them local – as in the case of Guinness, with its local non-alcoholic variant called Malta, popular in Ghana and many African countries.

8. Future market potential

Which countries do you see as having a strong marketing potential for the future, where the domestic market could be significantly expanded?

Brief worked example
Countries with a large population, even if not especially wealthy, can be seen as having good potential for the future – for example, Turkey, Malaysia and Indonesia. Unit sales can be large, even if margins are small. Rich countries with a small population, such as Kazakhstan – even though hard to penetrate – sound like interesting prospects, especially for luxury products. Russia is a huge market for these products, although they are often buying them from overseas. Countries with several billionaires – particularly India – have been targeted for years by Western luxury product retailers. These countries are now becoming better prospects as they open up and the diaspora sends money home, helping to expand the purchasing power of the locals. The potential for China to develop is still substantial, even if its economy is slightly contracting. South Africa is also becoming increasingly sophisticated.

9. Closed to the outside world

Which countries do you see as very distant prospects – that may remain so for some time?

Brief worked example
In Yemen, there seemed to be very few shopping malls or decent-sized supermarkets. Most stores were hole-in-the-wall affairs,

selling individual cheese spread triangles in foil from a Laughing Cow circular box one-by-one, or individual cigarettes or small pieces of chewing-gum. Most of the locals were wearing traditional dress. The homes had old-fashioned homespun Arabic furnishings. They smoked sheesha and chewed qat leaves. Not much sign of Western business here, although Yemenis in high office were very keen to drive Western cars: the Porsche Cayenne was especially popular. Even in the poorest countries there are wealthy segments, and there are always prospects in the bottom of the pyramid. Sometimes, however, difficulties of doing business and a high level of perceived corruption can be off-putting to Western businesses, except the most adventurous.

6 Entrepreneurship and Innovation

Technology, Innovation and New Business Ventures in Emerging Markets

Introduction

Opportunities for entrepreneurship exist in the BRICS and beyond in quite a different context from in the West. Entrepreneurs in emerging markets also face different (and sometimes forbidding) barriers, which they overcome in remarkable ways. Their approaches to **creative adaptation** and innovation reflect widely contrasting economic and social circumstances – and, thus, they have developed exciting new approaches as a result, including **disruptive innovation**, **jugaad**, and **polycentric** and **reverse innovation** (discussed below).

The fact that many emerging market businesses are new start-ups, have not experienced many years of development and are able to take advantage of new Western technologies without the trappings of old ways of operating – with a **springboard perspective** – can be a distinct advantage. As BRICS and beyond businesses gather more experience and market insights many are turning from **imitators to innovators**. New consumer segments can be targeted without considering old ones, such as the **bottom of the pyramid**. New products can be copied from old ones and then enhanced, modified and further developed without considering how the old products were created in the first place.

Also, having the experience of being a national from an emerging market and *then* being an expatriate or migrant in the developed world can produce positive effects back home. This can be an important source of new business ideas, adapted from the developed world to a developing scenario. Yet, overall, there is still a long way to go for the emerging markets entrepreneur – they have to stray far from the beaten path, and often there is more against them than for them – hence the value of their achievements and lessons for Westerners.

Over the last decade, businesses all over the world have set up in cyberspace without ever having been face to face with their customers and suppliers, and without physical premises, as discussed in the first section of this chapter, 'Leapfrogging the traditional path'. The advantages of online businesses have been embraced without necessarily undergoing the process of discarding more traditional approaches, which might never have been adopted in the first place. The second section, 'New businesses for the newly affluent', considers how new sources of wealth and, thus, new segments of customers have spawned new entrepreneurial opportunities of serving them.

Many countries known mostly for copying Western products – such as China – are now developing their own new products and investing heavily in R&D, described in the third section, 'From copying to creating'. This may be one of the ways in which entrepreneurship can help in the process of economic development, and how entrepreneurship can get started in new countries, as explored in the fourth section, 'Innovation for development'. Many emerging market countries experience an exodus of their people – a diaspora – sometimes seen negatively as a brain-drain, but that sometimes can result in more opportunities through entrepreneurial ventures, created by returnees. We consider this in 'Returnee entrepreneurs', the fifth section.

One of the overall questions we inevitably ask is – are the BRICS entrepreneurial and innovative, or not? Is there anything the West can learn here, especially from the most influential BRICS, such as the subjects of the sixth section, 'India vs China'? One of the most important issues is the attitude of the regulatory authorities. They might not be ready to cope with the challenges of managing entrepreneurship and innovation. This might be something they don't understand and could be potentially out of control and politically dangerous (discussed in the seventh section, 'Breaking down the barriers'). This may provide more opportunities for politically less-contentious foreigners.

The landscape for entrepreneurship in many emerging markets is great still mostly uncharted. However, in the penultimate section, 'The great unknown', we see that it is a territory there to be explored, enthusiastically by entrepreneurs and sometimes hesitantly by governments. Finally, some entrepreneurs risk life and limb in the interest of creating new business, illustrating the most daunting side of entrepreneurship – 'Do or die'. Clearly, Chinese entrepreneurs must be especially resilient and determined to pursue their opportunities – and in the West everything comes too easily.

1. Leapfrogging the traditional path

Several emerging market countries are at the forefront of innovative new business ideas, especially because they have not necessarily experienced the evolution of their business sectors in a traditional way, as in the West. Some emerging market businesses can reduce institutional and market constraints and overcome latecomer disadvantages by acquiring strategic resources from the West – especially by purchasing critical assets from mature multinational corporations – using a **springboard** approach. Many emerging market countries have suddenly opened up to modern, global business practices, reflecting rapid economic growth after a period of stagnation or the closure of the domestic market to foreign business. Many countries have jumped straight to using mobile phones and have hardly bothered with landlines. Banking by mobile phone has taken off in countries that had few banks and few telephones at all.

For example, in India, over half of the population earn less than a few thousand dollars per year, and the big banks are not interested in them – they are not seen as potentially profitable. Of the rural population, 70% have no bank account, but the technology now exists to serve the **unbanked** cheaply and easily. For example, a woman fruit-seller saves the equivalent of $1–2 per day, using her $10 mobile phone, through a local financial services provider. Every day she deposits her savings with the local 'banker', a villager who has a hand-held machine with a biometric thumb-print reader and card-swiping device. This inexpensive machine – like those used by airline staff selling in-flight duty-free goods – means that the **unreached** can be reached by branchless banking services. With $5 million a month saved by 40 million customers, through 21,500 transaction points in twenty-four states in India, the margins might be small but the volumes are huge. These 40 million customers would never venture into a big bank, which would take days of walking to reach, and the big bank wouldn't want them and their small deposits anyway. But the branchless bank has made a profitable business out of them, leapfrogging traditional approaches to banking and using easily-available and cheap technology.

In another example, the retail sector in Russia has developed several innovative approaches, not having necessarily developed a strong traditional retail sector over many years in the same way as in the West. In Russia, online shopping clubs offering heavily discounted high street fashion items and home goods have become increasingly popular. These clubs also operate online sites for offline stores, creating a wider market for these products and convenient selling mechanisms for those unable to visit physical retail premises. So, the Western investor should be looking out for opportunities at the entrepreneurial end of the market in Russia – and indeed, European and US venture capital firms have already invested $55 million in Kupi VIP, a typical Russian online shopping club.

Meanwhile, the use of the internet in China, especially in online shopping, has sprung up in places without any offline shopping opportunities at all. For example, branded cosmetics for women in China's more remote hinterland cities, where an entrepreneur spotted a gap in the market and not only sells cosmetics, but offers an email response-centre service explaining how customers can use these products. The more remote parts of China are seen as offering particularly good prospects for developing online retail businesses.

Such a service might not be popular in other countries, as more individualistic cultures might want to experiment with cosmetics by themselves, or discuss with friends and relatives, or consult women's magazines. But this is an example of entrepreneurship with Chinese characteristics, where the internet is more readily available than shops or magazines, and where friends and relatives might be equally ignorant.

2. New businesses for the newly affluent

Affluence is relative; it might not mean super-rich by global standards, just more well off than others. India, for example, can be divided into a small middle class – a growing aspiring group – and a massive number of deprived members of the population. The middle class, on annual incomes of around $30,000, number approximately 16 million, and total 1.3% of the overall population. These are high-achieving professionals, often dual-income couples, at work all day, and for whom time rather than money is the main consideration.

Many businesses have sprung up to serve them, such as lunch-box providers. One interesting new venture offers a laundry service street-by-street in the well-to-do neighbourhoods. From a small booth with a washing machine and ironing board, the laundry service accepts clothes in the morning and they can be collected at night, charged by the kilo. The modern washing machines use recycled water and access solar power from panels on the booth, and the franchise-holder pays commission each month to the owner of the laundry booths. As an alternative to the laundry man going to each apartment to collect clothes, washing them in the nearest river and bringing them back to each apartment at night, it's more efficient and higher quality for customers, and more convenient for the laundry man. There are already 600 franchises in Bangalore alone.

There's another angle, especially for the foreign company, too. With each booth serving around 200 families in one street, there's an opportunity for one washing-powder manufacturer to provide powder for one booth, rather than 200 households separately, in a competitive market with over fifty brands of washing powder available. There's also an opportunity for high-quality imported washing machines with dryers. A family might not be able to afford one alone, but 200 families can, via the booth. As more families reach a greater level of income, more businesses serving the newly affluent will emerge.

However, there are also, of course, the super-rich in emerging markets, and they are stimulating their own business ventures. In Russia, an innovative art fund has been listed on the Moscow Stock Exchange – purely focused on dealing in high-value artworks – and valued at $475 million. This can be seen as entrepreneurially cashing in on an attractive new business for Russian investors.

Building super-yachts, luxury cars and private jets are new targets for emerging market entrepreneurs – and if they don't know how to design and create them from scratch, they can buy in essential parts of the required technology. Advising newly-rich emerging market business people – with wealth management, real estate, how-to-spend-it suggestions and so on – has become another new business prospect.

So businesses designed to serve the newly affluent can be focused on services for individuals – but also for countries. Some entrepreneurs are driven by a need to do business with China and adapt their approaches accordingly – such as the richest man in Brazil, Eike Batista, who has developed the vision of a 'highway to China'. This mega infrastructure project is aimed at developing an ambitious super-port, deep enough to accommodate the ChinaMax – a new vessel capable of carrying 400,000 tonnes of iron ore from

Brazil to China. These are the lengths that developing country entrepreneurs will go to in order to attract business in the future – and these are highly tailored for a very specific market.

3. From copying to creating

China is not necessarily known for entrepreneurship – compared with the common me-too type products – but things are certainly changing in the biggest BRICS and world anchor economy. The perception has been that China just copies things very effectively. However, by making the transition from imitation to innovation and developing innovative services in cloud computing and small business networks – in a way more commonly seen in more mature economies that have supported a high degree of R&D for many years – telecoms giant Huawei is aiming to triple sales, from an expected $30 billion in 2011 to $100 billion during the second decade of the twenty-first century.

Chinese manufacturers have developed a reputation for always being quick off the mark to develop their own version of famous Western market-based successes. One example is Ren Ren, the Chinese version of Facebook. To what extent are these initiatives copying, or do they represent something more creative? Shares in Ren Ren soared 30% when the firm was listed on the New York Stock Exchange and it is now evolving into a new internet contact service with specifically Chinese characteristics. Arguably, the necessary cultural and technical modifications have made this service into something new. Also, the different approaches the Chinese may adopt in purchasing products (see Chapter 4) require different ways of operating. We could also say that the emailed make-up advice from Hangzhou mentioned above is an entrepreneurial new area in itself.

Africa as a continent has always been innovation-challenged, often lacking the know-how and investment – but South Africa has developed highly innovative retail financial products, especially with Investec. Other parts of the country are facing serious challenges.

Egypt – perhaps relating more to the Middle East than Africa – is technologically advanced and offers great IT and engineering outsourcing opportunities, but is yet to make its mark with new innovations. The same is true for much of Africa. Ghana, for example, has great food commodity products, but other countries and brands are marketing them.

4. Innovation for development

Areas of innovation in recent times in emerging markets are often focused on helping improve economic development. These innovations could include the impact of China's high speed trains on the development of the interior of the country. Other innovations could be seen as the need to reduce unemployment in the Middle East by creating new entrepreneurial businesses to provide jobs. Craft workers in villages in India are developing businesses thanks to a co-operative group bringing them together. The opportunities created by the foundation of brand new countries, newly independent, such as South Sudan, offer development-oriented new ideas. The need to create affordable, simple products to offset aspects of poverty in developing countries – such as housing and transport – has led to exciting new innovations. Development needs can be a strong impetus to entrepreneurship, and some initiatives here are highly innovative – in ways the West could pick up some new ideas from.

Let's look in more detail at China's railway network as a case in point. This service for connecting Chinese people is seen as particularly state-of-the-art, although it has suffered safety problems and will probably never recoup its costs, according to observers. But the innovatory aspects of having built the world's longest high speed network from scratch are impressive. The showcase project, the 1,318 kilometre (820 mile) Beijing–Shanghai line, reaches a speed of over 300 kilometres an hour, reducing the usual rail travel time between China's two most important cities by nearly half, to four hours and forty-eight minutes. The service is designed as a rival to air travel and the ultra-modern railway station facilities even resemble airports. The Beijing–Shanghai line took only three years to build, costing $34 billion, and the whole network certainly could bring significant productivity gains to China, fostering development away from the megacities and into the interior. The idea here is not necessarily to encourage migration to the big cities – which China is trying to control – but to enable cities in the interior to gain access to more consumer goods and services.

Entrepreneurship in the Middle East also has a developmental angle, often supported by governments anxious to promote enterprise because of high youth unemployment. More than a third of the region's young people are jobless, whilst others are stuck in dead-end jobs with no prospects. The labour force in the developing world as a whole (except China with its one-child policy) is set to increase by 50% by 2050. In sub-Saharan Africa it is set to increase by 100%. How to find work for all these young hands? The answer may lie with entrepreneurs. High-growth start-ups are widely seen as the best generators of new jobs. They are most likely to raise productivity, a strong basis for economic growth. The Global Entrepreneurship and Development Index, and many other developmental watchdogs, conclude that development and enterprise are correlated. Entrepreneurial businesses are seen as more job-creating and more wealth-creating, especially for countries with a large, young population.

Large rural populations – as in India – face the problem of the fragmentation of their skilled workers and a lack of access to marketing and distribution. An example of an entrepreneurial business addressing this problem is Fabindia – 51% owned by weavers – which operates as a holding company with thirty-five companies in different states. Hundreds of skilled people in the villages are provided with sewing machines and dyeing units, becoming Fabindia shareholders – their numbers have now reached 40,000. Their goods are sold in the Fabindia outlets across Indian towns and cities. Their products were much admired by the author, who saw these items as being made of simple, pure fabrics in basic styles and designs, more appealing to foreign customers than the overly-fancy goods made of artificial fabrics favoured by Indian city-dwellers.

Entrepreneurship in embryonic nations offers a range of opportunities to insiders and outsiders. One example is the new state of South Sudan, where local business people see themselves as 'starting below zero', referring to the lack of infrastructure and absence of roads in the landlocked country. 'Bars . . . are filled with Kenyan traders, Ethiopian waiters, Chinese engineers, American security contractors, Eritrean restaurateurs and Ugandan motorbike drivers', claimed a visiting journalist. Expatriate South Sudanese are returning home in droves after decades of civil war. The shortage of accommodation is such that many visitors sleep in furnished shipping containers at $150 a night. Entrepreneurs are active, with SAB Miller having built a brewery and oil companies checking out local possibilities. But South Sudan's ranking of 159th out of 183 places worldwide for ease of doing business suggests that considerable barriers exist. It's expensive, with the cost of sending a shipping container from a port in neighbouring Kenya reaching almost $10,000 and with 85% of the population illiterate, accessing the local market is not easy. And how long will South Sudan carry on attracting entrepreneurs? It may be fashionable and novel in its first few years, but this free-wheeling situation will not necessarily last, and business there may not be sustainable for the long term.

Yet developmental needs and how entrepreneurs and innovators respond to them are timeless and global, such as the $300 house. Why not apply the world's best business thinking to housing the poor? Why not replace the shacks that blight the lives of so many poor people, thrown together out of cardboard and mud, and prone to collapsing or catching fire, with more durable structures? A competition was launched in 2011 inviting creative business people to submit designs for a prototype of such a house, to be built of mass-produced and easily-available materials, which could nevertheless protect their inhabitants from a hostile world. To keep running costs low, they could be equipped with water filters and solar panels – or small solar units, which can provide at least ten hours of light without using kerosene. The houses would have to be capable of being easily enlarged or improved so that families can adapt them to their needs – all for no more than $300.

In a related example, entrepreneurs in India have developed a chain of inexpensive 'hospitals' especially for the delivery of babies. In three months since starting up, 12,000 babies have been safely delivered for low-income mothers needing a few days of care to have their babies – at a price of around $120. Each 'hospital' has between twenty-five and thirty-five beds, and is expected to reach over a hundred in number in the next few years. Supported by venture capital funding, the service enjoys developmental funding, looking to reduce infant mortality.

This can be seen as a form of **disruptive innovation** – the ability of emerging market businesses to disrupt their Western counterparts by innovating at a faster rate. Why go to an expensive Western-style hospital when this cheap and well-designed alternative exists? Other examples include $3,000 cars, $300 computers and $30 mobile phones that provide nationwide service for a few cents a minute. The techniques that have achieved this can also be applied in the West.

This kind of encouragement of entrepreneurship can be very effective, as long as the products or services are designed for the specific scenario and can appeal to the population, not being seen as hand-me-downs or old technology. This is where '**reverse innovation**' can also come in, representing a new business model based on the reinventing of products by Western multinationals to be affordable and appropriate for developing countries – such as GE Healthcare in India. Otherwise these leading emerging market players from the West are not accessing local markets effectively.

5. Returnee entrepreneurs

It used to be thought that 'the brain drain' of smart people from emerging markets to the West was necessarily bound to be negative, and would lead to slower development for the countries they left. But recent thinking considers the wealth and entrepreneurial inputs that these returning migrants can provide when they come home, temporarily or permanently.

Research on entrepreneurship reveals that many entrepreneurs have experience as part of a diaspora or being a migrant. Originally from poor countries, many have often become wealthy working overseas – and send the money home. According to a 2009 estimate, Indians, Pakistanis, Bangladeshis, Sri Lankans and Nepalis living abroad were worth $1 trillion. A 2010 estimate suggests that non-resident Indians own a further $500 million worth of gold, property and art. The 25 million Indians living and working overseas (far fewer in number than the estimated 60 million Chinese) send home huge amounts of money. India receives more remittances from expatriates than any other country, totalling over $50 billion a year.

This cash funds entrepreneurial ventures in emerging markets as well as providing experienced entrepreneurial talent. One example is that of a young African entrepreneur met by the author in Rwanda. Having left chaos, war and poverty with his parents as a child, he grew up as a savvy, street-smart teenager in London's East End. On returning to Africa he set up a chain of marketing and public relations-oriented event-management businesses, especially geared at cashing-in on the expansion of local telecoms providers. These countries – especially impoverished Rwanda, one of this particular entrepreneur's latest destinations – do not need cash alone but visions, missions and entrepreneurial energy.

6. India vs China

These two countries are among the most well-known of the BRICS – how do they compare in terms of entrepreneurship and innovation? Which one might be the best bet for the Western investor interested in entrepreneurial new ventures?

Entrepreneurship and innovation in China has often been adversely compared with India. India has many of China's advantages, such as its large size and plentiful, cheap labour, but India has outperformed China in a number of entrepreneurial areas. For example, when it comes to applying mass-production techniques to IT services, India can be seen as more successful and go-getting. India is also proving to be more imaginative than China when it comes to redesigning products for the mass market. China's Lenovo and Baidu produce low-cost versions of Western products or adapt Western innovations to the Chinese market. However, Chinese entrepreneurs are mostly investing in established industries, such as hotels and agriculture, or in copycat technologies. Many observers suggest that lax intellectual-property rights penalize cutting-edge research in China – but does it matter? If China is the world's most efficient workshop, perhaps it does not also need to be the world's most cutting-edge laboratory.

This might be seen as a useful contrast – to see China's entrepreneurship as resting in its efficient production, rather than its completely new ideas. By comparison, India's ability to mass-produce IT is the basis of its claim to be innovatory. These examples are seen all over India, such as in the mobile solar-powered automatic teller machines being set up in villages, cheaply built and able to take soiled and torn notes. This cashes in on Indian culture, with villagers too embarrassed to deposit small sums in smart city-based banks – and the slum-dwellers prefer them, too. China's culture is very different – everyone would think it was OK to go to a branch – the banks just need to build more.

Indian entrepreneurs in the more traditional vein are much admired – and not just in their own country – and the wealth they have amassed is known to be prodigious. Indian entrepreneurs are also much more international – as discussed in Chapter 8. One of the most famous is Mukesh Ambani, an Indian billionaire who has developed his own conglomerate and is now planning to create a new bank – to compete with India's largest private sector retail bank, ICICI. Meanwhile, Vijay Mallia, of Kingfisher Airlines and Kingfisher

Beer, is seen as an Indian version of Richard Branson. His airline in particular appealed to a rising middle-class consumer, who didn't want to be associated with cheap, budget airlines. The Ryan Air of India – Air Deccan – had a fleet of forty-six planes flying to fifty-six destinations but it failed after five years of operating, particularly due to the lack of secondary airports in India. Mallia, who took over Air Deccan, killed the budget airline but created a new glamorous carrier that is more attractive to aspiring, status-conscious Indians.

Arguably, China still needs input from Western entrepreneurs and innovators, but it could be suggested that India doesn't, with its own business tycoons fully established in the worldwide business scene. Entrepreneurship in India offers many opportunities, but it would seem that Indian business can respond to the needs more effectively than most businesses from outside.

7. Breaking down the barriers

In many emerging markets, entrepreneurs can be seen as a kind of threat. The regulatory authorities want to tax them and control them – but they don't always know how to.

For example, a kind of multi-brand retailing, a new phenomenon, has become popular in India. But should the regulatory authorities allow it? How should they handle it? This can be a hurdle to entrepreneurship and opportunities for Western businesses in more restrictive emerging markets where the authorities need a high level of control and don't like things they don't understand. Many of these countries are high power distant (as discussed in Chapter 4) and the senior government officials want to be in charge. Politicians don't always like very successful business people, who could be a threat to their power base.

For example, Muhammad Yunus, founder of Grameen Bank and many other micro-financing businesses, has been seen as a powerful supporter of local enterprise in Bangladesh and elsewhere, but is not necessarily popular among politicians in his own country. In Bangladesh, Yunus has faced ongoing criticism, despite his almost saintly demeanour and reputation. Accused of evading taxes, and at the age of seventy, officially five years beyond the retirement-age limit for bank managing directors in Bangladesh, the central bank wrote to Grameen's board in early 2011 that he had been relieved of his responsibilities as managing director of Grameen. The government ministers of Bangladesh may actually be envious of Yunus and Grameen because they won the 2006 Nobel Peace Prize, and did try to set up a political party back in 2007. Business success in a country with jealous and protective politicians, especially if you once tried to get into politics yourself, is a challenge and can pose an unlikely but real barrier to continuing as an entrepreneur. The biggest losers from the government's bullying of Yunus would be Grameen's 8.35 million clients, almost all of them poor Bangladeshi women, whose barriers to doing business he was helping to break down.

Meanwhile, the barriers to entrepreneurship in some countries are more cultural and historical, such as in many parts of Africa where donor funds are plentiful and can encourage a putting-your-hand-out attitude rather than realizing that entrepreneurship is hard work and risky. Rwanda – especially because of the genocide in 1994 – receives a good deal of European funding, but corner shops there are run by Indians and souvenir and craft-goods factories by Chinese. There is a lot of money being pumped into the economy, but the Rwandais are still largely in employee roles, rather than playing a part in the development of their country as entrepreneurs.

In Vietnam, there are hundreds of small entrepreneurs, with tiny retail outlets and one-man-band services. Ho Chi Minh City, previously known as Saigon, is one of the main centres. But the authorities are nervous about the shift from communism, and almost none of these businesses are big enough to attract FDI or produce exportable products. Small entrepreneurs are struggling to make a living, against the odds, and with government suspicion rather than active support.

8. The great unknown – especially the private sector in China

How do we know what the contributions of entrepreneurship and innovation are to an emerging market's economy? We don't, most of the time, especially in countries where private business lacks clear regulations and where published financial returns are not easily available, like China. The extent of entrepreneurship also varies by district in China and – as we will see in the final section – is sometimes conducted outside the law, posing one of the strongest barriers of all.

China is often held up as an example of state-directed, tightly-controlled capitalism, yet the economic dynamism of the country owes much to those outside the government's sphere of influence. Many small-scale Chinese entrepreneurs are making a significant contribution to the expansion and diversification of the economy, but the regulatory environment faced by China's private companies is by no means clear. Private companies with more than eight employees began to emerge only in 1981 and were not officially sanctioned until 1988. Many observers see China as having a brutal history of ideological retreats. Today's entrepreneur can be tomorrow's convict, as discussed below.

The government in China owns most of the biggest companies in the country, and this is likely to continue. This is also true of many other BRICS and beyond countries – vast state-owned enterprises are climbing the world's economic and business league tables in every industry, as seen in the *Financial Times* compilations, for example. These are not just Chinese, but many Russian industries too. These organizations may not be particularly profitable, with the average return on equity barely 4%, despite cheap financial leverage by government-controlled banks. The returns of unlisted private firms in China especially can be ten percentage points higher – but no-one knows quite how much these private companies contribute.

Many observers feel that China's strong economic performance owes more to its entrepreneurs than its bureaucrats, but the precise meaning of 'capitalism with Chinese characteristics' remains unclear. Many Chinese entrepreneurs operate outside of the ambit of the powerful state-controlled companies, but also outside the country's laws. As a result, their contribution cannot be tracked by the state-generated statistics recording China's economy, although one estimate puts the share of Chinese GDP produced by enterprises that are not majority-owned by the state at over 70%. In Zhejiang province, it could be that more than 90% of companies are private, but it would be difficult to confirm this officially. For foreign businesses looking to make inroads into China, it could be well to venture into the provinces known to be more entrepreneurial.

9. Do or die

The perilous legality of China's private companies was highlighted by the early 2011 revelation of a death sentence, handed down to a young businesswoman after a five-hour hearing. This prominent twenty-nine year old entrepreneur was charged with committing fraud – but before her arrest, Wu Ying had seemed to personify the miraculous business success that could be achieved by people from even the most humble background in modern China. She had started a string of beauty parlours, and her net worth had reached $576 million, before being convicted of 'illegal fund-raising'.

The case obviously struck a nerve across China. Not just because of the severity of the sentence and the fame of the accused, but because she was convicted of raising and pooling money outside the official system, an approach common amongst Chinese entrepreneurs and one of the principal ways in which entrepreneurs operate all over the world. With this obvious entrepreneurial fund-raising strategy now declared illegal – and punishable by death – the prospects for developing new business in China are looking less attractive, and foreigners may see this as a particular minefield.

Executive lessons on emerging markets

• Western entrepreneurs looking to cash in on emerging markets can often ignore traditional development paths, as many newly-empowered emerging market consumers are not used to traditional scenarios, and are open to embracing new technologies, so there is no point expecting them to respond to a development route based on that experienced in other countries.

• Western countries could themselves learn from the innovative business models and use of technology being used in developing countries, such as branchless banking.

• Respect for longevity and tradition may be less effective in many emerging market countries, which are now challenging usual norms, and consumers can accept new ideas more readily – such as internet marriage-broking.

• What do rich people in poor countries want? This is very different from what rich people in rich countries might want. How can we make it easier to do business with them? These needs may be driving entrepreneurs from elsewhere looking to cash in on new opportunities.

• Countries known for copying – such as China – have significantly moved on to a higher level of entrepreneurship and innovation, this time with Chinese characteristics – so don't underestimate their newly-found confidence in being creative, even though it may be more of a form of adaptation and modification.

• Entrepreneurship that helps in development generally rather than just enriching the few is obviously a much-desired goal, but can be hard to achieve – especially when challenged by pricing and distribution.

- New markets are opening up all the time, as new nations gain independence and can offer first-mover advantages to the brave and risk-taking – but the novelty might not last long.
- Returnees from the West to emerging markets can be a good option to team up with, as they know both environments – but the problem can be one of balance. If they are too Western their ideas might not be accepted, but if they regress to being very local again they might lose their entrepreneurial zeal.
- Many Western entrepreneurs don't realize the extent of the diaspora to the West of people from emerging markets, and the amount of cash they remit home – which offers many business opportunities of itself.
- Two of the most significant BRICS are India and China – but they have a very different approach to entrepreneurship and innovation, and we can't necessarily say that one is better than the other – India is great at scaling up IT, China at efficient and low-cost production – each innovatory in its own way.
- It could be that in many emerging market countries the regulatory authorities cannot keep up with entrepreneurs, fearing the loss of control, and that somehow they fear that the entrepreneurs may be gaining political power and threatening their positions.
- Many entrepreneurial businesses are not recorded or quantified by statistical bureaux in their own country, so we don't know much about them, and cannot assess their role in an economy.
- Entrepreneurs in some countries can be taking bigger risks than just losing their money – especially if they are really against the system. So be careful when doing business with a private firm (especially in China) that might already be in big trouble.

Entrepreneurship and Innovation: Workshop Activities

1. Leapfrogging the traditional path

How can companies from emerging market countries capitalize on the fact that many are starting from a low technological base and have no need to follow a Western-style route to providing modern goods and services?

Brief worked example

In many parts of Africa, people don't have landline telephones at home, and it's not necessarily economic for them to have landline phones installed – pay installation fees, line rental and so on. One thing I noticed in Rwanda was that there were barefoot kids roaming around the streets with landline phone handsets. I initially thought they were selling these, but then saw a passerby give the boy – aged around nine years old – a few coins, and then the handset was hooked-up to a nearby telephone pylon line. After the phone call, the customer returned the handset and the boy carried on touting for business. It was not clear who was making the money here – and it may not have been the telephone line provider – but it was an entrepreneurial idea with non-traditional characteristics. So, ways of providing business services in many emerging market countries are quite different. Imagine a barber shop set up on the street, tapping into the electricity lines of a nearby hotel to plug in an electric shaver, with just a plastic chair and pair of scissors? This is an emerging market approach – and convenient and cost-effective.

2. New business for the newly affluent

In terms of your own business area – the products and services you offer – how could you cash in on newly-rich people in emerging markets? What adjustments might you need to make to be successful?

Brief worked example

When I was working in Arab Gulf areas, and particularly when I was in the Yemen, I noticed that wealthy individuals were rather constrained by their religion to wear simple clothes, and men were not supposed to wear unnecessary decorations, such as bracelets and necklaces. The idea was that everyone would look the same wearing these simple clothes, and you couldn't tell who was rich or poor. But in reality, people who were wealthy wanted to flaunt it, so they wore very expensive fabrics, they carried a pricey gold pen – like a Montblanc – in their top pocket, they fiddled with gorgeous prayer beads made from precious stones, and drove the smartest and most highly-priced off-road vehicles. These are obvious areas for entrepreneurs to tap into – and many of these products can be supplied by Westerners. Say you make basic jewellery from semi-precious and precious stones, with nice silver or gold clasps – how about branching out into prayer beads? Or into pens with rather fancy casings? Or even jewel-encrusted copies of The Koran?

3. From copying to creating

In your experience, what is the difference between these two approaches to manufacturing products?

Brief worked example

In China, we were consulting to an Italian firm making white goods. Two engineers came to China to assess potential market demand – and saw one of their own branded water heaters for sale in a hardware store! Funny, they thought, we don't export to China. They bought a unit and took it apart in the hotel room with their screwdrivers. They discovered it was 99% faithfully copied, with just one or two unrecognized components. All the labelling

(continued)

was copied exactly. So this is obviously copying, and very effective, at a fraction of the price the Italians needed to charge to break even and make a profit.

But how about the 'Thank Goodness it's Saturday' restaurant next door to TGIF in Beijing? It serves more traditional Chinese food and Western food with Chinese characteristics, at a much cheaper price. The broad concept was copied, but not necessarily the local execution of it. Then there is the example of Shanghai Sally's English Pub, created by a Chinese visiting the UK and 'importing' the idea back to China before real UK pubs arrived. It is not clear if this is copying or creating.

4. Innovation for development

Which innovatory new idea related to your current business interests, possibly helpful in the development process for emerging markets, could you suggest?

Brief worked example
I've seen very simple cheap computers and radios, requiring no power but operated by a wind-up handle, which can definitely help develop new business in emerging markets. And simple washing machines, also low-tech and hand-operated, which can cut down on the time it takes to do the laundry and enable women to get out of the house and take up paid employment rather than spending all day on domestic chores – especially in India. One of the most useful tools at the **bottom of the pyramid** in emerging markets – which has been around for centuries – is, of course, the bicycle! So high-tech is not always the answer.

A country announcing independence can get a lot of publicity and attract more entrepreneurs, and especially give opportunities to consultants advising companies on how to enter these new markets. So, being a proactive business entry consultant can be profitable, but it might have a limited window of opportunity as certain countries go in and out of fashion. South Sudan became independent in 2011 and many Western businesses are rushing in to make a fast buck, but their offerings must be tailored to local needs. The same is true for businesses targeting the new post-revolutionary Libya – they are hoping to cash in on present business interests in a new land of opportunity.

5. Returnee entrepreneurs

Discuss ways in which returnees – leaving their countries and coming back – can come back and make a difference, and how Western companies could benefit from this.

Brief worked example
Many returnees from the US to China could get jobs with US companies because they could speak good American-style English and relate very well to the Americans trying to hire Chinese staff – but they often didn't work out as they were not good team-players, and thought they were superior to the other, more local Chinese. They were only interested in getting rich on an individual basis, and many became compulsive job-hoppers, until they ran out of luck.

However, I met with some Peruvian returnees from the US, who had been college students in North America, and they came back with all kinds of ideas, including about recycling, and started up a business in the local university's small business incubator. With their US-style business background they were able to make a convincing business plan, and raised finance quite easily. The timing seemed to be good, as Peru was starting to get into green initiatives at this point.

6. India vs China

Contrast your understanding of the differences in entrepreneurial approach between these two countries.

(continued)

Brief worked example
In India, there seem to be many entrepreneurs on different levels, from corner-shop operators to mega-millionaires – and they have been around for centuries. But in China they seem to be fewer and more recent. In India I remember meeting business people who had been on the wrong side of the border with partition in 1947, lost everything and had come to India with nothing. They had started from scratch, selling jars of home-made pickles by the roadside. By contrast, in China, especially when the economy was really just opening up in the mid-1990s, everyone seemed to be an employee working for a state-owned work unit, and entrepreneurs were the exception – seen as very daring, even slightly traitorous to Communism. This was private business and, twenty years later, the authorities are still not quite sure how to deal with this. Indians continue to be highly entrepreneurial, overseas and in India, targeting wealthy segments and the **bottom of the pyramid**.

Both nations have produced successful entrepreneurs outside their own countries, and especially in terms of serving the needs of their own fellow countrymen. The scale of the Indian entrepreneurs' business would seem to be greater and less connected with their government, and they are able to quickly adapt and integrate on arrival overseas. The Chinese do not integrate so much and tend to keep themselves separate, but work all over the globe supporting Chinese investment, and don't seem to mind where they go.

7. Breaking down the barriers

Give an example of an entrepreneur in an emerging market with whom you did business, especially one who achieved success against all the odds.

Brief worked example
In China, I remember meeting an entrepreneur in the mid-1990s who came from Beijing but discovered that in Mongolia they

made really good thick coats for the winter. He travelled north in the goods van of the train, because he couldn't afford a passenger ticket, and brought back four coats. He sold them for double what he paid for them and went back for more. What a hard struggle to make a living! Then he opened underground retail stores using the underground cities built by Chairman Mao when the Chinese revolution appeared to be threatened by the West. When I met him he was a competitor to our own business, running training businesses across China. We tried to develop a partnership, as he was very good at marketing and very in tune with local Chinese customers. He travelled the world looking for new ideas, taking an interpreter with him as he never learned English or any languages except Chinese. At that point in China, we tried to run courses on entrepreneurship, but most people didn't know what the word meant! And most Chinese were comfortable with the state-sector mentality. You had to work for the state sector to get any benefits. You could not even buy a monthly season ticket on the train unless you had authorization from your work unit, which I discovered as an expatriate working for a foreign company in Shanghai.

8. The great unknown

If you were doing business with a private firm in an emerging market, and there were no legally-available records of this business and no necessary filing of returns, how would you find out about it and make a decision about continuing this business relationship or not?

Brief worked example
The only way to find out information would be to ask customers and suppliers, but probably in a very informal way through your local staff discreetly asking around. Were they reliable? Did they offer reasonable quality? Did they pay bills on time? Who were their staff members? How long did they stay? Any published

(continued)

information, such as websites and brochures, are unlikely to be useful. The word on the street would be the most valuable input. Perhaps the best idea is to start small with this particular private firm, test the water and build up the relationship over time.

9. Do or die

How can you find out the rules of doing business in a certain country? Do rules applied to locals also apply to foreigners – even the most serious ones?

Brief worked example
The death sentence for foreigners may be unlikely, but not impossible. To keep safe you need very strong relationships in high places – *guanxi* in China – not usually available to foreigners. An entrepreneur like the one quoted above in this chapter was 'the fall guy' for many others who got away with it, but her well-publicized case was designed to scare business people from breaking the rules, and to enhance Chinese government control. Most foreign businesses operate in a more transparent way than the locals – due to pressures at home and in the country of operating – and so may not be exposed to such an extent. But this is a sobering moment for all entrepreneurs – there can be worse things than going broke! Such as being hanged or shot.

PART III

PRACTICE

7 Strategy and Operations

Changing Business Strategies and Operations in Emerging Markets

Introduction

The strategies and way of operating of businesses in emerging markets can be quite confusing for the Western business executive. Decisions made by BRICS and beyond companies are influenced by a number of factors and considerations – and can be fairly opportunistic – or at least flexible, sometimes described as like a **chameleon**. So what might motivate an emerging market business to make new strategic moves? Many influencing factors are externally driven. What if the home government is offering incentives and **regionalization** and **internationalization** can be seen as bargain-basement short-cuts to expansion? And what if there is a possibility of attracting investment from China and the European Union might be especially amenable to providing support? What kinds of **entry strategies**, export modes and supply chain approaches might be considered, and are such methods as **off-shoring and near-shoring** interesting possibilities?

Internally-driven factors can also be important in shaping strategies. What if businesses are feeling left behind and need to catch up? Diversification can be a popular strategy in the West – emerging market businesses can approach it in the same or different ways. They may want to change their target market, and aim at achieving a primary positioning from a previously low base. Finally, many companies are concerned with filling in perceived gaps in their operating competencies – whatever these might be.

Many BRICS and beyond businesses practice **vertical integration** – even without realizing it – as there's always a necessary ability on the part of emerging market businesses to manage without a network of reliable suppliers in their supply chain, and, therefore, they do not necessarily focus on core competencies, a popular strategy of Western multinational corporations. This can be a strength, as it enables the emerging market businesses to build related expertise and, thus, stronger foundations and more autonomy.

The first section, 'Support from the top', describes how the encouragement of key industries by governments, with protection and subsidies, can be an important consideration for a growing business. The opportunity for expansion offered by the availability of low-priced acquisitions from targeted countries, and other possibilities for growth, are discussed in the second section, 'Expansion – in different ways'. These two aspects of a growth-oriented strategy can include expanding into other emerging markets (especially through technology partners) and responding to a perceived need for consolidation for strength and sustainability in uncertain times. Businesses responding to these drivers may be ones to watch for the Western executive.

As examined in the third section, 'Attracting Chinese money', strategies for many companies often revolve around cashing in on China as the world's money-pot, so this opportunity to utilize capital from China is explored here. For Chinese companies, the chance to enter a market not already dominated by another Chinese company, to score points off them, can be attractive – and some companies can benefit from this perceived need.

In the fourth section, 'BRICS investing in Europe – rather than the US', the point is made that many emerging market companies are more attracted to Europe when considering their future strategies. This is discussed further in Chapter 8. There are important insights here for Western businesses looking for inbound – as well as outbound – investment. Meanwhile, the success of China in some markets is inspiring other countries and companies to emulate their progress, or is at least making them feel they need to catch up, as discussed in the fifth section, 'India – and other also-rans'.

As in the case of many Western businesses, the strategies of several emerging market companies include diversification, explored in the sixth section, 'Diversity – not keeping all your eggs in one basket'. 'Moving upscale – and downscale' (seventh section) and 'Going for gold' (eighth section) look at businesses changing their focus or deciding that they want to try to be number one. In the process they might practice 'unbundling' – in which emerging market businesses break down traditional clusters of businesses, avoiding legacy thinking, textbook approaches and established taboos, to create new 'audacious solutions' to achieve their objectives. In the final section, 'What's missing?' we look at the need for emerging market companies to continuously pursue '**creative adaptation**', to further develop their business and technological capabilities in order to decide which way they are going for the future – as something may be missing.

These approaches and ways of operating are obviously not the sum total of the strategies and operation modes of companies in emerging markets. Many BRICS and beyond businesses are pursuing rather inexplicable strategies, without apparent rationale. But should a strategy and operational approach always have a specific mission behind it? Perhaps opportunism and flexibility are more effective, given global uncertainty?

Some BRICS countries promote high-level, government-supported strategies for their companies – even if they are private – so the question of company directors controlling and planning how they might see the future of their businesses is not necessarily relevant. As discussed in Chapter 2, business in some countries – such as China – is to an extent dominated by the state, and their strategies are nationally decided or at least nationally influenced. To a degree, Brazil is also impacted by this factor. For example, China wants to export finished goods and only import raw materials, but Brazil doesn't want to play this game and is trying to achieve more reciprocity. These issues can make a big difference in company strategies, whereas they may be much less of a consideration in the West.

1. Support from the top

Many businesses in emerging markets enjoy a form of protection and support from their governments that can be unusual in more developed economies, and this can shape the strategies of companies able to capitalize on this protection and encouragement. For example, the telecoms regulatory authorities in India, in trying to ensure that local telecoms businesses can reap the benefits of growth in this sector, are insisting that Indian telecoms operators purchase 80% of their network equipment within India. They can buy from foreign vendors, but the equipment must be manufactured in India. So, this incentivizes local producers and only those foreign manufacturers who have taken the step to set up factories in India.

Government subsidies and the unclear (or lack of) separation between church and state – referred to in Chapter 2 – often help BRICS and beyond companies to expand and take advantage of new business opportunities. Petronas of Malaysia is building a $20 billion refining complex – reflecting increased demand globally from petrochemicals and plastics – backed by the state. The refinery is being built on the border with Singapore – a strategic positioning likely to further boost sales.

Chinese telecoms giant Huawei in particular has been seen as long enjoying government support. Widely respected for providing impressive state-of-the-art communications equipment on a massive scale, the company is now opening up and becoming more transparent, especially to counteract complaints of strong and even unfair levels of government support. Although the company is seen as reflecting the best of China's manufacturing prowess, it is also a prime example of Chinese secretiveness – and many think this is to cover up the existence of huge support from the authorities. At least now the company is publishing more data, such as on its revenues, 185 billion yuan ($27.4 billion) for 2010, having grown 29% in the past four years, and profits, having grown 56%. But there are still concerns, expressed by many governments who are customers of Huawei, that this company has strong links to the Chinese state security apparatus. However, for the first time, Huawei's directors are named, the financial help Huawei gets from the Chinese state is discussed, including its receipt of plentiful cheap loans at only 1.7% interest, and its research grants are detailed. The firm's accounts do not contain all the information needed to meet full international accounting standards and corporate governance requirements, but they are more open than ever before.

Many Western businesses see such government-supported activities as protecting Indian telecoms, developing Malaysian refineries and providing contracts and cheap loans to Chinese industrial giants (especially where the founder was a high-ranking army officer) as unfair competition. There is a need to accept that there is no level playing field in doing business in emerging markets. Support by governments of specific industries and some favoured companies, to a greater degree than in the West, is unlikely to change soon.

2. Expansion – in different ways

Strategies for expansion can take several forms. Companies from emerging markets are often interested in buying up businesses within their own country, within other emerging markets and especially from developed countries. Other strategies for low-cost expansion can include buying businesses cheaply when affected by the economic downturn, but when credit becomes more easily available and when a business can persuade neighbours to become ready customers – and cut down on distribution costs.

An example of an emerging market company buying a developed-country business is the Chinese acquisition of a majority stake in

Preh, the German auto supplier, by Joyson, the private auto electronics business in Ningbo. The new business is expected to make future sales of $725 million–$1 billion. As described in Chapter 8, Western executives wanting to offload recession-hit assets can look to emerging market giants like China – but they must be win–win deals, not just bail-outs – as we saw with the abortive attempt by Spain to raise funds in China discussed in Chapter 4.

Credit is becoming more easily available in China and, hence, Chinese companies are keen to expand despite government restrictions and the nationally-planned and controlled economic slowdown. Many are on an unprecedented borrowing spree, especially property developers who are generally starved of credit by state-owned banks in China. A sign of the expansion of these companies was that they had already borrowed $12.2 billion by mid-April 2011, when only $15 billion was available for credit for the whole of 2010. For companies starved of credit, this presented a real opportunity.

Another way of expanding in a fairly cost-effective way is to try to interest your neighbours in your products and services. For example, Russian leaders are trying to get the Ukraine into a Russia-led customs union – and have offered an $8 billion annual discount on Gazprom natural gas prices. This would be like an EU free-trade agreement, reflecting Gazprom's aim to expand and ensure continued control of supplies – and, therefore, influence.

Also expanding into nearby countries is South African brewery operator SABMiller – which posted a massive $3.6 billion profit by early 2011 – based on enjoying strong growth in many other parts of Africa, and in emerging markets generally, rather than looking for expansion in developed countries. SABMiller has been able to lift beer sales worldwide through growing sales in Africa and Asia. This leading brewer of the BRICS countries has experienced a growth in sales everywhere except in North America. With 80% of sales in emerging markets, the strategy to focus on this area is obviously paying off. Why would they want to push more into developed countries when these markets are so remunerative?

Emerging market companies often acquire other emerging market companies to diversify their businesses, and Indian organizations are increasingly following this path. Wipro, the Indian software services exporter, signed a deal to acquire a majority stake in RKM, a Brazilian-based hydraulic cylinder manufacturer, to create an infrastructure engineering division. But, we may ask, what is the nature of the synergy here? What is the thinking behind this? Similarly, Tata has been buying businesses in Gabon, acquiring a 25% stake in the Olam International urea manufacturing project for $290 million – whilst the Gabon government holds 12%. An Indian capital markets company has been buying brokerages in Nigeria and South Africa to increase access to foreign investors – a new strategy for Religare Capital.

And why would a BRICS country allow another BRICS company to supply it with manufactured goods beyond the capacity needed? This would appear not to make sense. For example, Tata Steel in China, regularly increasing its investment to maintain market share, is seen as having overcapacity in China, with production exceeding demand. This overproduction is expected to decline as the industry develops more energy efficiency. So, if we may conclude that there is a need for more energy efficiency in steel-making in China, do the Chinese have another motive here? Are they really using the steel produced? What is the real story?

Consolidation is another tactic for expansion, with the second and third largest steel companies in Brazil increasing their shareholdings in each other and welcoming an investment from Japan's Nippon Steel – safety in numbers can be the name of the game for companies who are not number one in their market. Brazil's $1.4 billion HEP dam project is also being 'kept in the family' in terms of the major investor being Vale, the Brazilian copper ore mining giant.

Finally, some emerging market businesses are working with more developed country companies to further expand, such as Mahindra and Mahindra – an Indian business, in talks with Japanese giant Mitsubishi to source the latest farm equipment. Mahindra is the largest tractor manufacturer in India, but recognizes the need to keep on innovating. Sourcing the newest and latest farm equipment from Japan is one answer, so capitalizing on Japanese R&D can be a win–win situation, as the Indian business can help the Japanese to capture new markets.

Mahindra wants to buy technology from Mitsubishi and then incorporate this in future sales to other emerging markets. In this situation, the emerging market unit looking for more business – Mahindra – can target other emerging market companies – its customers – more successfully than the Japanese can directly. Mahindra – possibly because of stronger on-the-ground knowledge of customer needs – can be more effective here. This emerging market-based strategy can work in terms of distributing added-value technology – as long as the financing is in place.

3. Attracting Chinese money

The strategies of many businesses in emerging markets are increasingly driven by the dominance of China in providing investment dollars for their economic growth and expansion – but at a cost. China's powerful position among the BRICS is enabling it to exert an increasingly strong influence in emerging markets – without many checks and balances, and often without much experience of dealing with the Chinese on the part of the recipients. Beijing is seen as being able to push its evolving global agenda without the overbearing presence of the USA – especially as the Americans are bogged down by long-term domestic economic problems. So many emerging market strategies are largely based on how to attract Chinese money. But some of them are facing the problem of not 'giving away the shop', i.e., not compromising their national sovereignty – as discussed in more detail in Chapter 3 – and this can create ethical issues.

Chinese money can certainly make a difference to an emerging market business trying to expand, in terms of a substantial injection of capital in a slow-moving or failing business. One example, of many, is the Chinese takeover of a Hungarian chemicals business – Borsodchem – acquired by Wanhua in a $1.7 billion deal in early 2011. But at what cost to the Hungarian chemicals industry and its future? Many developing emerging market businesses don't always think this through, they are anxious to get the money now.

Although India sees China as an overwhelming competitor in many arenas, the country is not averse to attracting Chinese money for itself. China's leading truck manufacturer Beiqi Foton Motor signed an MOU with the Indian state government of Maharastra to manufacture trucks on the ground, representing an investment of $400 million – starting small but potentially getting larger in the future.

Attracting Chinese money by making a listing in China is a popular strategy. The London-listed Kazakh copper miner Kazakhmys also made a secondary listing in Hong Kong for this purpose. Many resources and commodities companies want a stock market presence in China, especially as 48% of Kazakhmys' sales are from China. Attracting Chinese money is easier if you are geographically nearer, or at least this is the perception, and Hong Kong is still more popular than the Chinese mainland for this purpose.

Chinese companies are often interested in investing in other emerging markets in order to compete against each other and build greater sales growth. Hence, China's second largest telecoms equipment provider ZTE, arch-foe of Huawei, is trying to boost revenues from its dominance of the terminals market – and Indonesia is a good place for this. Indonesia itself can capitalize on the war between these two companies, especially with its huge domestic market. So, in a plan to double terminal sales to Indonesia, ZTE wants to achieve an overall 50% growth in worldwide sales. In 2006–7 ZTE increased sales from $200 to $400 million and has been steadily achieving 25% annual growth in this market, seeing this as helping it in its war against Huawei. It might look like Indonesia is the winner here, dividing and ruling, but it may just be a pawn in the game between these two Chinese business rivals.

Meanwhile, both Huawei and ZTE want to aggressively push into Europe, at all costs – and are prepared to ignore efforts by European countries to keep them out. Both Huawei and ZTE have been involved in IP-related battles in the US and Europe, and the latter insisted that a temporary injunction issued by a German court would not stop its expansion into Europe. In an unusual move, ZTE discussed its IP problems with arch-rivals Huawei. The Europeans appear to have lost an opportunity for divide and rule tactics, and seem to allow some very strong BRICS companies to ride roughshod over European rulings. The cost-effectiveness of the offerings of ZTE and Huawei and their ability to win bids are giving them the chance to get away with it, such are the attractions of doing business with China.

Divide and rule is a popular Chinese policy, especially in terms of containing foreign competition, where foreign firms are isolated and confined to specific areas, preventing them from getting too big and powerful, and letting them know who's in charge – China. Hence, in the 1990s, British Airways was given landing slots at Beijing Airport, and Virgin was given Shanghai. Chinese money remains attractive and can influence the strategies of both developed country and emerging market business – but there is always a price. As the non-Chinese recipient – do you still have control? Did the Chinese get a better bargain than you realized? What is their real agenda? Are you thinking in the short term but they are thinking in the long term? Are you just a pawn in their game? Are they making a mockery of your ways of operating?

4. BRICS investing in Europe – rather than the US

Many BRICS businesses – especially China – find Europe more attractive than the US for several reasons. It's more welcoming, dollar-based assets are seen as not being the best place to park money, some acquisitions are denied by the US authorities and companies are being accused of being copycats of US companies – such as Groupon imitator Lashou.com, launched in a $1.1 billion valuation – much criticized in the US.

Capital and companies from China are increasingly moving into Europe, such as London's black taxi cabs, owned by Manganese Bronze, part-owned by Geely, a Shanghai-based carmaker that also owns Volvo – and there are hundreds more examples. Europe is feeling the force of China's outward expansion earlier and to a greater extent than America, as Chinese feel more welcome in Europe. Investments by China into Europe are made by the state, by private individuals and by Chinese companies. Around a quarter of China's $3 trillion reserves are now in euro-denominated assets, and leading investor CIC was reportedly given another $100–200 billion to invest during 2011. Chinese investment in Europe is often made through third-party managers. Where it does hold direct stakes, it has so far shown little inclination to interfere in the running of companies, which can be attractive for the Europeans.

One of the reasons for not investing in the US for BRICS companies can be seen in the example of Huawei, already widely quoted above. China's biggest maker of telecoms equipment reversed course and accepted the recommendation of the Committee on Foreign Investment in the US that it revoke its acquisition of assets owned by 3Leaf, an American technology company. Huawei had already bought the assets, but officials at the Pentagon asked the CFIUS, which considers the national security implications of takeovers, for its opinion. If Huawei had persisted in wanting to keep 3Leaf, the White House would have had to rule on the deal, and Huawei thought it wise to step back. These problems are not impacting Huawei and other emerging market companies investing in Europe in quite the same way – the Europeans are seen as less paranoid, or perhaps they are more in need of the injections of cash.

However, some BRICS and beyond companies need to expand into developed countries, including possibly the US, because they can no longer easily identify attractive investments in their own countries, and are not necessarily seen as attractive in other emerging markets. For example, Reliance Industries is now seen as too big for India, and there is concern that Indian investors have fallen out with India's largest firm. A large acquisition abroad could be its next move. Today, Reliance is a conglomerate active in energy, refining and petrochemicals, with a market value of $55 billion, representing a tenth of India's total stock market valuation. Ambani family and friends own 45% of the business. Reliance's share price rose from less than 20 rupees in 1991 to 1,610 rupees in 2008, but has since slumped to 770 rupees, and the return on capital has drifted down to single figures. Yet, the company still maintains a large market share in petrochemicals. The way forward for Reliance is now seen as making the leap from Indian champion to global blue chip company.

Although the US might be less attractive for investment, it is still much sought after for stock market listing, especially for internet-based operations. Web companies from China, Russia and elsewhere have rushed to list on American exchanges. Yandex, Russia's largest search engine, floated its shares on the NYSE, where its price rose by more than 50% on the first day of trading. Renren, the Chinese social network site, also with a listing in the US, enjoyed more publicity than it could get in China or elsewhere when the news media in the US covered the rapid rise in their share prices.

Other companies are still interested in US investments, however, but for highly specific reasons. Wipro, trying to make a statement about being 'green' and forward-looking, is investing $15 million in Vinod Khosla's clean technology fund in the US – the biggest fund in Silicon Valley. State-owned Banco de Brazil is to acquire a US retail bank – reflecting surging profits in Brazil, and a strong local currency – so Eurobank in Miami, with three branches in Florida, now has Brazilian owners, and with this investment could offer remittances to the US for Brazilians. Investec – from South Africa – sees Africa, as many countries, having dispersed political risk. There have been some political improvements in Africa but the country is still not seen as stable, so Investec is now more global, operating in London and across the UK, New York and Hong Kong. The company must do business in the US to be seen as successful in global fund management. With $94 billion in funds under management, the company still sees the US as an essential market, but not exclusively.

Besides Europe and the US, there are other popular developed country markets, such as Australia. India's GVK – a power and infrastructure business, building airports and running utilities – is borrowing $850 million to buy two Australian coal mines – so BRICS and beyond are not just investing in Europe and the US.

Emerging market companies playing on the world stage must learn to play by the rules. Treating European and US organizations in the same way as they may at home doesn't always work, as many BRICS companies are finding to their cost, and they can be reluctant to change their strategies and ways of operating accordingly.

Cosco – the Chinese shipping firm – is an example of a BRICS company trying to change the rules of a game created by developed countries; and we are yet to see the outcome. Cosco wants to operate in Europe, but is not willing to operate in the way that many European companies expect. When contracts are signed in Europe, there is a high level of expectation that parties will abide by the terms and conditions (discussed in more detail in Chapter 4). Shipping rates went down in the summer of 2011 and, although Cosco could pay the higher rates to which it originally agreed, it won't, simply because the rates have gone down since it signed the contract. Cosco, a substantial owner as well as charterer of dry bulk vessels carrying a range of raw materials, signed long-term contracts a couple of years ago, when rates were around $50,000 a day, four or five times their current levels. To try to force the ship-owners to let it off its obligations, Cosco has started withholding payments, seeing this as a 'market-based' approach for a company, trying to maximize its shareholders' returns. Meanwhile, the Greek ship-owners concerned are willing to help Cosco with any short-term cash-flow problems the company may experience – but this is not the point. Cosco doesn't need to borrow the money to pay – it has the money – it just doesn't want to pay. The Greeks are ready to seek worldwide seizures of the shipping firm's fleet – a handful of vessels were already arrested by the autumn of 2011.

So, many BRICS and beyond businesses favour Europe as a target for their investments, and they are generally welcome there, especially in contrast with the more onerous requirements insisted on by the US authorities. Most emerging market businesses don't want to change their strategies and ways of operating in line with the regulations of foreign jurisdictions, and often have cultural reasons for these strategies. This clash can be a cause for concern for Western business partners, especially if the behaviour of the emerging market company is pushing for a compromise, to which Westerners might be reluctant to agree.

5. India – and other also-rans

The dominance of Chinese businesses in expanding across emerging markets and the developed world is sometimes challenged by India, but apparently less successfully and in a less determined fashion. In Kazakhstan, Indonesia and Africa, Indian businesses are lagging behind China – but may be seen as much more successful in Western markets (seen below in the examples of Reliance and Glenmark). Other BRICS are further behind – such as South Africa, even (or especially) in its own continent. However, we must not ignore the battle going on in their own countries – Chinese businesses in India and Indian businesses in China. In terms of different companies' strategies, perhaps spread of interests and range of activities are more important than which company from which country is apparently 'winning' in different markets.

Examples of India as an also-ran to China are rather obvious in several countries. India is definitely interested in buying into Kazakhstan for oil, but already 25% of Kazakhstan's oil is owned by China, so Indian businesses looking to secure their oil supplies need to be faster off the mark. Not only the Chinese, but the Russians are also here in force. Meanwhile, Indian tycoon Anil Ambani is investing in Indonesia – in infrastructure, mining and railways – but is another also-ran, as China is there big-time already!

India is also pushing into Africa – but has largely missed the boat compared with the existing dominance of China. Reminiscent of the battle for possessions in Africa of the colonial powers of the nineteenth century, the major economic powers of the twenty-first century are jostling for position. Not so dissimilar to their much earlier predecessors, companies from these countries are especially concerned with increasing sales and taking advantage of cheaper manufacturing opportunities. India's Jain – a manufacturer of drip-irrigation systems – evaluated many sites in Africa to set up its first factory there, which it hopes will expand local and overseas sales. Non-China investors are popular and encouraged in Africa, as many African countries are trying to offset the perceived stranglehold by China, especially when the Chinese import their own workers and do not necessarily offer jobs to Africans – and there are issues with retaining sovereignty (see Chapter 3).

Overall, many Indian companies are trying to make their way into Western business spheres. Reliance has found that its natural gas output is dropping and its profit growth is slowing – and has created credit default swaps as part of the cost of protecting its debt. The firm is negotiating with American Express to create a joint venture for forming e-payment gateways – seen as another way of trying to catch up, but in many ways Indian businesses are more comfortable in the US and Europe, especially as a result of long-term immigration.

Similarly, Glenmark – a pharmaceuticals business in India – has come to an agreement with European operator Sanofi to grant a licence for the development and commercialization of its new mono-clonal antibody. Glenmark expects to gain $613 million and double-digit royalties – hence trying to overcome being an Indian also-ran by teaming up with a European provider, rather than in the domains more dominated by China.

Even further behind in the battle against Chinese company domi-nance and especially in the scramble for Africa, but still determined to make inroads, is South Africa and its increasingly dynamic com-mercial sector. The Standard Bank of South Africa has announced its willingness to sell its operations in Turkey and Argentina to refocus investment efforts in the African continent. This strategic flexibility could appear inconsistent compared with the early commitment of China in Africa, and looks like the Standard Bank is not paying due attention to opportunities on its own doorstep. The Western business observer may find it difficult to appreciate that the Standard Bank is from the same continent, being the only BRICS country, or near-BRICS country, in the region.

Meanwhile, Chinese and Indian companies are entering each others' markets – so the picture of national strategic competitiveness is quite muddied. Huawei is betting big on India, having set up new business units costing $2 billion in 2010. The company was expecting $100 million in sales by the end of 2011, and is hiring 100–500 new staff for India – a clear recognition that India is not far behind in China's perception of where it should be at. In reverse, Infosys of India is investing in China, putting $135 million into a delivery centre in Shanghai in an effort to build up market share. Perhaps the main difference is the scale of investment from China and its willingness to take big risks.

6. Diversity – not keeping all your eggs in one basket

Many BRICS and beyond companies tend to focus on developing a wide range of businesses in order to hedge their strategic bets. They are more interested in clustering different businesses together than offering a mix of products and services from one company in one business area – even if this apparent lack of focus doesn't make much sense to the market analysts, who think these companies look like old-fashioned and unstructured conglomerates whose holdings are too thinly spread. Here, we look at two examples from India – Tata and Godrej – which, despite criticism, have their own ways of operating from which Western businesses might take some lessons.

So, diversity is the name of the game for many emerging market businesses, some of which – as a result – might look like throwbacks to old-fashioned Western multi-functional, rambling mixtures of haphazard companies thrown together, especially by analysts looking for a sophisticated strategy where one does not exist. One of the most remarkable of these conglomerates is India's Tata group, active in everything from hotels to steel. Tata is so big that several of its companies are important multinationals in their own right. These kinds of organizations are seen by many Western observers as the most common business form in emerging markets. In India about a third of companies belong to wider entities and, also, many of them have thrived because of their close relationships with their national governments – which is easier to access if a company is part of a leading national player, presumably.

Yet, clearly there is more to these groups and their success than just cronyism. The rise of diversified global conglomerates has been identified as one of the five trends worldwide – in both emerging and emerged markets – that will shape the future of business. Many observers have reflected that success for businesses all over the world in the years to come may depend on their ability to operate effectively and profitably around all kinds of markets – especially currently underdeveloped ones – rather than an ability to manufacture a particular product or provide a specific service, particularly if this product or service becomes redundant.

Let's return to the Tata Group, as an example of such a diversified conglomerate. With cars and consulting, software and steel, tea and coffee, the group earned $67.4 billion in revenues in 2009–10, operating in over eighty countries. One of the stars of India's globalization drive, Tata is more diversified than Western firms, more engaged in the life of the community and, if its employees are to be believed, better equipped to prosper in both developed and developing markets. It's not completely rambling, as Tata has implemented liberalization, streamlining, and focuses on six core industries: steel, motors, power, telecom, IT and hotels. Tata Management Training Centre selects high-flyers who move regularly from one company to another as their careers develop. This builds the integrity of the whole and the strong inter-relationships between the companies, so the appearance of disconnection is not necessarily borne out by reality.

The Godrej Group, a Mumbai-based family-controlled conglomerate, is much smaller than Tata but there are some similarities between the diversification strategies of the two groups. Godrej suffered a false start experimenting with joint ventures with foreign firms, which often failed to work out, and has settled on creating clearly-defined divisions. The group has reached overall sales of $3.3 billion. The largest division is Godrej Consumer Products, a sort of mini-Unilever, with deals in Nigeria, Indonesia, Argentina, Britain and South Africa, worth $1 billion – a third of the group's sales are outside India. Western fund managers would say this all looks too thinly spread, but for Godrej, the key is to pick niche products with sizeable local market shares that pass under the radar of big global rivals. They have reached critical mass to be profitable and self-sustaining, and Godrej grants the acquired and existing firms a good deal of autonomy.

So, a diversification strategy BRICS-style can look opportunistic and may not look stream lined, but if it can crack entry into the kind of emerging markets not yet successfully penetrated – there may be advantages here over some Western strategies.

7. Moving upscale – and downscale

In most emerging markets, manufacturers are eager to produce more sophisticated products to compete with the West – but this is not always the case, and strategies and operational approaches can vary according to the state of local economies, and the perception of the needs of local consumers. So, even though Chinese companies – and firms in other emerging markets – are mostly keen to upscale, they are willing to downscale, too.

Although the typical Chinese consumer mostly prefers luxury products produced in the West by famous brand names – they are increasingly interested in buying luxury products made at home. 'Made-in-China-super-yachts' sounds like a contradiction in terms – an oxymoron – but Xiamen Hangsheng Yacht Building in Fujian Province is now one of six luxury yacht builders in China. Making luxury yachts is really stretching the manufacturing capacity of a country, so this may be an opportunity for the Chinese to show their capabilities.

Sophisticated manufacturing is becoming more and more widespread throughout the BRICS. More and more technologically complex businesses are becoming the new domain of emerging market manufacturers – even the building of modern passenger aircraft. One day, Boeing and Airbus could lose their dominant position in aircraft production. Embraer in Brazil is moving onto building bigger jets; Russia's Irkut and China's Comac are entering the international market for single-aisle airliners. Irish-based budget airline Ryanair has signed orders with the Chinese company to use it as an alternative to Boeing. Wherever you look, newcomers are muscling in on what was once a Western domain, especially as the market for air travel is widening and changing. The Asia-Pacific region already accounts for 40% of the air-cargo market and 26% of passenger travel, and by 2014 the region is forecast to have 30% of the world air-travel market, adding 210 million passengers from China alone. So, why should emerging market countries look to the West for aircraft when they are increasingly able to build their own?

Meanwhile the well-controlled and well-orchestrated planned slowdown of the Chinese economy has impacted domestic service offerings here – one example being that the high speed rail network developed as a prestigious and efficient form of transportation was being slowed down by late 2011. Expenditure on further development is expected to be cut by $31 billion, and projects not yet started may not get off the rails, as it were. As discussed in Chapter 5, small and relatively inexpensive cars and vans – such as the BYD

and Wuling microvan – do not represent the peak in Chinese technical brilliance, but they do show a willingness to relate to consumer
needs, which can go down as well as up in terms of sophistication
and technological development.

8. Going for gold

Some emerging market businesses have a strategy to be number one
in the world in their products – and are getting there. But others are
trying to run before they can walk, and their attempts to build market
share to position themselves in a more dominant way don't always
work. Reliance, Tata and JSW of India, Chinalco of China and Vale of
Brazil are showing strong progress in going for gold – but the same
can't be said for other companies, of which Chinese company Covec in
Poland is an interesting example. However, on the world stage, every
year sees more emerging market companies in the worldwide listings
of top companies, and details of the 2011 results are given below.

Certainly a top player worldwide is Reliance of India – especially in
rubber and chemicals, and increasingly in applications for hygiene
and healthcare products. Reliance has invested $12 billion in building
massive plants in India. Meanwhile, also in India, Tata steel is selling its Australian-based mining company to Rio Tinto. Tata decided
it didn't want to remain a minority investor without a joint-venture
agreement with the majority owner. If you are going for gold, you
can't be in a weak position. JSW India paid $2.3 billion for Bengal
Steel – using the strategy of buying another plant to become the largest steel producer – as a means of achieving the number one position.

In a Chinese example, Chinalco has taken a controlling stake in the
rare earth subsidiary of Guanxi non-ferrous metals – involved in rare
earth mining. China wants to ensure constant supplies of essential
ingredients in its businesses. It wants to be number one here – in these
essential commodities – to make sure that the country is in a controlling position for its most valuable supplies for the future.

Brazil's Vale – involved in mining – is also consolidating its position, and also wants to become a leading agricultural producer by buying a leading fertilizer plant. So, this firm is trying to be number one in more than one sector, and this strategy is becoming more and more popular among the large South American conglomerates.

Acquiring businesses is one route to going for gold – gaining market share and increased profits through attracting customers is another. In Poland, a Chinese construction group put its price so low it was like dumping, but it won the business. In a large European highway project, the Chinese company winning the project through this very low bid then ran into difficulties, and stopped work. The Polish authorities involved then cancelled the contract. The Chinese company had come in at less than 50% of the 2.8 billion zlotys or $1 billion budgeted by the Polish government. The Chinese company – named Covec – said that raw material prices had gone up in the meantime and made the whole project much less profitable. The Poles want their road finished for a major soccer tournament in 2012 in June, and many local companies wanted the work, which Covec won. It was obviously trying to be number one, but expanded beyond its ability, and did not allow provision for increasing costs.

Yet, overall, the policy to be number one for many emerging market businesses seems to be working. The *Financial Times* Global 500 publication for 2011 – in which companies are listed based on market value as a measure of size – now has many BRICS as number one in their sector. These sectors include banking, life insurance and mobile telecoms – all of them dominated by Chinese organizations. Other BRICS businesses are coming up fast, such as beverage manufacturer Ambev of Brazil, after Coca-Cola, PepsiCo and Anheuser-Busch InBev. Brazil's Vale is second only to BHP/Billiton. PetroChina is second only to ExxonMobil in oil and gas, PetroBras of Brazil is third, and Gazprom and Rosneft of Russia are rapidly moving up the ranks of the oil majors. Mexico's AMX is third worldwide in mobile telecoms and Reliance – mentioned several times in this chapter – is already in the top twenty worldwide in oil and gas alone.

In the Global 500, companies from the BRICS are making themselves felt, with firms from Mexico, South Africa, Thailand, Saudi Arabia, Argentina, Czech Republic, Indonesia, Chile, the UAE, Malaysia, Qatar, Kuwait, Turkey and Poland entering the rankings, some for the first time in 2011.

9. What's missing?

The pace of development has been so fast for many probably still fairly immature businesses, that they don't always know what they need to have in place before completing deals with other businesses. Many emerging market companies find themselves in triangular deals, sometimes with other emerging market businesses bidding for Western companies' holdings in a third (usually yet another emerging market) country – and the first-mentioned company might be bidding against another company, too. But they may not have all their capabilities in place, so they might not be able to fulfil the contract. The approach might be to go for it anyway, and worry about that later, but this approach can backfire.

An example of such a tangled plan might be the bidding by Indonesia's national oil company Pertamina for ExxonMobil's $3.5 billion stake in an Angolan project, especially after a major dispute with CNOOC, the Chinese state-run oil company. Whilst Pertamina wants to go ahead with purchasing the ExxonMobil stake despite problems with the Chinese (who have now withdrawn), the Indonesians lack the deep-sea exploration expertise, and also need financing. So there are still many pieces missing here.

Many emerging market companies have ambitious strategies to become involved in new developments opened up by Western companies, but they have not always lined up the capability to take on these deals if they win them. There is a good opportunity for Western businesses to add experienced input here, especially as the world is becoming more interdependent, as discussed in Chapter 8.

Executive lessons on emerging markets

- The idea of fair competition and a level playing field does not exist in doing business with most emerging market companies, so there is no point complaining about this – they often enjoy government subsidies and protection, and Western businesses have to work around this if they want to do deals in the new world.
- Emerging market investors may be interested in acquiring Western businesses – but although they are often looking for a bargain, it must somehow make sense to their strategy. However, often that process can be difficult for Westerners to discern, as there may be a different rationale at work. They may be looking for prestige, technology, people.
- For a Western business, providing essential technology for an emerging market company can help leverage that company's business in another emerging market to which it has access. It can mean big licence fees or another form of commission to the technology-owner, as the emerging market company is in effect using the Western firm's R&D expertise – as long as there is something beneficial for each party.
- Focus on emerging markets and consolidation within emerging markets can be seen as a popular and profitable strategy – so what value can Western businesses offer in these scenarios? This might be mostly technology and marketing ideas – often service-based and consulting-oriented.
- BRICS can be better than non-BRICS at tapping into investment money in each other's regions – especially when it comes to dipping into Chinese funds – but Western investors need to learn about the strings attached – the agenda of a Chinese investor might not be entirely clear.

(continued)

- Most Chinese companies compete against each other rather than co-operate, it would seem, but they do protect their competitive advantage in certain products and certain geographical areas, allowing each other to 'own' certain territories rather than competing head-on, and expect to treat foreign companies the same way.
- Europe can be seen as more welcoming for BRICS and beyond for investment than the US – so Europeans need to focus on the pull factors and avoid the push factors already identified by the emerging market investors as unattractive.
- Many non-Chinese BRICS companies – especially from India – are trying to attack the strong position of China in expanding across the world. Sometimes this can be an advantage, as some markets are becoming nervous of China's dominating and controlling influence. So Western companies can partner with non-Chinese businesses to appear less threatening, and they may be more receptive than the overly-controlling Chinese.
- Diversification is a popular corporate strategy everywhere, and some Western analysts see emerging market company strategies as old-fashioned, unstructured and lacking depth – but maybe the lesson here is don't knock it, as it may be working, especially in the developing world.
- Upscaling and trying to enter more and more sophisticated industries is often a plan for emerging market businesses, to prove that they are not so emerging and more established – and with access to technology, they can do it – but it's not for everyone.

- Downscaling is also possible when BRICS businesses feel they may have over-stretched themselves, and this can particularly apply to China – perhaps unsurprisingly, the world's richest country can also draw back from development in specific economic circumstances.
- Being the best in its field is now a viable possibility for an emerging market business that knows what it's doing, and more and more Western companies are being knocked off their perches. Being number one is no longer the preserve of the West, so Western businesses need to avoid complacency.
- Emerging market companies can be opportunistic when it comes to the availability of deals, and can go ahead even if their ducks are not all in a row – they will worry about that later. The strategies of some emerging market companies can be hard for Westerners to discern, and they may be known only to a small, inner sanctum – who may not have thought through everything they need to have in place.
- This opportunism is of some concern when the Western companies themselves are part of the deals but are not really sure what is going on. The deals among emerging market companies are even more complex and indecipherable – so all the more reason for Western companies to try to get to the heart of the matter.
- Western companies can often look inconsistent because they publish strategies and missions and then abruptly change them. BRICS are less transparent, their strategies may seem inscrutable. When they change them this is not always apparent and the rationale may be almost entirely unknown.

Strategy and Operations: Workshop Activities

1. Support from the top

Give an example where an emerging market company with which you were competing, or at least doing business, enjoyed government support that caused problems for you, and how you dealt with it.

Brief worked example

A contact of mine in China was operating a business making rubber handrails for escalators, and other rubber-based industrial applications. His was an Austrian company, and was highly visible to the Chinese authorities, who were always inspecting his operation. In particular, he had to strictly enforce the minimum wage regulations for his workers. However, nearby factories – local Chinese, Taiwanese and Hong Kong Chinese – disregarded many local laws, especially about worker pay and benefits. Although they did not necessarily enjoy direct Chinese government support or subsidies, the government turned a blind eye to their way of operating – so in effect they had many advantages over my Austrian friend. There was not much he could do except promote his foreign branding, better quality and more attentive customer service and follow-up. He always tried to be co-operative and above-board in all his dealings, to give the authorities no reason to give him a hard time. Meanwhile, his competitors enjoyed a lower cost structure as a result of their ability to avoid Chinese government supervision.

2. Expansion – in different ways

How could you, as a Western business, offer attractive expansion possibilities to an emerging market business, in a mutually advantageous way?

Brief worked example

A major training and educational institution in Peru was looking to expand across Peru – away from just operating in the capital, Lima – and also into other Latin American countries. A European training and educational business had something they needed – a track record in research and publications, and much stronger English-language capabilities, as well as an internationally-recognized brand name. So, even though the Peruvian operation was much bigger, they were happy to team up with the European outfit to help in their expansion. This was good for the European business too, expanding its scope and bringing in much-needed revenues to offset losses due to the downturn in educational funding in Europe.

3. Attracting Chinese money

Give an example of how a Western business successfully gained financial support from China to help with its own objectives, whilst still controlling the outcomes.

Brief worked example

A European consulting business operating in Tanzania was looking for sponsors to fund a series of projects aimed at making clusters of small businesses that could help stimulate entrepreneurship and, thereby, economic development. These projects were in agriculture, handicrafts, fisheries and light manufacturing. The Chinese could see the value of supporting this initiative to further their own economic pursuits in Africa, and the European firm were able to protect their interests by clearly limiting the Chinese involvement, keeping them as sleeping partners but well-informed about the progress of the clusters, which they called 'Round Table Africa'. This needed strong, centralized management, whilst at the same time providing the Chinese with something they could see the value of.

(continued)

4. BRICS in Europe

Explain how, as a European business (or a business from other developed countries) you can form part of the strategy of an emerging market company looking to enter developed markets – as an investor, supplier or customer.

Brief worked example
A South African investment company was interested in going global, and found the UK attractive as a target for overseas expansion into the developed world. The South African management saw the UK business environment as more flexible and less heavily regulated than many others, and felt the UK was more knowledgeable about local country risk. This UK business, which has become a major customer of the South African firm, was interested in doing business with a firm from South Africa – they knew about the country, they were open to perhaps a larger degree of risk than US businesses might be and, as long as they could monitor the performance of their investments in a fairly transparent way, they were happy to consider putting their money here. Banks, building societies and investment firms in the UK have become so internationally oriented in terms of ownership that the thinking in the UK has become – I'm doing business with Spanish and Germans and Dutch – why not South Africans?

5. India – the also-ran

How can Indian businesses expand and grow to try to catch up with the example of China? Explain how a Western business might contribute to this process.

Brief worked example
I was managing a small recruiting business in New Delhi – it was a branch of a firm headquartered in London – and our clients included both Western multinationals and local Indian firms.

One of the things that really impressed us was the quality of the candidates we were recruiting. Even bank tellers seem to all have MBAs! They were bright, go-getting and very hard-working, had great language skills and always fitted in very well in the UK. So I suppose our contribution was encouraging Indian entrepreneurship overseas. We recruited Indians for jobs in the UK, and these were often stepping-stones for these smart people to then set up businesses and expand the worldwide presence of Indian companies in the process, in the UK at least. It was very good for our recruiting firm too, because these candidates never let us down and didn't disappoint our clients.

6. Diversity

'A company's success may depend on its ability to operate in and around underdeveloped markets rather than having an ability to manufacture a particular product or provide a specific service'. Explain how your company could benefit from understanding and capitalizing on this particular strategy.

Brief worked example
Our consulting business in the Netherlands is a good example of a firm having developed an almost unique ability to navigate around many different emerging markets. For the last sixty years we have worked all over Africa, the Middle East, Asia – you name it. I was working in the Yemen – typical of the sort of place where we operate, a kind of final frontier – and was at the airport at Sana'a. I was probably the only other non-Yemeni in the place, when this other European came up to me and asked if I worked for this particular firm, by name! We won a huge amount of business because of our long-term on-the-ground knowledge, our willingness to go to and work in these places and our cultural

(continued)

affinity with the locals, which became our point of focus and unique selling point.

Some individual nationalities are very good at functioning in several local markets – such as the Egyptians all over the Gulf and Saudi Arabia – and Kazakhs and Ukrainians all over Russia. They are very adaptable, speak the language and are prepared to work for almost anyone, anywhere. They are immensely resourceful and autonomous, and are savvy and street-smart wherever they go.

7. Moving upscale and downscale and 8. Going for gold

In order to cash in on the strategies of emerging market businesses, we need to understand their objectives. So, are they trying to improve quality and move into a different and higher-placed market segment or downsize their operations to cope with reduced business or rising costs? Or are they trying to achieve a really dominant position in their particular sector? Provide an example of a Western business cashing in on these strategies.

Brief worked example
One of our consulting clients was a shipyard in Turkey, trying to go upscale by attracting super-yachts with (hopefully) super-rich owners. The shipyard had some good, highly-skilled workers and a lot of experience in ship repair, but they were more used to downscale vessels – tourist boats, patrol vessels and fishing trawlers. We prepared a consulting report for them showing them the way forward – how to look the part, develop skills for the future and market themselves more effectively, especially by painting a picture of an ideal scenario and helping them to understand the gap between that and where they are now. As a Western business, we were probably more effective than a local consulting firm, which might have felt uncomfortable being so confrontational.

9. What's missing?

Give an example of an emerging market business with a vital ingredient missing, impeding its strategic progress, and how this was rectified, especially with the involvement of a Western company.

Brief worked examples

I – I was working as a consultant to a tea business in India – it was very large, over a hundred years old, and had tea gardens in some of the most prized areas of India. Its teas from Darjeeling were especially sought-after. Whilst I was helping them with training and public relations, the price of Darjeeling leaf tea broke all the records on the Calcutta tea exchange. But the ironic thing was that they could not sell their tea directly to upmarket retailers like Harrod's in London. Lipton's and Twining's, the famous tea brands, would buy their teas and make loads of money, but my tea business in India couldn't, even though it was their tea. The problem was packaging and marketing – mostly packaging. They could not achieve the quality and consistency of packaging to attract top buyers, who would notice smudged printing, labels falling off, dented cartons and so on. I've seen the same with saffron in Iran and lemon grass in Bhutan. There is no problem with the quality of the product – which is top class – it's mostly the packaging, followed by a lack of professional marketing and distribution. It takes a long time to build up expertise here, so probably the best idea is to outsource these functions, and I recommended a Western marketing consultancy, which came up with super ideas.

II – Similarly, some businesses in Vietnam seem to lack a far-sighted strategy for the future, and this could be their vital missing ingredient. Here, they can get valuable help from Western consultants helping them to develop strategic plans, but the experience of being a highly-centralized politically-managed economy means that many businesses don't know where to start, and how to plan for the future.

8 Strategic Alliances

*Western Business and Emerging Market
Business – Working Together*

Introduction

Like it or not, the BRICS and beyond need Western businesses, and
the feeling is mutual. But many emerging market companies only
reluctantly do business with the West – they want their business but
they don't want their restrictions and other unattractive features,
and they ultimately want their own control – and the same is true in
the other direction. Western businesses are increasingly interested
in partnering with opposite numbers in emerging markets, but
are worried about many of the country risk and CSR issues
mentioned in previous chapters, and may still have '**corporate imperialism**' attitudes.

So, as a result, many of these relationships are not based on con-
vinced and sincere foundations from the start, and this may be one
of the reasons why they don't last, or fail to get effectively started in
the first place. Maybe one party is not offering unique value to the
other, and this can work either way in the equation.

Some strategic alliances reflect historic relationships between
countries – although power and influence may have subtly shifted
in the meantime – there may even be **reverse imperialism**. Alliances
can become deeper and more established with the setting-up of

manufacturing operations on the ground in each others' countries, and depending on the need for essential raw materials present in each others' lands.

The latest phenomenon in the process of the creation of strategic alliances between companies in developed and those in emerging markets is that they are moving down the food chain. These alliances are no longer the preserve of the largest and richest businesses, such as the traditional **leading emerging market players** from the West like Unilever, Coca-Cola, McDonald's and so on. This kind of partnering is now the concern of companies of all sizes – and of all kinds of business sectors. Inevitably this process will continue.

The first section of this chapter, 'Marriages of convenience', looks at problematic relationships, which would seem to have limited prospects. Indeed, many Western businesses in emerging markets are having negative experiences, bailing out after investing large sums with little to show for it; this is considered in the second section, 'Dipping a toe in the water'. The third section, 'Not getting off the ground', examines why some business relationships fail to get started at all, despite the best of intentions.

Companies in the BRICS and beyond want something special from Western companies, something they can't easily provide for themselves. We ask, in the fourth section, 'What's so special about what you are offering?' The objective for Western businesses here is identifying their own unique value-adding proposition – especially targeted for emerging markets – and profitably supplying it. Elements to emphasize here are prestige, unique technology, luxury branding – something different and sometimes unexpected – and this could be constantly changing.

Looking at the other side of the coin, many Western companies are seeking the possibility of 'Riding on the back of the BRICS' (fifth section), looking for new sources of growth, especially to offset saturation in their home markets, cashing in on a higher level of opportunity. So they want something special for themselves in emerging market business scenarios. For this mutual benefit to happen, these

Western companies have to address the issue in the sixth section, 'What makes a BRICS country attractive to a Western firm?'

Many countries have long-term relationships, even over the centuries, but in a number of cases the boot is now on the other foot, in so far that a degree of reverse colonization is now taking place. The seventh section, 'Reverse colonization', discusses this phenomenon in the relationship between BRICS companies and the West – in the case of India in particular, now moving into the UK in a very significant way.

Through manufacturing and the signing of long-term deals, the relationship between many Western companies and some emerging markets is becoming deeper, with more and more companies setting up on the ground in each others' countries, shown in the eighth section, 'Getting grounded'. East and West are becoming more and more inextricably linked in many different kinds of strategic alliances, with the need for essential commodities becoming an important driver, discussed in the ninth section 'Commodities – the name of the game'.

Many organizations in the BRICS and beyond are contemplating opportunities to bail out sick Western companies, but themselves can catch the Western recession sickness through a drying-up of Western export markets for their products. BRICS companies can provide cost-effective and attractive products to the West – meanwhile tying up with Western companies can help with their own diversification plans. Western companies are buying up businesses in the BRICS and are copying their strategies – and the other way around.

In the final section, 'East meets West – there's no escape', we see that the West can be a battlefield for competing BRICS companies – and again, this also works in reverse. To a large extent, some kind of Western–BRICS relationship has become inevitable, even for small and medium-sized businesses, and in a wider span of kinds of operations, products and services. Even quite small Western businesses are venturing into relationships with companies from emerging markets, sometimes responding to approaches by the latter, rather than seeking them out for themselves.

1. Marriages of convenience

The interaction between emerging market businesses and those from the West can be combative but can ultimately settle for a peaceful co-existence, due to a realization of mutual need. For example, Chinese telecoms giant Huawei complained at the proposed move by Nokia Siemens Networks to acquire Motorola's wireless assets; in return Motorola expressed popular US concern that Huawei's founder is an ex-army officer and very close to the Chinese military – so there are security issues for the Americans here. Yet, neither side can manage without the other.

Strategic alliances between businesses from developed and developing countries – especially the giant and high-profile ones – can be a reluctant better-the-devil-you-know kind of relationship. We don't like each other, we don't trust each other, but we need each other. Most Western companies are nervous about country risk, as discussed in the previous chapters. But the thinking of both sides can be that 'we could both damage each other if we wanted to, but this won't get us very far'. Western executives need to understand this point in negotiations of 'marriages of convenience'.

These relationships involve give-and-take on both sides. They fulfil certain needs, but can break up when reservations on one side become too great. For example, Indonesia wanted to import Australian beef and a lively trade ensued, but government restrictions brought this particular 'marriage' to an end.

The difficulties between Australia and Indonesia in the past had improved after East Timor became independent and trade had exploded between the two countries as a result – between 2003 and 2009 annual exports of live cattle to Indonesia nearly doubled, and exports of Australian boxed beef grew nearly six-fold. Indonesia's 240 million population were particularly attracted to spicy beef rending, made from Australian beef, but the Indonesian authorities insisted that their country needs to be self-sufficient and restricted imports. Their drive to increase the supply of domestic Indonesian born-and-bred beef would be achieved when it reached 90% of the market. Australian live cattle exports immediately dropped 30% in this initiative on the part of Indonesia to resort to a form of agricultural protectionism.

2. Dipping a toe in the water

Many strategic alliances between Western multinationals and major emerging market businesses are short-lived – and it would seem that the Western businesses involved are more likely to be opportunistic and lacking a long-term strategy than the emerging market ones. The UK-based Virgin pulled out of the Virgin Mobile deal with Indian group Tata (initially a marketing success, as described in Chapter 5) – Virgin decided to sell their 50% stake but continue receiving royalties. Meanwhile, Tata planned to integrate their telecoms businesses under one umbrella. Not only did Virgin face sliding market share, but also suffered an exodus of senior management and closed their offices in light of the sale.

Another short-lived deal was that of HSBC in Russia, which reached the status of being the second foreign bank after Barclays, but then had a rethink of the company's global strategy and decided to pull out, seeing Russia as a drag on its profitability.

The 'suck-it-and-see' approach of many Western companies doing business in emerging markets smacks of a lack of preparation, research and long-term thinking – criticism that needs to be forestalled and countered in business negotiations for them to be taken seriously and achieve longer-term outcomes.

The BP and Rosneft debacle may be seen in the same light, especially in terms of BP thinking that a previous agreement could be ignored, and that it could go ahead with new deals whenever the possibility arose. The arrival of Exxon on the scene may lead to a longer relationship, especially because of a shift in the balance of power. The failed strategic alliance between BP and Rosneft has many lessons for the Western organization seeking to dip more than a toe in the water. BP wanted to gain access to the Russian Arctic's vast reserves, and had agreed in January 2011 to swap shares with Rosneft. However, by doing so, BP effectively violated an agreement with their existing Russian partners in a previously-formed joint venture, TNK-BP, by which BP agreed that it could only pursue further business in Russia through this venture. As a result, the deal was then blocked and the Russian authorities were annoyed that BP went behind their backs, especially as BP had fully assured Rosneft that it did not have any third-party obligations. The approach to Rosneft was widely seen as misjudgement on BP's part, although the company insisted that it had no idea that its deal with Rosneft would result in such legal issues, saying it felt no need to mention the previous deal.

Clearly, when Western multinationals find themselves competing for the same deal, the reasons for the success of one party can be instructive to others – so why is Exxon so much more attractive to the Russians than BP? The latest deal is seen as a triumph for Exxon, giving it access to one of oil's richest frontiers, with none of the problems that tripped up BP. Exxon has given the Russian firm 5% of its shares – BP couldn't do this, as its existing Russian partner objected to and successfully blocked the deal. Exxon, in contrast, is neither swapping shares nor violating any previous agreement. Exxon's total investment in Russian Arctic oil could run into hundreds of billions of dollars. It looks more promising than BP's offer and so far has not shown a misjudgement of Russian politics and corporate culture. For BP, a lot was at stake; but observers consider that to Exxon's great advantage, its deal is more important to Russia than it is to Exxon.

To dip more than a toe in the water, and to create a lasting deal, there must be a win–win situation for both sides, a perception of entering the deal on a fairly equal footing showing respect for each other, with a high degree of transparency – and without arrogance or assumptions.

3. Not getting off the ground

Some strategic alliances between Western companies and emerging market businesses just don't get started at all, and the reasons may be similar to that described in the previous section. It can be due to a lack of preparation and planning, and also to protectionist restrictions in the local market, as described in the first section above.

For example, Carrefour's plan to merge with an upmarket food chain in Brazil, seen as being in the long-term interest of the French supermarket, backfired as the Brazil chain was already substantially owned by a Carrefour rival. Casino, an arch-rival of Carrefour and also based in France, already owned 37% and was poised to take control of the Brazilian business. There was also an outcry against further concentration of the Brazilian retail market by the authorities, which helped break up the deal, especially when the Brazilian Development Bank withdrew its backing. Observers considered that it did not make sense for Carrefour to imagine that Casino could be excluded from the discussions – sounds like BP and Rosneft again.

Brazil – one of the most exciting and fast-growing of the BRICS – is showing itself hard to penetrate, so, as a result, many foreign businesses are not getting off the ground. Foreign law firms are finding it especially difficult, especially after 2010, when formal alliances between foreign-trained and local lawyers were declared against the rules of the Brazilian legal authorities. This ruling also proclaimed that alliances between foreign and Brazilian lawyers were unethical. Observers felt that the real problem was the threat of foreign lawyers to the status quo, in which a half-dozen big law firms advise on the Brazilian end of most big deals. Foreign companies setting up in Brazil, or Brazilian businesses buying or merging with foreign organizations, have to seek legal advice from entirely separate Brazilian and foreign firms. Brazil is, therefore, moving against the trend in the globalization in legal practices around the world. Only India is also holding out against change and reform, banning foreign lawyers in India completely, even to advise Indian businesses on the law of their own foreign countries.

4. What's so special about what you are offering?

Western organizations, to win the opportunity to work with major emerging market businesses, must offer something special – and something that the emerging market businesses lack or have not yet developed. These unique selling points include having a prestigious and respected name (especially in finance); help with providing a listing in a major financial centre in the West; offering specialized advisory services; having technology adaptable to local needs; possessing advanced technology in a specific area – such as in arms manufacturing; offering luxury goods and attractive brands; and being a source of popular entertainment content, such as movies.

This may be why high-status Goldman Sachs has often been chosen to advise Indian companies, and especially in the high-profile BP–Reliance deal, for example. India's oil and natural gas businesses hired Rothschild and Citigroup to help in the acquisition of a stake in Russia's Bashneft energy business, as part of a plan to secure overseas energy assets to fuel the planned double-digit growth of the economy.

This may be because the Indian and Russian businesses think they can raise more funding with such a prestigious name, particularly to counteract the occasionally negative publicity they receive, related to unreliability or corrupt practices. Many Western businesses are put off dealing with India and Russia, hearing so many horror stories. For example, Vodafone of the UK is considering an India listing, but only if the company is able to win its difficult $2.6 billion tax battle, already discussed in previous chapters. Foreign businesses in Russia are always worrying about the moving of the goalposts. The presence of well-known international advisers can allay their fears somewhat.

Having a listing in a major financial centre in the West is also seen as highly prestigious for a BRICS company needing a stronger reputation to support its ability to attract investors. A Russian helicopter business targeting a $2.6 billion valuation through an IPO found it a good idea to list in London, as well as Moscow. $500 million was raised in Moscow-traded shares offered at $19–25 per share, and in London the company traded global depositary receipts, raising another $250 million in the first round.

China is also keen to attract interest in the yuan – also known as the RMB – in the US and the UK, to support their currency and help them raise capital. Wall Street banks are responding to this by launching yuan funds, cashing in on China's need to build relationships with leading financial centres. London-based banks also want their city to become a hub for trading in the yuan. China now allows the yuan to circulate freely outside its borders, but not across them. Foreigners must earn yuan by selling goods to China or, in some cases, through direct stakes in Chinese companies. Most of this offshore business is currently in Hong Kong but, with yuan deposits totalling almost $90 billion in July 2011, there is little to stop other financial centres competing for a smaller share of this big offshore business, especially given that London can boast a great depth of experience in foreign exchange.

Advisory work is another important area in which Western companies can provide unique value to BRICS and emerging market companies. Thus, a Western firm specializing in engineering software to design oil and gas installations – including power stations, oil rigs and fleets of seaborne oil and gas carriers – set up a business in Brazil, and immediately experienced a 10% growth in demand as a result. **Investment entry** into BRICS can raise corporate profits for the Western business – but it must be in a value-adding area, above and beyond the capability of companies in the BRICS and beyond to easily provide for themselves.

The Danish company Vestas – the world's largest manufacturer of wind turbine machines – is much in demand as emerging market companies realize an increasing need for this technology as they become more aware of the advantages of 'green' energy – or at least power not based on fossil fuels. Vestas was able to win a large contract from China Datang Corporation Renewable Power – who else can entice the Chinese as customers, and not just as suppliers, except a provider of unique technology? There is clearly a need for the Westerners to provide something special.

One of the ultimate measures for Western companies being able to maintain competitiveness through their own value-added is by beating the Chinese at their own game. Being able to stand up to Chinese competition is now seen as a great achievement in itself for a Western firm. German medium-sized family firms, in particular, are benchmarking themselves against the Chinese economy and Chinese competitors, especially in terms of producing products that are well-engineered and built to last, even if comparatively highly priced. These German companies are reducing their manufacturing processes to their leanest, ensuring that all components are available when needed, so that products can be delivered at least a month quicker than any Chinese competitor. A medium-sized German firm producing pumps and pump-motors observed that their high quality was an attraction, and that in an uncertain world, many clients opt for German reliability.

Medical equipment from the West can be attractive in emerging markets – but must be adapted to their needs, and affordable. GE has been successful here, with cardiac monitoring in rural India. A technician or nurse can be quickly trained to use it, and the price of an electro-cardiograph can be reduced by 70%. Portable and battery-operated, 15,000 have been sold in India to date. Similarly, a Western-designed eye-screening device has also been distributed in India, which can diagnose cataracts, glaucoma and other preventable eye diseases. There are 12 million blind people in India, a quarter of the number worldwide, and 80% could be saved with early screening. The small machine is also cheap and easily transported. This can be seen as an example of '**reverse innovation**', based on a new business model representing the reinventing of products by Western multinationals to make them affordable and appropriate for developing countries.

Western arms manufacturers are also seen as attractive to emerging markets. Building jet fighters is not yet well-developed in the BRICS and beyond – so a country such as India, anxious to build up defences, can choose between US and European suppliers. The Russians also have a finger in this pie, but are not always front-runners in the race to supply arms. With a budget of $11 billion to spend on the Indian air force and looking to buy 126 multi-role fighter jets, India has been favouring European rather than American suppliers. Two US defence companies have been dropped by India as bidders – the US government is disappointed, but hope they can sell the Indians other defence products instead. This situation could change depending on political allegiances – a country risk factor in many strategic alliances.

Luxury products and services from the West have a strong appeal in the BRICS and beyond. The Mandarin Oriental hotel management chain, known for fabulous properties across Asia and especially in Hong Kong, is to manage a second Oberoi-owned hotel in Mumbai. Talks with newly-listed Oberoi Realty in India have confirmed that the Mandarin Oriental will gain not just a hotel management contract but will run 200 residences in a branded, mixed-use development occupying 3.1 million square feet. Strategic alliances that capitalize on unique corporate competencies seem to work well, as this applies not only to Western companies but Western to BRICS and BRICS to BRICS.

Classy brands appeal to consumers in up-and-coming middle-class markets in India and China because their own brands have not yet taken off, or there is still a 'grass-is-greener' or 'prophet in your own land' mentality. Hence, luxury brands such as Aston Martin have targeted India because they have a critical mass of super-rich – in fact, the largest group of billionaires outside of the US reside in India. In China, the luxury brands market continues to expand, and subtle shifts are taking place, as discussed in Chapter 5. Even fine-dining establishments have been targeting India – including London's Hakkasan and Carluccio's, US chain Trader Vic's and Las Vegas' La Cirque.

Sales of all luxury goods are increasing in China, despite heavy import taxes, and are expected to increase by at least 25% a year. China is the largest market for Louis Vuitton, for example, representing 15% of the company's global sales. More than half of the luxury goods bought by Chinese people are bought outside mainland China, partly because counterfeiting is rife. If an obviously wealthy Chinese lady is asked about her new handbag, she will point out that she bought it in Paris. This tells you not only that she is rich enough to travel, but also that the bag is genuine. Other brands are also booming, with Burberry China up by 30%. Chinese people are clearly much less shy about flaunting their wealth than people in other countries.

Fine wines are becoming more and more popular in China. Anecdotal evidence suggests that wine buyers often look at the right hand side of wine lists and buy the most expensive bottles, not knowing very much about them. They go for the most famous names, and as a result keep pushing the prices up for Western consumers. Moet et Chandon has become the most popular champagne in China, but many cynics think it's because of the name recognition, rather than it being the best.

The provision of top quality branded services is also increasingly attractive. The rising number of wealthy businesspeople in India continues to attract Western service providers, including US health insurer Cigna, keen to partner with local players to access this lucrative market.

Sometimes a Western product's popularity can be unexpected. For example, the Russians have developed a keen interest in Hollywood movies, with *Pirates of the Caribbean* being a big hit. Box office revenues in Russia's multiplex outlets have risen 27% in the half-decade 2006–11. Hollywood movies are now looking increasingly for foreign viewers, especially young people in countries such as Russia, China and Brazil, where box office spending is increasing, even doubling, at a time of falling DVD sales. Some films that flop in the US are big hits outside, such as *The Prince of Persia*, *The Chronicles of Narnia*, and *Gulliver's Travels*. *Avatar* alone made \$2 billion outside North America. In Russia, cinema-building is increasing and more supply has created more demand. Growth is even quicker in China where cinema screens are going up at a rate of three a day, but receipts for Western film-makers are a fraction of those elsewhere, as only twenty non-Chinese films are allowed each year. However, in Russia and in many other BRICS and beyond, there are no such limits.

5. Riding on the back of the BRICS

Many Western businesses want to ride on the back of the economic growth of the BRICS, especially those businesses who can help companies in the BRICS to be more successful, so Western firms who can play a part in this process are rapidly moving in. This can take place through Western companies setting up on the ground in the BRICS; through buying up emerging market businesses, selling Western brands to the BRICS (see previous section), investing in BRIC organizations in strategic sectors (especially in countries where foreign businesses are restricted), offering specialist products in specific growth areas (especially when prospects in Western countries are flat), selling franchises and attracting investment into your home patch in the West from wealthy BRICS investors.

Hence KKR and TPG – US private equity groups – are setting up operations on the ground in Brazil to tap the emerging markets for more growth in the future. The chance to purchase an emerging market business, and gain an important foothold in a market, can be attractive to Western businesses – and possibly a more reliable form of FDI (foreign direct investment) than investing in a wide spread of stocks and shares. Indian company Larsen and Toubro – an electrical supplies and automotive business – was put up for sale at \$3 billion, attracting great interest from Eaton in the US and Schneider Electric of France. Many Western multinationals see BRICS as good scope for manufacturing, for domestic customers and for export – such as

Siemens in Brazil. But the strong local currency is crushing exports – hence, Siemens' exports from Brazil are down from 20% to only 12% of their production.

Dublin-based financial business Experian is expanding in Latin America through buying credit information provider Computec, based in Colombia, for $400 million, having already bought a similar business, Serasa.

The drinks business is a scene for many strategic acquisitions, such as Western beverages giant Diageo taking over Mey Icki, Turkey's largest maker of raki – an aniseed-flavoured spirit – for $2.1 billion. More than 35% of Diageo's revenues come from emerging markets, with a strong presence and many brands in Africa, India, China and Brazil – and Red Stripe in Jamaica, for example. By 2020, Diageo expect that more than half of their revenues will come from businesses acquired in emerging markets. Another acquisition by Diageo was of Shui Jing Fang, a well-known *baijui* (or 'white spirit') label in China. Diageo's majority stake in a well-known Chinese alcohol producer is seen by some as an indication that China is more open to foreign takeovers than had been thought, especially after Coca-Cola's attempted acquisition of a juice company was blocked in 2009.

Diageo is also riding on the back of the BRICS by selling traditional European and American brands to the developing world's growing middle classes, particularly champagne. In China, Moet Hennessy (34% owned by Diageo) has 47% of the global market for cognac – where well-off Chinese have acquired a taste for luxury Western spirits, especially to impress their friends.

Another route to taking advantage of the BRICS is to invest in local businesses ahead of them gaining major contracts. India is spending a lot on infrastructure and is inviting bids to redevelop their roads, ports and housing during the period 2012–17. They want Indian companies to cash in on the business possibilities – but it's acceptable also if Western companies have invested in the Indian businesses concerned beforehand. This presents a strong opportunity for Western businesses to buy stakes in Indian businesses, knowing that there are good prospects for profitable projects and major sales opportunities in the pipeline. Hence Swiss cement maker Holcim is strengthening control of two of India's largest cement companies, owning up to 50% in each of ACC and Ambuja. With India spending $1,000 billion on construction and manufacturing, these companies will be well set to win big contracts.

Another savvy Western company – Kone, a major manufacturer of lifts and escalators – has been able to cash in on the increasing spread of urbanization in China. The boom in construction in the smaller cities of the PRC and towards the west of the country have given the firm another opportunity. The sheer size of China makes its development look almost infinite, good for Western companies with saturation and lack of growth at home.

When one door closes another door opens, and this scenario is faced by foreign tobacco companies, looking to maintain sales, when facing multiple restrictions all over the world. They see South-East Asia as the final frontier, as countries struggling with widespread poverty and unemployment can be reluctant to clamp down on an industry that provides so much revenue and so many jobs. So far, anti-smoking lobby groups are relatively weak in South East Asia, whereas 'Big Tobacco' – the Western tobacco industry – has lots of friends in countries such as Indonesia (population 238 million) and the Philippines (population 96 million), where cigarette advertising is unrestricted. Even one in four children aged between thirteen and fifteen smokes. Growing and selling tobacco contributes perhaps 10% of the Indonesian government's revenues and provides millions of jobs. It is, thus, of great interest to 'Big Tobacco' firms such as Philip Morris and British and American Tobacco.

Major Western fast-food joints have penetrated many BRICS and beyond – such as McDonald's in South Africa, where local business-man Cyril Ramaphosa has won a twenty-year franchise with 132 outlets. This doesn't guarantee success, as this is a very competitive environment, with Famous Brands, McDonald's main rival, having already opened more than 1,100 outlets, operating under such names as Wimpy. Ramaphosa has benefited from the ANC government's black economic empowerment policies, building an empire in mining, energy, property, banking, insurance and telecoms. With investments worth $224 million, Ramaphosa is a member of the thirty-one-strong club of rand billionaires. As well as serving as executive chairman of his own group, he has several non-executive chairmanships and directorships of some of the country's best-known companies – he is also a member of Coca-Cola's international advisory board. So, obviously choosing the right partner in a franchise is a plus, even though the results might not be there yet.

Finally, many Western businesses are looking to attract BRICS money to redevelop declining areas. For example, the city of Liverpool in the UK is trying to attract investment from around the world – and from China in particular. The municipality has set up a dedicated office in Shanghai for the purpose. China is seen as a much more promising source of funds than Britain. A Liverpool-based group has already secured Chinese cash for a development in Birkenhead, across the Mersey from the main city, and this firm sees their two already-secured foreign-financed projects as test cases for gaining others. This firm, focusing on infrastructure and real estate, hosted a pavilion at the Shanghai World Expo in 2010, and is continuing to try to attract Chinese sovereign-wealth funds to develop Liverpool's derelict northern dockyards, including a sixty-storey Shanghai Tower.

6. What makes a BRICS country attractive to a Western firm?

Western multinationals are looking for countries in the BRICS and beyond who are happy to welcome them, and appear to offer stability, security and transparency, without undue restrictions and not too much competition. In particular, Western companies – like GE – are looking for BRICS who will accept a larger on-the-ground presence and with whom they can build a significant relationship over many years; other Western businesses are looking for good prospects for export sales in growing domestic markets in the BRICS. These can include both manufacturing exports and services businesses on the ground. However, although some BRICS countries look attractive, there can be problems behind the scenes, especially when the Western firm looks like it might take a heavy-handed approach. Many Western firms have set up in Egypt in the past, but now political instability associated with the Arab Spring revolution has made the country temporarily less attractive, and private sector business is much reduced.

GE likes Brazil for its large domestic market, and the company is ramping up its presence each quarter, especially with the upcoming World Cup in 2014 and the Olympic Games in 2016, seeing Brazil as an attractive strategic base in Latin America for the future. GE is popular in Brazil too – prestigious, a well-known brand, investing for the long term and with a reputation for straight dealing.

The attraction of many Western firms is being able to use abundant raw materials in their own country (as well as find employment for local people) whilst supplying a very big market in a BRIC, such as a factory in rural Georgia, USA, which supplies chopsticks to China. Chinese consumers use billions of disposable wooden chopsticks each year, but the country is relatively short of timber. A former scrap metal exporter in the US saw an opportunity and began manufacturing chopsticks for the Chinese market in late 2010. The chopsticks are made from poplar and sweet-gum trees, which have the requisite flexibility and toughness and are abundant throughout Georgia. The area suffers from an unemployment rate of more than 12%; Georgia Chopsticks now employs eighty-one people turning out 2 million chopsticks a day, and is on track to increase the workforce to 150.

The size of BRICS markets themselves and their openness to internet-based services are an attraction for many Western businesses, especially as many BRICS consumers have eagerly taken to new technology-based services. Groupon in China is a case in point, entering with a joint venture with Tencent, China's biggest internet company. Chinese consumers are rushing to take advantage of Groupon's offers, as they have in many other parts of the world. With its unique ability to consolidate deals, Groupon has become the world's fastest-growing company. Consumers subscribe to receive offers from local firms by email each day, ranging from restaurant meals to pole-dancing lessons, at discounts of up to 90%; in China, Groupon offered 75% off the regular price to an indoor hot-springs resort. The company sees China's massive domestic population as a great opportunity for expansion. By the end of 2010 Groupon employed over 4,000 staff, and had gained 51 million subscribers in 565 cities worldwide – China's interest in online shopping is a real attraction to continue growing the business.

South Africa's relative prosperity, sophistication and openness are increasingly attractive, hence a significant interest by Walmart from the US in this country's retail sector. Walmart made an acquisition of a 51% stake in South Africa's Massmart for $2.3 billion, purchasing 265 wholesale and retail stores in South Africa and twenty-five more in thirteen other African countries. But South Africans fear that Walmart will then source cheap products from China instead of buying locally, as well as confronting unions and cutting staff wages. Massmart insists that with the Walmart acquisition it has no plans to make any lay-offs, but will open fifty-four new stores over the next three years and add 6,300 new hires to its 27,000 employees. But the restrictive labour policies in South Africa (which is also the case in India) can be a deterrent to a Western business looking for an attractive BRICS investment possibility.

7. Reverse colonization

Many emerging market countries – especially those with an experience of imperialism in the past – are anxious to avoid 'the colonial experience' of being milked for raw materials and forced to buy manufactured products to keep the national engine of economic growth going in the 'colonizer'. India, a well-known example of having been through this experience, wants to prevent a repeat of the nineteenth century. This is seen in Indian companies' attitudes to Western interests – and India is not the only country taking this line.

Tata – one of India's largest and most successful businesses – has proactively invested in the UK, not just in a tit-for-tat move but through the attraction of the UK as a familiar environment. In a surprisingly forgiving and upbeat gesture, Ratan Tata described the investments in the UK as 'coming home'. With its takeover of Jaguar Land Rover – formerly of the UK – Tata is arguably contributing more value to the UK than the former colonizing power ever did for India. Tata plans to invest $8.2 billion in 2012–17 to: 1) ensure that the product quality of Jaguar Land Rover is fully comparable with that of BMW, Mercedes and Audi; 2) increase production through three UK plants, employing around 17,000 people; and 3) develop a planned new factory in China to continue to expand the Asian domestic market.

Indian businesses in Britain are seen by some observers as more than an isolated phenomenon. Britain is seen to be at the leading edge of an important global trend. In the past decade, Tata in particular has invested $15 billion buying up famous British firms, and is now Britain's biggest industrial employer and biggest manufacturer. What does Tata seek from Britain, which now accounts for 60% of Tata group revenues? The firm opened an outpost in London in 1907 through Tata Consultancy Services, which pioneered the outsourcing of computing to India and now employs 4,900 people in Britain and has roughly three times that number in India servicing British-based clients. In 2000 Tata Tea bought Tetley as a template for the future purchase of Jaguar Land Rover and Corus Steel – in each sector Tata was buying a bigger, established firm. Big acquisitions have been a way for Tata to reach the required scale quickly, and are a shortcut to gaining more name recognition and know-how. Tata sees its strategy of having a low cost base and rapidly-growing domestic market in India, coupled with a strong technical presence in the UK, as a potential winner for the future.

This strategy of Tata's can be seen as one of **'polycentric innovation'**, where their strategy is based on multiple centres, where innovation might come not just from the home headquarters but different places around the world where the company has built an operational culture and defines its go-to-market strategy. So, Tata's Nano car is also being adapted for Western markets. This helps test new business models as part of its **'disruptive innovation'** approach.

To some extent, this is the British chapter of a wider story – the rise of the emerging market giants and their interest in the West. Britain is seen as particularly attractive, and has become the destination for $129 billion of emerging market acquisitions. Only the US gained more (with $193 billion). In proportion to the size of its economy, Britain actually received four times as much as America, possibly due to its open economy, expertise in many fields and strong, well-established brands. Investment in Britain also brings easy access to the City of London. With its multicultural population, including many of Indian origin, and economic challenges, Britain does not fear reverse colonization, and the emerging market businesses from India and elsewhere will probably keep coming as long as Britain welcomes them.

There is still concern in India to avoid a repeat of perceived colonial hardships, so in their deal with South Korean steelmaker Posco, the Indian government has insisted that there must be no exports of raw materials, including iron ore – so that the Indians can try to ensure that they make the potential profits here.

India is not the only proponent of **'reverse colonization'**. Another, on a smaller scale, is that of Angola and Portugal. Seen by observers as the case of an ex-colony getting the better, in economic terms, of its old master, Angola has taken advantage of Portugal's declining economy, suffering from the worldwide economic downturn. Many Angolan professionals have been returning to the former colony, marking an increase from 45,000 in 2007–8 to 92,000 in 2009, and the numbers continue to rise. Angola has successfully gained Chinese credit total-ling $14.5 billion, and its **GDP** (gross domestic product) grew by 7.8% in 2011 and is expected to grow by 10.5% in 2012. Portuguese banks have long dominated Luanda's financial sector, but now Angola's state and private investors are looking at Portugal itself, including buying a major bank in Portugal for $58 million, a fifth of the original asking price of $260 million. The IMF (International Monetary Fund) made the sale a condition for Portugal's recent bailout of $113 billion, offering an attractive bargain for the former colony.

8. Getting grounded

Western multinationals may have started off their emerging market strategies by trading with BRICS and emerging markets in a hands-off way, but have increasingly moved towards an on-the-ground presence, for a variety of reasons. These include economies of scale, accessing a domestic market more successfully, strengthening rela-tionships to improve ease of doing business generally, and to be truly global in reach. But some Western businesses are pulling back in their on-the-ground presence, failing to keep up with competitors or taking the conscious decision to go back home, especially reflect-ing changing cost–benefit scenarios.

Swiss pharmaceutical giant Roche made the decision to set up its third worldwide strategic operations centre (after Switzerland and the US) in Shanghai, representing an investment of $75 million. The strategic reasons for doing so were based on asking questions like:

Will this save us money through cheaper operating costs?
Will this help us develop more domestic sales in China?
Is it seen as putting forward the message that Roche is truly global?
Will the benefits offset the country risks of operating in China?
Will Roche keep this operation forever or sell to another multina-tional or to the Chinese themselves?

Western companies often see having a presence in China as fundamentally important, hence Japan's huge efforts to resume Toyota production in China despite earthquake-related disruption. Toyota's China plants re-opened two months earlier than expected.

Getting grounded is not just a phenomenon of Western companies operating in China. J.P. Morgan in Brazil added another 150 staff to its existing workforce of 630 – especially to help cash in on economic growth and increased investment activity – with perhaps more obvious motives than Roche. Citigroup in Brazil hired 780 new staff in early 2011, on top of 500 in 2010. Spanish fashion brand Mango – already selling popular casual clothes in India for over a decade – decided to finalize a licensing deal in India with a local real estate giant, further cementing its involvement in the subcontinent.

Not all Western businesses are expanding in terms of the 'getting grounded' strategy. HSBC is an example of a basically Western organization with a long connection with emerging markets, which has always sought to have businesses on the ground. The bank has huge operations in the US, Britain and France, but thinks of itself as an emerging market specialist, especially since it was formed in Hong Kong in 1865. However, observers have noted that it has only made three small and insignificant acquisitions in emerging markets since the financial crisis began in 2007. By contrast, J.P. Morgan Chase and BNP Paribas have made big strides forward, whilst HSBC has lost market share on the ground in many countries. Opportunities missed in emerging markets have arguably diminished HSBC's reputation for emerging market businesses. A proposed move by HSBC headquarters back to Hong Kong might be seen as providing an opportunity to turn the bank's leading position in Hong Kong into a more powerful operator in China, and reverse the trend.

Western businesses on the ground in emerging markets are not always successful in the long-term in this policy, often due to changing conditions in the BRICS and at home, and depending on whether the manufactured products are designated for Western or BRICS markets. For example, many US manufacturers have become discontented with operating in China and are moving back home. They have realized that, in many cases, the economics of globalization are changing fast. As emerging economies boom, wages are rising. For instance, pay for factory workers in China soared by 69% between 2005 and 2010, and wage growth is expected to continue to increase at around 17% a year in China. At the same time, wage rates are expected to stay fairly constant in the US. American manufacturing firms planning today for production tomorrow, for consumption in the US, are increasingly looking closer to home. Also, importing from China may require 100 days of inventory due to shipping times, which can be reduced if the goods are made nearer to home.

However, it should be emphasized that this view does not necessarily apply to businesses manufacturing for local emerging markets. It is expected that many multinationals will continue to develop most of their new factories in emerging markets, not to export back home but because that is where demand is growing fastest and they can sell locally – making the most of local labour and reduced transportation costs.

9. Commodities – the name of the game

One of the most in-demand businesses to invest in for both Westerners and BRICS investors is the commodity sector – especially as rising commodity prices are impacting economic growth across the globe. If a country lacks a vital commodity essential to manufacturing – and especially if that country wants to be self-sufficient and independent – it will go to great lengths to ensure a regular supply. Local communities where valuable commodities are located are becoming increasingly savvy about the value of their treasures and what this can mean for their own enrichment.

This growing strategic importance of commodity provision has inevitably been part of the thinking behind Swiss-based Glencore's continuing dominance of commodity trading worldwide, controlling significant chunks of the market in zinc, copper, lead, aluminium and thermal coal. Controlling trading is one aspect – another is acquisition. An example of the latter has been Glencore's $3.2 billion deal to buy a Kazakhstan mining group. So Western executives are keenly focused on unique products – especially if they can realize high prices for basic commodities, the value of which might not have been heavily exploited in the past. BRICS like China are also most concerned with not relying on others for vital supplies – so commodities are a battlefield for all businesses.

In another example, where Western businesses previously dominated high-value mining, such as of diamonds, local companies are getting the message. Well-known long-term operators such as Rio Tinto and de Beers have played a major role in this sector for many years. However, Indian corporate leader Reliance – India's largest company by market capitalization – is acquiring diamond mining areas in India, breaking away from relying on Western firms and seeking profitability and freedom from dependence.

A lower-priced but equally valuable commodity could include pulp – in the case of one example, viscose staple fibre. The Indian group Birla bought a private Swedish pulp maker for $340 million, with the intention of lowering the cost of production of viscose staple fibre through supplying the pulp more easily and cheaply – as a vital ingredient in the fibre. The strategic relationship between the Indians and the Swedes in this case was heightened by ongoing competition from China, anxious not to be squeezed out from the lucrative pulp business. So, the Western business executive must realize that there can be multiple agendas at work here, in this sensitive area of commodities.

Western businesses seeking vital commodities can sometimes have a negative impact in emerging markets, which above all need stability and are facing continued political uncertainty. For example, Papua New Guinea, dominated by a 'grand chief' for decades, suffered a long-term lack of leadership and disruptive power-broking, but finally was able to appoint a new prime minister. One of the constituencies of this new politician is in the Southern Highlands, where ExxonMobil and the state are creating a $16 billion LNG project, due to come on-stream in 2014. This new development has led to the country's elite of society becoming wealthy and powerful. The Southern Highlands has a history of tribal in-fighting, which was once settled with bows and arrows but is now fought with high-powered weapons bought with the proceeds of locally-grown cannabis. The local landowners and other well-to-do residents are expecting to make profits from the ExxonMobil investment, and this might be a further cause of conflict.

10. East meets West – there's no escape

Western and BRICS companies need each other – in good times and in bad. Western businesses are looking to the BRICS and beyond to offset declining demand at home, and for new sources of investment when they hit hard times. BRICS and beyond businesses that depend on the continued expansion and prosperity of developed countries are facing reduced profits due to the economic downturn or other problems in many richer countries. Other emerging market businesses have found their own local ways of operating cost-effectively and building profits – and attracting Western businesses in the process. Symbiotic relationships are seen in many strategic alliances, but sometimes Western businesses are hunting the same prize – and the other way around – and markets are becoming battlefields for rival firms. The variety of East and West combinations is endless, and the way forward for the benefit of both sides of the equation would seem to be to smooth the path and reduce the obstacles in the way, and to fulfil mutual needs for mutual advantage.

Some BRICS are successfully bailing out 'sick' Western companies – when the reverse used to be the case. For example, automaker Saab – well-known for safety and producing safe and reliable cars for generations – was forced to halt production when suppliers stopped deliveries after their bills were unpaid. Saab's liquidity crisis led to a strategic partnership with Hawtai China, but then Saab was in turmoil as the China rescue deal collapsed, and it then turned to Russia.

Saab management then moved to forming alliances, and signed new distribution deals in China and Russia, two large markets for well-known foreign car brands. Saab is now owned by Spyker Cars, with a Russian co-founder, which is trying to stabilize Saab's finances.

Political issues in more developed countries can negatively impact BRICS and beyond business. For example, well-known Brazilian airline manufacturer Embraer faced a volatile political and economic situation in their usual markets with the outbreak of conflict (or at least the Arab Spring) in the Middle East. This has resulted in high oil prices and uneven global economic growth – to the extent that the airline maker expects only 5% revenue growth for all of 2011. There may be a boom situation in many emerging markets, but with a gloomy outlook in many developed countries, this boom may be difficult to sustain.

Western companies are frequently finding BRICS suppliers to be more cost-effective and attractive in providing value-added. For example, Chinese telecoms giant Huawei has been hired to upgrade the UK mobile network in a four year deal for Everything Everywhere, the UK's biggest mobile operator, especially to make it more energy efficient and reduce the number of base stations. Spanish fashion chain Zara also uses emerging market suppliers in Turkey and Asia to reduce manufacturing costs. Zara opened eighty more stores towards the end of 2011 in China alone, benefiting from the fact that 34% of its manufacturing is outsourced to Asia and 14% to lower-priced parts of Europe including Turkey. The high-fashion items, less than half of Zara products, are cut and finished in Spain but often based on raw materials sourced in emerging market countries. However, Zara has to worry that it's not **cannibalizing its cash cow**, a phenomenon that refers to a Western company setting up in an emerging market country and reducing capital and operational expenditure to enhance business margins there, but with the danger of eating into the profits enjoyed by its same-branded products from sales in Western countries. Zara's products in developing countries are significantly cheaper than in Europe – and this is a real danger with global retailing.

Some BRICS are using connections with Western businesses to diversify and expand their services in their home base. Thus, David Brown Systems – a 150-year-old maker of industrial gearboxes – has developed a relationship with Indian auto gearboxes company Kalyani. The idea is that David Brown helps Kalyani to win exports outside the auto sector and increase their access to their domestic market of India. This can be seen as following the trend started by the relationship between Jaguar Land Rover and the steelmaker Corus.

There are cases where two or more Western companies are both looking for a stake in a BRICS company, which then is able to attract multiple shareholdings – such as India's Telenet Global Services – an attractive business outsourcing company, already 66% owned by Blackstone, the US private equity group. Now Serco, a FTSE 100 services groups wants to buy a controlling stake in Telenet. It would appear that BRICS businesses with a high profile always find more investors – but Western investors seem to follow the pack, and don't always look for new, well-kept secret acquisitions, which could be more of a bargain.

We have seen two Western companies both trying to buy into the same BRICS company – and we can also see two BRICS trying to buy into a Western business. Sometimes this reflects competition between two rival BRICS organizations. For example, coal mining is fiercely competitive between China and India – hence Yanzhou Coal – the fourth largest in China – and India's Aditya Birla group – another emerging market giant – are both interested in Australia's famous Whitehaven coal company. China offered $3.7 billion against the Indian company's earlier bid. This begs the question, which is more important – beating the other BRICS or winning the bid and purchasing the company?

Multinational companies can be seen as copying the strategies of some Chinese businesses, especially when it comes to trying to penetrate the China market. For example, General Motors started going into inland villages as the new sales frontier – as even in the more

remote parts of China, people are becoming sufficiently well off
to buy a basic car. Wuling Microvans – with a 44% stake owned by
General Motors – were designed specifically for this market. Of course,
there are many cases of BRICS companies copying the approaches of
Western multinationals, but always with their own characteristics.

Emerging markets are becoming battlefields for multinational
companies competing against each other. Firms trying to reach dominant positions are realizing that they need to build their presence in
the BRICS and beyond, especially to capitalize on growing domestic demand and low-cost manufacturing bases. For example, BMW
is targeting Brazil and Turkey to set up new factories, and is also
looking to build up its presence in India, mainly because it wants
to establish and extend its lead over Audi. Fighting on home turf
is not enough anymore. The same can be said for BRICS companies battling it out in the West, such as Huawei and ZTE, discussed
in previous chapters, already competing head-on in several European
markets.

Some attempts to build East–West relationships – despite their
attractions and benefits – are still taking their time. For instance, the
advantages for India of opening up to more foreign investment are
potentially great, but currently the country is seen as being too inac-
cessible – and is failing to attract FDI. The latest figures are going in
the wrong direction for India. In 2010, India gained just $24 billion
in FDI, down by almost a third on 2009 – reflecting the many reasons why foreign companies are reluctant to go into the Indian subcontinent. India's apparently primitive and wasteful retail industry
is seen as an obvious example of the need for foreign investment.
Dominated by tiny 'mom-and-pop' stores, the near-absence of
supermarket chains means there is no 'chill-chain' of transport and
storage to keep fruit and vegetables fresh, so around 25% is wasted,
whereas in more advanced retailing the statistic is less than 10%.
Vietnam is also unable to attract enough FDI to emerge out of this
highly locally-oriented phase – big retail stores are still heavily out-
numbered by streets and streets of tiny outlets.

And some countries in the West are more successful than others in attracting emerging market interest. Given this mutual need of Western firms and BRICS and beyond companies to co-exist and work together, the US would appear to be lagging behind Europe. Observers feel that America needs to worry about the contrast between the attitudes shown by many in the country to China, compared with that of Europe. In Europe, most emerging market businesses, and especially China, attract red carpet treatment. In America, it's more like a red mist. European leaders, caught up in the euro area's crisis, want China to buy more of their debt; American politicians worry that it owns too much of theirs already. Chinese money has already gained visibility in Asia, Africa and Latin America, but the next stage in China's emergence is expected to centre on Europe. China, in its further development, will be looking for new sources of advantage like Western brands and marketing expertise. Many Chinese business people regard the US as hostile to them. Observers feel that 'scaremongering' about China could cost the US around $1 trillion of Chinese FDI by 2020. At the same time, more of that cash is being invested in Europe.

Executive lessons on emerging markets

- Many Western executives have problems with potential partners from the BRICS – there are many things they might not like – but there is a sense of mutual need. As in a marriage of convenience, you must know your partner's attractive and unattractive features, and know that the divorce rate is high here.
- Some Western businesses in BRICS countries are short-lived or don't even get off the ground, so it's important to

(continued)

think through the long-term strategy and consider potential problems more seriously. Worse-case scenarios are often not thought through – and then they actually happen.

- BRICS countries want something special if they are going to buy from the West – so Western executives must not only package their offerings to appear unique and different, but must emphasize that they have something that the BRICS countries can't easily make or provide for themselves, and fill an important gap in their needs.
- The BRICS represent a range of important opportunities for many Western businesses – but you must identify the pros and cons offered by each BRICS and beyond country venture and be savvy to get it right – the risks are as great as the opportunities.
- Emerging markets don't want to be colonized anymore but they don't mind colonizing their old imperial masters – India has been especially successful here. This offers an opportunity that Western executives are now getting used to.
- Chinese entrepreneurs in Africa – for example – will also have to be mindful of the way they appear – as neo-colonialism is definitely unfashionable, and they are facing many criticisms here.
- Setting up on the ground in a BRICS country can be an ultimate plan for a Western company used to a trading relationship with emerging markets – but there is a need for deep pockets here, and the situation for both will not stay the same.
- One of the most important areas in East–West deals is that of commodities – and this can be one of the most profitable routes to co-operation and creates an urgent need – it all comes back to offering something special and unique.
- There are many ways in which emerging market companies and Western businesses build alliances – and most are for

mutual benefit and convenience and work both ways – it must be a win–win deal.

- The world is now a battlefield for all kinds of businesses competing – and now there is no such thing as a level playing field – the kind of competitive rules common in the West hardly exist in the BRICS.
- Western companies are now just as likely to find themselves competing against BRICS companies in the reverse scenario, and must prepare their approach accordingly.

Strategic Alliances: Workshop Activities

1. Marriages of convenience

Explain a scenario where your Western business worked with an emerging market company that provided you with opportunities, but you felt uncomfortable about working with them, for a variety of reasons. What happened and why? What did you learn from this?

Brief worked example

We were running a consulting business in China and normally just worked with other foreign businesses, but the opportunity came up to work with a Chinese company – this was a shipping business in Shanghai. We thought if we worked successfully with them, we could get into consulting to the Chinese company sector. We weren't very keen on working with their managers as their English was poor, we depended too much on our local Chinese staff to negotiate with them, and they didn't seem to

(continued)

understand the way we went about our business – research-based headhunting. But I suppose we thought we could educate them and convince them. They were rude to our candidates (asking them why they were disloyal and looking for another job, when they had been headhunted – they had been approached by us and persuaded to come for interview). In the end they didn't pay our invoices, because they could only see the point of paying for tangible things, not advice-based services. So we decided to stick to serving foreign companies in China only, and after more than twelve years, this headhunting business is still going strong!

2. Dipping a toe in the water and 3. Not getting off the ground – failed alliances

Why can strategic alliances between BRICS and beyond businesses and Western companies fail? Give an example.

Brief worked example
Our training co-operation in a central African country has been very difficult, mostly because we have not been able to collect our share of the money. We know they've got it, because it's from the World Bank, but they are not handing it over – we are concerned that they have invested it to get the interest payments, or – even worse – someone in the organization has run off with the funds and we'll never get it. The last director of this local African organization ended up in jail for this very reason – misappropriation of funds. We do the work and commit ourselves and trust them to pay up, but at the last minute they make excuses and we don't see the money. But this doesn't always happen – we had a very profitable co-operation with an Iranian company, and an Egyptian client – and they paid up straight away, in cash, before we got started with the training. The availability of money and getting paid would seem to be a central issue here. A successful alliance is where neither company feels disappointed – especially financially. Some African

countries are seen as getting better in terms of transparency – especially Botswana, Rwanda, Namibia, South Africa and Ghana – and their Transparency International scores are a source of some pride in the government. But this doesn't mean that their alliances with Western multinational corporations will go without a hitch.

4. Our special offerings

Discuss why your products or services, being offered to BRICS and beyond customers, have unique selling points for them in particular, adding to their acceptability.

Brief worked example
A business I know offers extremely high-end luxury individually-tailored holidays on a super-yacht for discerning and wealthy customers who would probably like to have their own super-yacht, but in any case can afford over $100,000 a week to have a gorgeous ship all to themselves and go wherever they please. Recently, this super-yacht has attracted a Brazilian family, who were very demanding and critical but nevertheless wanted to show off their wealth and extravagance and hire a Western-owned and manned yacht. This was way beyond anything available in their country. They invited their well-to-do friends on board so they could really make the point about how rich they were, and make sure they were mentioned in the gossip columns at home.

5. Riding on the back of the BRICS

Explain how a Western company can expand by cashing in on an emerging market opportunity, to the benefit of both.

Brief worked example
Our consulting firm in London was looking to expand but we didn't know quite how to go about it. We had a number of consultants with an emerging market background – one had worked

(continued)

in Turkey, another in the Czech Republic, another was a Pole. When we had a client from one of these countries, we matched them with the consultant familiar with their environment and situation. If the project went well, we would open a local office, send our consultant there, and develop new business through referrals from our client. So all we needed to set up the new business was a client and a consultant with experience and knowledge of his or her country. This was a relatively low-cost and low-risk way for a Western business to enter a new, developing market.

6. An attractive BRICS country

Discuss how you went about or would go about selecting a particular country in the BRICS and beyond in which to operate your business.

Brief worked example
In the experience of a Western company I know operating in Peru, the main factors were business opportunities and the availability of established contacts. The entrepreneur behind this company – an Australian – lived in Peru for many years and came to know the people and the country well. He has even married a Peruvian lady! His business was in satellite communications, and he was able to make use of Peru's high mountain ranges, and the industry in minerals and mining across South America. His satellites enabled unmanned vehicles to be operated and all kinds of vehicles fixed and serviced from a distance. Through his wife he came to know of customers and other shareholders, as well as staff members to hire. He also operates in Europe, but his cost base is much cheaper in Peru.

7. Reverse colonization

How and why can this phenomenon take place? What can go wrong?

Brief worked example
In Tanzania, whilst on a business trip, I attended a church service
on the Sunday I was there. I was approached by an African cler-
gyman who told me about how his great-grandfather had been
converted to the Anglican faith by British missionaries in the nineteenth century. He made the point that the Anglican faith (and religion generally, of many denominations) was much more popular
in Tanzania and most of Africa than in Britain. His small church –
with a capacity of around fifty or sixty only – would receive well
over the equivalent of $1,000 in offerings on a Sunday. Much big-
ger churches in Britain – even cathedrals – would be glad to get
a few hundred. But I was not confident about his plan to come
to Britain and reconvert lapsed British former churchgoers. His
sermon was too intolerant and high-church, based on instilling
fear into the congregation, who blindly accepted and embraced
everything he said. I just didn't think people would buy it in the
UK, with their cynicism and attitude of challenging and question-
ing everything, and the fact that so few can be persuaded to go to
church at all. Religion is big business in much of Africa, but it just
isn't in Britain, and is not likely to be in the near future.

8. Getting grounded

Why would a business want to set up manufacturing and distribution on the ground in an emerging market country? What
would be the attractions of the idea, and what would be the pit-
falls in reality?

Brief worked example
One of my customers in the past was working for a UK company
making high-mast lighting. She explained that their products
were very large and bulky, and shipping them from their plant
in England to China (one of their biggest sources of business)
was costly and inconvenient. Also, they could easily import raw

(continued)

materials directly to China, and recruit lower-cost labour. My job was to head-hunt a Chinese manager to work for her – and finding the right Chinese manager who could be trusted and was competent was going to be the biggest job. It was difficult to find a technical person who could speak English – this was in the 1990s – but luckily my customer was a Chinese scholar, having studied Chinese at university in the UK. When I hired a very good local manager for her, it didn't matter that his English wasn't great, as they spoke together in Chinese. Negotiating with all the state-owned enterprises was challenging, but the Chinese manager we recruited learned quickly how to represent this UK business quite effectively. After several trips to England, he got to know the head office team well, although he found the tea too strong to drink! This Chinese manager is still in place, and the UK high-mast lighting company is still doing well, fifteen years down the track.

9. Commodities

Explain how a focus on the value and importance of specific commodities can drive a Western company's relationships with emerging market businesses.

Brief worked example
I – The ongoing need to source tea from India as a mature market for a range of teas meant that the company I used to work for – a trading and shipping business – kept its old tea gardens going – but actually they were a drain on our capital, because they employed so many thousands of workers and also had many thousands of pensioners. In the end we had to let them go, and instead buy teas on the tea exchanges like everyone else did. Owning commodity-producing plants is not always an advantage.

II – However, a friend of mine managed an industrial business in Kuwait that needed supplies of vital commodities, because when they were invaded by the Iraqis their manufacturing operation ground to a halt without one particular chemical they needed. So, they acquired a source of this commodity from a nearby emerging market country to ensure a permanent supply.

10. East and West – no escape

Discuss how Western businesses are finding themselves inevitably connected with emerging markets, in the day-to-day pursuit of their operations, without necessarily seeking them out.

Brief worked example
A friend of mine works in a small-scale and specialist UK-owned company making defence equipment, specifically designing and manufacturing prototypes of armoured vehicles resistant to landmines. These vehicles are also useful for civilian applications, especially in very rugged terrain, and in the mining and oil and gas sectors. The company usually sells these vehicles to other Western businesses – in Australia, for example. But they received enquiries from Kazakhstan, and are now shipping vehicles to oil companies there, with their customers helping in the difficult process of getting import licences. You actually don't have to seek opportunities to do business in emerging markets – sooner or later they may come to you if you have something they want, even if you are a fairly small, specialized and even obscure business.

Lessons for Global Business

What We Can Learn from the BRICS and Beyond

Introduction

Doing business in the BRICS and beyond – as we have seen – involves trying to offset risks but maximize opportunities, and meanwhile the experiences of many other Western executives and organizations in the past provide useful indicators of what to do – and what not to do. This chapter summarizes practical lessons and ways forward – with these three elements in mind.

RISKS

Leadership

The leaders in many emerging markets are wealthier, more powerful and less tolerant than in many Western countries. Populations are much poorer, are generally 'high power distant' and are often easily intimidated and socially controlled, and their businesses nationalized without explanation or compensation. The liberating influence of the Arab Spring movement shows just how much many nations were being ripped off by their dictators, and the potential of each country for improvement in wealth in the future.

Government intervention

As a result of a higher degree of government intervention in the BRICS and beyond than in the West, there is a greater need to build relationships with politicians – who must be carefully chosen for influence, permanence and being on the right side. They can help you understand a country's regulatory environment and how to prevent expensive fines, paying too much tax and so on. But once you have a well-connected relationship, the regime changes and now your man is in bad company or behind bars. When an election is being held, keep a low profile, or your business might become ammunition used by one interest group against another. Is this country free to make up its own mind or is it dominated by another country behind the scenes?

Western business people must understand that some governments are paranoid about civil unrest, especially in view of the many uprisings of 2011. Keeping a low profile as a foreigner may be the safest policy. Many emerging market countries expect complicity from their high power distant populations. Foreigners are high profile and under scrutiny, so you mustn't do anything that might put your complicity into doubt. This also applies to post-Communist societies despite their claims of a new era of capitalist freedom – a high level of state control can still persist.

Financial risks

These are significant in most of the BRICS, due to high levels of inflation and the inability of many governments to control this, and banks can be notoriously unreliable – so you will need to check minimum capital requirements, government guarantees and other measures. How accurate is this information? How can you avoid dealing with dodgy local companies? Do you know what is happening to your investment in a BRICS company? 'Show me the money' is a popular phrase from the movies – sometimes the money involved was there – but no more, and no-one knows where it's gone.

Corruption

This can take many forms and governments throughout the BRICS and beyond are trying to crack down – keen on reducing their high corruption ratings and attract more FDI. However, the Western executive may encounter a mind-boggling prevalence of corruption almost everywhere. Corporate governance and transparency are not necessarily widely understood in the BRICS and beyond – and the pressures for adopting them may be reduced in the worldwide recession and lack of availability of FDI. Therefore, there is less need to make an effort here.

Risk of working with local people and businesses

Loyalty is a major concern when hiring staff – whose side are they on? Intellectual property is another fairly alien concept, so for the Western executive you are probably only as good as your latest idea, as the previous one may have been copied and stolen already. Monopolies are not necessarily seen as negative in emerging markets, where business people will happily go on enjoying them as long as they last, and may be supported by governments. Your 'impartial' and 'independent' bidders may be colluding behind the scenes. Gaining respectability is often a major ambition for a business from the BRICS and beyond, and this may be an attractive perceived outcome from dealing with a Western executive – but at whose expense?

Censorship, information and keeping your head down

Don't put anything negative in writing on the internet – even if your internet account is not blocked or your BlackBerry hijacked. If your privacy is invaded – your emails are read and your phone is tapped as a Western executive when working in an emerging market – and the contents get you into trouble, this is your problem, not theirs. Don't loiter in the streets looking like a foreign journalist or potentially subversive activist. Watch out for 'tit-for-tat' activities if your country has offended another. Don't assume everyone must be united against the regime and against 'human rights abuses', so be careful what you say. Don't spread rumours as they might be believed – in some countries people feel vulnerable and need guidance on how to feel and think, and they are looking to authority. If their own authorities are weak they are at a loss.

Cultural risks

The need for agreed clarity over signed business contracts may seem obvious, but many executives from the West make unfounded assumptions. They expect local business partners to abide by agreements through changing circumstances, and fit in with the Western partner's needs, oblivious to previous arrangements and in an approach smacking of corporate imperialism – so cultural risks through arrogance and ignorance can go both ways.

Many emerging market executives have a more collective and less individualistic outlook than most Westerners, so they must not be expected to accept individual blame. They may need to know the exact requirements and expectations of their bosses in completing a task, so ambiguous instructions and the assumption on the Western boss' part that they are understood won't work. There's a much stronger sense of obligation to family and friends than in the West, so local executives are not being rude if they change appointments at short notice for family reasons. Many senior managers in emerging markets may not have much idea about their jobs and may entrust a lot of work to deputies – but this fact should not be revealed – they gained their position through status and others do their jobs.

Workplace behaviours in the BRICS and beyond can be quite different, especially in terms of levels of emotion shown – which can be much more or much less. The separation of work and non-work activities can be less clear, and there can be a much greater need to build relationships before business can be transacted. Attitudes to time management, planning and queuing can be very different – it doesn't mean being disorganized and out of control, it is just the normal way of working.

Commodity risk

Your ability to grow a business in an emerging market country has a lot to do with the absence or presence of commodities. You are suffering from shortages, or trying to obtain your own where there is abundant supply. The weakest countries must make the difficult choice between exporting for survival and looking after local interests. The newest imperial battles are about vital commodities to keep economies going – both developed and developing.

All kinds of risks

Particular countries charge foreigners more for everything; their populations lack purchasing power; there is high unemployment; an ageing population; too much bureaucracy; sanctions against some countries are still in effect; there is protectionism; dumping; and punishment of local business people, who might be the partners of Western firms – and all kinds of perhaps unexpected tendencies. Risk assessment is a number one priority for Westerners doing business across most emerging markets – they are all risky in different ways – but which?

OPPORTUNITIES

Marketing strategy

Creating a sustainable long-term marketing strategy includes more than a launch plan – and especially not underestimating local competition, who could become future strategic partners. Many developing countries are changing so fast that marketing strategies must keep changing – what consumers wanted last year may now be no longer in fashion, creating more opportunities. Some products designed specifically for emerging markets can be uniquely successful – and may have potential for transfer to more developed markets – so we can learn from developing consumer environments.

The luxury segment

The appeal of certain luxury products varies culturally, so the marketing approach must be modified accordingly. Advertising directed at the customer in the target market might be quite different from in the home market. More on the ground market research can lead to competitive advantages, so some luxury firms from the West are more successful than others overseas.

Brand consciousness

The collectivist culture of many BRICS and beyond can mean that customers may want a me-too look recognizable as a specific brand. The middle class may deliberately emulate high-class consumers in admired developed countries – which might also be Asian, like Japan – and are focused on copying a desired lifestyle making use of many well-known brands rather than trying to do anything different, new or individualistic.

Advertising

Due to 'high power distance', the opinions of an authority figure can count for more than personal experience, even if it conflicts with it – so advertising must be targeted to reflect cultural norms. Again, on the ground knowledge can help the Western marketer to steal a march on slower competitors.

Spending power

The concept of disposable income and purchasing power may be different too – so splashing out on hugely extravagant items may bear no relation to income. Spending a month's salary on one fashion item is commonplace. And what do rich people in poor countries want? Very different things from what rich people in rich countries might want. These needs are driving marketers and entrepreneurs to cash in on new opportunities – and many of these are Western influenced.

Foreign franchises

These can be popular in developing countries – but only to a limited extent. They may be used as a stepping-stone and opportunity for a learning experience for gaining credibility on the part of local businesses, so foreign franchise-owners should not expect their foothold in the local markets to go on forever – but they can have a profitable window of opportunity.

Links with local businesses and brands

These are important for tapping into the energy of local entrepreneurs, their deep market knowledge, their patriotic ideals to develop their countries, and their willingness to accept new technologies. It can be a useful approach for the Western marketer and entrepreneur. Western companies can learn from the new local business models developed in emerging markets – such as **creative adaptation, disruptive/reverse/polycentric innovation** – and the use of technology in developing countries, such as branchless banking. Westerners must not underestimate the newly-found confidence in being creative, even though it may be more of a form of adaptation and modification, or even **jugaad** – or making do with basic raw materials and cast-offs that are to hand. Many entrepreneurial businesses are not recorded or quantified by statistical bureaux in their own country, so businesses from developed countries don't know much about them – but this should not always be seen negatively – they can be more influential than we think!

New markets

These are opening up all the time, as new nations gain independence and open up to foreign investment, and can offer first-mover advantages as an entry strategy to the brave and risk-taking. Returnees from the West to emerging markets can be a good option to team up with, as they know both environments. Many Western entrepreneurs don't realize how many people from emerging markets are in the West, the skills they are gaining and the amount of cash they remit home – which offers many business opportunities in itself.

PRACTICE

Competition

Fair competition and a level playing field do not exist in most emerging markets – they often enjoy government subsidies and forms of protection – and sometimes certain products and certain geographical areas are 'owned' as territories rather than local businesses competing head-on with foreign companies in the same way as in the West. So, competing on the ground in domestic markets can be challenging.

Now, developed country businesses are just as likely to compete against stronger BRICS companies as in the case of the reverse scenario, as some BRICS companies are more powerful and have gained more market share. Being the best in its field is now a viable possibility for an emerging market business, and more and more Western companies are no longer market leaders – being number one is no longer their preserve. Western companies can partner with BRICS companies to compete against other BRICS companies to maintain competitive position, so the world has become an open battleground – but there's no such thing as 'fair' anymore.

Inbound investment into the West

Emerging market investors interested in acquiring Western businesses are often looking for a bargain, but it must somehow make sense to their strategy. They may be looking for prestige, technology and people – and **reverse imperialism** can be a tactic. Different developed countries can be seen as more welcoming for BRICS and beyond for investment, rather than others, and BRICS can be better than non-BRICS at tapping into investment money in each other's regions – especially when it comes to dipping into the funds of the biggest BRICS to then venture into developed countries. BRICS countries want something special if they are going to buy from the West – so Western executives must not only package their offerings to appear unique and different, but must also emphasise that they have something that the BRICS can't easily make or provide for themselves – filling an important gap in their needs.

Outbound investment from the West

The BRICS represent a range of important opportunities for many Western businesses – but they must identify the pros and cons offered by each BRICS and beyond venture and be savvy to get it right. Emerging markets don't want to be colonized anymore, and have noticed that some Western businesses in BRICS countries are short-lived or don't even get off the ground. Setting up on the ground for a Western firm in a BRICS country can be an ultimate plan for a Western company used to a trading relationship – but there is a need for deep pockets here, and the situation for both will not stay the same.

Technology transfer

For a Western business, providing essential technology for a developing country company can help leverage that company's business in another developing market to which it has access. It can mean big licence fees or another form of commission to the technology-owner, as the local company is in effect using the Western firm's R&D expertise. An expansion plan for a local emerging market business in its region can be seen as a popular and profitable strategy – so what value can Western businesses offer in these scenarios? This might be technology and marketing ideas, and is often service-based and consulting-oriented.

Diversification

This is a popular corporate strategy everywhere in emerging markets, and some Western analysts see emerging market company strategies as old-fashioned, unstructured and lacking depth – but maybe more effective in their own context. Upscaling and trying to enter more and more sophisticated industries is often another plan, especially using Western technology – as above. But downscaling is also possible when BRICS businesses feel they may have over-stretched themselves, and refocusing on local markets – even targeting the **bottom of the pyramid** – is still very challenging to most Westerners. Seen as opportunism (see below) this might also be indicative of **chameleon**-like agility and flexibility.

Opportunism

This can be seen in a more rapid response to available deals, even if an emerging market company lacks all the necessary capabilities – they will worry about that later. These strategies can be difficult for Westerners to grasp, and they may be known only to a small, inner sanctum – who may not have thought through everything they need to have in place before rolling them out. Opportunism is of some concern when the Western companies themselves are part of the deals, but are not really sure what is going on.

Yet, the same can be true the other way around. Western companies can often look inconsistent because they publish strategies and missions and then abruptly change them. BRICS are more **anony-mous**, less transparent, their strategies may seem inscrutable, and when they change them this is not always apparent – the rationale may be almost entirely unknown. It can be difficult to see what is more difficult for which party concerned. However many problems Western executives have with potential partners from the BRICS, and despite there being many things they might not like, their sense of mutual need is increasing as this book goes to press mid 2012.

Glossary

Anchor economy: A term used by Antoine van Agtmael (see Reading List quoted in Goldman Sachs reports) to identify a country in the world economy seen as one around which other countries revolve – a dominant economic force that attracts would-be suppliers and other partners. Previously seen as the US and possibly Europe, many observers see China as occupying this role in the future – see Chapter 2.

Anonymity: A term used by Antoine van Agtmael (see Reading List) describing unknown companies from emerging markets 'which aspire to be the largest company no-one has ever heard of' that tend to avoid transparency (qv) and might buy brands rather than building them – see Chapters 2, 3, 7 and 8.

Barriers to entry: The problems encountered by a business trying to set up in its own or a foreign country, including costs and the need to navigate the regulatory environment, which can relate to the need for vertical integration (qv) because of the absence of a network of local suppliers – see Chapters 7 and 8.

Bottom of the pyramid/base of the pyramid: A concept formulated by C.K. Prahalad (see Reading List) identifying business opportunities among the poorest strata of society, at the lowest level of the socio-economic pyramid, missed by the corporate imperialism (qv) of the West – see Chapters 5 and 6.

BRICS and beyond: The BRIC term – originally coined by Goldman Sachs in 2001 – was widely used for the last decade, with the 's' (BRICS) signifying South Africa added more recently. It is used interchangeably in the current text with emerging markets (qv), referring to countries not regarded by *The Economist* as developed countries (qv), although relatively little attention is given to countries with high per capita incomes that are nevertheless relatively under-developed, such as the Gulf States. BRICS are expected to contribute around a third of the global economy by 2020 by purchasing power parity (qv).

Cannibalizing your cash cow: Refers to a Western company setting up in an emerging market country and reducing capital and operational expenditure to enhance business margins there, but with the danger of eating into the profits enjoyed by this product from sales in Western countries (see Cisco Report in Reading List) – see Chapters 6, 7 and 8.

Chameleon: A term used by Antoine van Agtmael (see Reading List) referring to the agility of emerging market companies in constantly evolving, especially moving up the value chain (qv) and changing their strategies and portfolios – see Chapter 7.

Copyright piracy: Defined as the unlawful usage of intellectual property in a variety of forms without payment of royalties – seen as a problem for Western businesses in emerging markets because of culturally contrasting attitudes and spending power – see Chapter 3.

Corporate imperialism: Referred to by C.K. Prahalad (see Reading List) in terms of the end of this phenomenon, in which arrogant Western multinational corporations assumed that emerging markets were hungry for modern, Western goods and targeted only affluent segments resembling Western consumers, missing the bottom of the pyramid (qv) and failing to achieve a deeper understanding of the unique conditions of emerging markets – see Chapters 5 and 6.

Creative adaptation: One of Antoine van Agtmael's terms describing the reasons for the success of emerging market companies against adversity and prejudiced thinking of Western companies, also including 'unconventional thinking', 'audacious solutions' and the 'leapfrogging' of well-established industries (see Reading List) – see Chapter 6.

Developed countries: Defined by *The Economist* (see Reading List) as (based on 1990 data) Australia, Austria, Belgium, Canada, Denmark, Finland, France, Germany, Greece, Iceland, Ireland, Italy, Japan, Luxembourg, Netherlands, New Zealand, Norway, Portugal, Spain, Sweden, Switzerland, the United Kingdom and the United States (see also G7) (qv).

Disruptive innovation: The ability of emerging market businesses to disrupt their Western counterparts by innovating at a faster rate – from cheaper products such as $3,000 cars, $300 computers and $30 mobile phones that provide nationwide service for a few cents a minute – and the techniques that have achieved this can also be applied in the West (see Cisco Report in Reading List) – see Chapter 6.

Emerging markets: Used in the current text interchangeably with the BRICS and beyond (qv), differentiated from developed countries or the G7 (qv).

Emerging Market Index: A regular survey of the economic performance of twenty-six emerging market countries researched and published by Morgan Stanley, widely quoted by the press and useful for analysing future prospects. A similar survey is provided by *The Economist* and the *Financial Times* – see Chapter 8.

Emerging market multinational: Also referred to as EM MNCs, contrasted with developed country or Western multinational corporations. Unlike the Western multinational corporation, this company knows its own country and usually its own region, and can get to know the Western environment through higher levels there of transparency (qv) and governance (qv).

Entry strategies: These can include investment entry modes (qv) and export entry modes as well as setting up actual manufacturing operations in another country – see Chapters 7 and 8.

Foreign Corrupt Practices Act: US-enacted law that penalizes US citizens and companies for engaging in activities defined as involving corruption, such as paying bribes – see Chapter 3.

G7:   The leading developed countries of the world, used by Goldman Sachs and other analysts to benchmark against the BRICS and beyond (qv), N-11 (qv) and developed countries (qv) – namely, Canada, France, Germany, Italy, Japan, the UK and the US.

GDP: Or gross domestic product, seen as rising faster in the BRICS than in most developed countries and, therefore, enabling emerging markets to attract FDI from the West – see Chapter 8.

GNP: Or gross national product, closely related to GDP (qv).

Globalization: A process of becoming global, i.e., in every important country, such as in the case of the largest Western multinational corporations, and to which some of the largest emerging market multinational corporations are aspiring. Globalization is beyond internationalization (qv) and much beyond regionalization (qv) – see Chapters 7 and 8.

Governance: Often referred to as corporate governance, this term is seen as related to transparency (qv) and considers processes especially concerned with accountability. Companies with robust governance have independent and accountable board members, fair compensation policies, independent control functions, adequate risk management and long-term horizons – see Chapter 3.

Imitators to innovators: A phrase quoted by Antoine van Agtmael looking at emerging market companies who have moved away from 'cheap brawn power' to 'cheap – and not so cheap – brain power' by moving into capital intensive industries; moving into technology-oriented businesses; and moving from 'small-time to prime-time' in terms of creating new products previously seen as a monopoly of Western multinational corporations. Agtmael argues that Western protectionism has created a false sense of security, which has turned into an advantage for emerging market businesses – see Chapter 6.

Innovative distribution model: A concept whereby emerging market products can overcome distribution difficulties by adopting modular designs that can be distributed in kit form and then assembled locally by entrepreneurs who then sell them on, such as in the case of the Tata Nano, which sells for $2,500 (see Cisco Report in Reading List) – see Chapter 5.

Institutional voids: Concept discussed by Khanna and Palepu (see Reading List) referring to the absence, in many BRICS and beyond, of the expected range of institutions available to facilitate the functioning of markets and establishment of new businesses – see Chapter 2.

Internationalization: A process of a company leaving its original base and setting up in other countries, usually seen as beyond regionalization (qv), but not to the extent of globalization (qv) – see Chapters 7 and 8.

Investment entry modes: Such as setting up marketing subsidiaries (see Chapter 5), joint ventures or as foreign direct investment exercises, which can be inbound or inward into emerging markets, or outbound or outward. China and India are well-known for outbound FDI into Europe, for example – see Chapter 8.

Jugaad: Especially in India, a way of 'making do' with what's available, or creating 'what we need from what we have' – such as a *jugaad* car used in rural India made from leftover spare parts as a form of 'frugal engineering' – see Chapter 6.

Leading emerging market players: A term used to describe the Western multinationals that are most active in emerging markets, such as Coca-Cola, Unilever, Colgate, Danone, Walmart, GE, Nike and Pepsico – see Chapter 8.

Maritime piracy: A term describing the dangers encountered by merchant shipping in specific emerging market areas of the world – including the Middle East and Africa – whereby ships are captured by pirates and held to ransom – see Chapter 3.

Multi-polar: A descriptor of a new world order, used by the consulting firm Accenture, discussing the 'seismic shift in the world economy' represented by the rise of the BRICS and beyond, which present a 'counterbalance to the McDonaldization of the world' – see Chapter 7.

N-11: Or the 'Next 11' – a term coined by Goldman Sachs in late 2005 encompassing a diverse list of countries with long-term and highly varying prospects, but already seen as promising. They include Bangladesh, Egypt, Indonesia, Iran, Korea, Mexico, Nigeria, Pakistan, Philippines, Turkey and Vietnam – see Chapter 10.

Off-shoring and near-shoring: Widely-used terms relating to the supply chain (qv), the latter producing less risk from hyper-extended operations, enabling Western businesses to benefit from lower-priced labour and relatively cheap brain power in emerging markets – see Chapter 7.

Polycentric innovation: Based on multiple centres, where innovation might come not just from the home headquarters but different places around the world where the company has built an operational culture and defines its go-to-market strategy – such as Tata's Nano car, which is being adapted for Western markets too. This helps test new business models as part of disruptive innovation (qv) building on a culture of collaboration (see Cisco Report in Reading List) – see Chapters 6, 7 and 8.

Purchasing power parity: A termed used by many economists and illustrated by The Big Mac Index – coined by *The Economist* – in which the relative purchasing power of consumers in different countries may be compared – see Chapter 5.

Reconnoitring for adversaries: A term referring to the search for local competitors by Western multinational corporations, many of whom are off the radar screens, because of anonymity (qv) and a lack of transparency (qv).

Regionalization: Often the first step in an internationalization process, but not necessarily – some emerging market businesses might sidestep their original regions and go wider afield, even to more developed countries – see Chapters 7 and 8.

Reverse imperialism: The tendency of former colonies to invest in their previous overlords, such as the investment of Indian-based companies in the UK, and Angola in Portugal – see Chapter 8.

Reverse innovation: A new business model based on the reinventing of products by Western multinational corporations to be affordable and appropriate for developing countries – such as GE Healthcare in India – used by Goldman Sachs (see Reading List) – see Chapter 6.

Springboard perspective: A term used by Antoine van Agtmael (see Reading List) describing how emerging market businesses can reduce institutional and market constraints and overcome latecomer disadvantages by acquiring strategic resources from the West – especially by purchasing critical assets from mature multinational corporations – see Chapters 6 and 8.

Supply chain: The process by which products are sourced, processed and delivered to the company selling them to the end user – in India the milk supply chain is referred to as 'from pail to lips' and is problematic, due to poor roads, inadequate transport and a lack of refrigeration. This issue includes environmental responsibility and sustainability, and the creation of agile, scalable supply chains – see Chapter 5.

Transparency: A descriptor of the tendency of a business to reveal and publish details of financials, ownership and so on – or not. Western businesses, especially those publicly quoted, tend to have a much higher level of transparency (seen as an important part of governance (qv)) than most emerging market businesses, including for cultural reasons, hence the difficulties in reconnoitring for adversaries (qv) because of widespread anonymity (qv) – see Chapters 2, 3 and 4.

Unbanked: A term relating to the lowest segment of the socio-economic pyramid, which are excluded from traditional banking services, but may wish to invest small sums on a regular basis. They can utilize banking providers with existing technology such as hand-held finger-print readers and card readers – see Chapter 6.

Unreachable, reaching the: Term referring to the drive of emerging market businesses to do business with consumers at the bottom of the pyramid (qv) who previously were ignored by Western businesses who targeted segments more similar to their home markets – this can include consumer products, telecoms and banking (see unbanked (qv)) – see Chapter 5.

Value chain: A process related to the supply chain (qv) where value can be added to a product at each stage of production. Leading to economic development, it can involve adding new producers and other value-adding contributions. Emerging market companies can move up the value chain to retain more control, ensure higher quality, make greater profits and cut out the dominance of Western multinational corporations and build partner ecosystems – see Chapters 3, 4 and 7.

Vertical integration: Or vertically integrating, a term used by Antoine van Agtmael (see Reading List) emphasizing the necessary ability of emerging market businesses to manage without a network of reliable suppliers in their supply chain (qv) and, therefore, not necessarily focusing on core competencies, a popular strategy of Western multinational corporations, which enables the emerging market businesses to build related expertise – see Chapters 5 and 7.

Reading List

References

Economist, The (2010) The World Turned Upside Down: a special report on innovation in emerging markets, 17 April.

Economist, The (2011) Extracts from relevant articles in weekly edition (see below, February–September).

Financial Times, The (2011) BRICs daily emailed report, March–September.

Goldman Sachs (2010) Governance Report.

Goldman Sachs Global Economic Group (2007) The BRICs and beyond.

Jones, S. (2011) 'Security concerns: piracy at sea and the carriage of essential commodities by merchant shipping – the impact on commodities', Annual Partners' Conference, 11–12 November 2011, Maastricht School of Management: 'Resource Scarcity, Natural Disasters and Business: Present and Future Challenges for Management and Entrepreneurship'.

Moazami, M. and Lavergne, E. (2010) Momentum Now: Emerging Markets – innovations East-West – which way is up? CISCO IBSG.

Prahalad, C.K. (2005) The Fortune at the Bottom of the Pyramid – eradicating poverty through profits, London: Wharton School Publishing.

Transparency International (2011) Corruption Perceptions Index.

Wall Street Journal (2009) Editorial in Indian Edition, Jugaad, 13 July.

Extracts quoted from *The Economist*

(In introduction – reference to (6–12 August 2011) Economics focus – why the tail wags the dog)
1. (26 March–1 April 2011) – China's authorities – The faithless masses – A lack of trust in officialdom triggers panic buying, and a rare ballot-box backlash.
2. (6–12 August 2011) – China's train crash – Curiouser – The angry response to the Wenzhou crash continues.

3. (25 June–1 July 2011) – Saudi Arabia – The brrrm of dissent – Even the most conservative of monarchies is facing change.

4. (12–18 March 2011) – Brazil's labour laws – Employer, beware – An archaic labour code penalises businesses and workers alike.

5. (2–8 April 2011) – Business and insurance – How to become politics-proof – Businesses can get cover against some, but not all, political upheavals.

6. (26 February–4 March 2011) – Uganda's elections – Rambo reigns – The president of 25 years increases his share of the vote after playing a little fairer.

7. (5–11 March 2011) – Jasmine stirrings in China – No awakening, but crush it anyway – The government goes to great lengths to make sure all is outwardly calm.

8. (12–18 March 2011) – China's security state – The truncheon budget – China boosts spending on welfare – and on internal security, too.

9. (26 March–1 April 2011) – The world this week – Business – Google claimed that China was again interfering.

10. (26 March–1 April 2011) – Censorship in China – Leaping the wall – Authorities with the jitters.

11. (28 May–3 June 2011) – Liberalism under attack in China – Boundlessly loyal to the great monster – But at least the liberals are fighting back.

12. (25 June–2 July 2011) – Leaders – China's future – Rising power, anxious state – Tensions between China's prosperous middle classes and its poor will make it a harder country to govern.

13. (11–17 June 2011) – Botswana – Not so perfect after all – Belts are being tightened and whips cracked in one of Africa's richest places.

14. (14–20 May 2011) – International justice in Africa – The International Criminal Court bares its teeth – Many Africans resent the ICC, but recent events suggest that they may now be less able to ignore it.

15. (6–12 August 2011) The future of natural gas – Coming soon to a terminal near you – Shale gas should make the world a cleaner, safer place.

16. (6–12 August 2011) – Angola and Congo – Bad neighbours – Rape and rows over oil have hurt relations between two big countries.

17. (16–22 April 2011) – Conflict and poverty – The economics of violence – Are countries poor because they are violent or violent because they are poor?

18. (19–25 February 2011) – Population control in Beijing – Air-raid warnings – As the leaders see it, a plague of human rats in the capital.

19. (21–27 May 2011) – Censorship in India – see caption to map.

20. (12–18 March 2011) – Press freedom in Turkey – A dangerous place to be a journalist – More arrests stoke fears that the government is intolerant of criticism.

21. (6–12 August 2011) – Leaders – Dissent in China – Of development and dictators – When the story of Chinese democracy is written, a train crash in Wenzhou will deserve a special mention.
22. (23–29 April 2011) – China abroad – Bang a Gong – China's critics are being silenced in South-East Asia.
23. (19–25 March 2011) – China – Don't worry, be happy – The government introduces the country's new mantra.
24. (23–29 July 2011) – India's economy – The half-finished revolution – India's liberalisation began with a bang in 1991, but two decades on the unreformed parts of the economy are beginning to drag on growth. Time for another bang.
25. (9–15 July 2011) – Gujarat's economy – India's Guangdong – A north-western state offers a glimpse of a possible industrial future for India.
26. (23–29 April 2011) – Huawei – Interesting reading – A Chinese industrial champion opens up a bit on its way to world domination.
27. (2–8 July 2011) – China investment in Europe – Streaks of red – Capital and companies from China are sidling into Europe.
28. 26 February–4 March 2011) – The world this week – Business – Trade secrets – Huawei.
29. (13–19 August 2011) – Reliance Industries – Too big for India – Investors have fallen out of love with India's biggest firm. A large acquisition abroad could be its next move.
30. (11–17 June 2011) – Internet companies – Welcome to IPOville – Social-media firms see champagne; others see bubbles.
31. (27 August–2 September 2011) – Cosco – Can't pay, won't pay – A big Chinese shipping firm takes shareholder value to extremes.
32. (5–11 March 2011) – Leaders – Tata sauce.
33. (5–11 March 2011) – The Tata group – Out of India – Under Ratan Tata, the business group that bears his name has transformed itself from an Indian giant into a global powerhouse.
34. (30 July–5 August 2011) – Indian firms abroad – Under the radar – Godrej, an Indian conglomerate, goes global in its own way.
35. (9–15 July 2011) – Aviation – Climbing through the clouds – Airlines and the aircraft industry are belatedly being buffeted by globalization.
36. (6–12 August 2011) – Indian consumers – The other Asian giant – Companies are scrambling to decode the Indian consumer.
37. (9–15 July 2011) – Consumer goods – The mystery of the Chinese consumer – In the first part of a two-part series on Asian consumers, we ask what makes the Middle Kingdom's shoppers tick.
38. (26 March–1 April 2011) – China's carmakers – Dream deferred – A Chinese car company carrying great expectations stalls.

39. (9–15 April 2011) – Mobile telecoms in Africa – Digital revolution – Makers of mobile devices see a new growth market.
40. (30 April–6 May 2011) – Advertising in Africa – Nigeria's mad men – What ads say about doing business in Africa's most populous country.
41. (16–22 April 2011) – India and foreign investment – Fling wide the gates – India should throw off its caution about opening up to foreign investment. The benefits would be huge.
42. (2–8 July 2011) – Electric cars – Highly charged – The future of electric cars is in China.
43. (21–27 May 2011) – Retail in China – All eyes on Chinese aisles – Who will conquer China's rampant retail market? Probably no one.
44. (18–24 June 2011) – Indian mobile telecoms – Happy customers, no profits – India's mobile industry is magnificent but also a mess.
45. (23–29 July 2011) – Indonesia's middle class – Missing BRIC in the wall – A consumer boom masks familiar problems in South-East Asia's biggest economy.
46. (21–28 May 2011) – Chinese gambling – The high-roller's guide to the Galaxy – Why does Macau have no mainland Chinese rivals?
47. (14–20 May 2011) – Africa's growing middle class – Pleased to be bourgeois – A third of Africans now live on at least $2 per day.
48. (7–13 May 2011) – Monopolies in Mexico – Compete – or else – At last, a crackdown.
49. (2–8 July 2011) – High-speed rail in China – Tracking slower – A showcase line, but throttling back.
50. (26 February–4 March 2011) – Schumpeter – Uncorking enterprise – Policymakers are desperate to promote enterprise. A new index could help.
51. (9–15 July 2011) – Doing business in South Sudan – Ready, steady, invest – Welcome to one of the world's whackiest economies.
52. (30 April–6 May 2011) – Schumpeter – A $300 idea that is priceless – Applying the world's business brains to housing the poor.
53. (23–29 July 2011) – Banyan – Diminishing returns – What South Asia's diaspora can do for the lands of their forefathers.
54. (7–13 May 2011) – Schumpeter – Bamboo innovation – Beware of judging China's innovation engine by the standards of Silicon Valley.
55. (5–11 March 2011) The battle for Grameen – Halo, goodbye – Attacks on the sainted Muhammad Yunus escalate.
56. (12–18 March 2011) – Leaders – China's economy – Bamboo capitalism – China's success owes more to its entrepreneurs than its bureaucrats. Time to bring them out of the shadows.
57. (12–18 March 2011) – Entrepreneurship in China – Let a million flowers bloom – China is often held up as an object lesson in state-directed

capitalism. Yet its economic dynamism owes much to those outside the government's embrace.

58. (16–22 April 2011) – Chinese business – When fund-raising is a crime – A death sentence for a young businesswoman chills entrepreneurs.

59. (12–18 March 2011) – Leaders – Corruption in India – A rotten state – Graft is becoming a bigger problem – And the government should tackle it.

60. (26 March–1 April 2011) – Business in India – The price of graft – Investors have gone off India. Blame, in part, uncertainty over corruption.

61. (6–12 August 2011) – India's politics – Dust in your eyes – Politicians of all stripes buckle under the weight of corruption.

62. (26 March–1 April) – India's corrupt politics – Singh singed – A Wikileak is a long time in politics.

63. (12–18 March 2011) – Corruption in India – A million rupees now – Congress drags its feet over tackling graft. It may pay a high price.

64. (20–26 August 2011) – The world this week – Politics – Hazare hazard.

65. (7–13 May 2011) – A novel way to combat corruption – Who to punish – India's chief economic adviser wants to legalise some kinds of bribe-giving.

66. (28 May–3 June 2011) – Nigeria's prospects – A man and a morass – Can the new government of Goodluck Jonathan clean up corruption and set enterprise free in Africa's most populous country?

67. (19–25 March) – Corruption in Sierra Leone – Rich pickings – Bad apples are still in the barrel.

68. (30 April–6 May 2011) – Cuba's cigar industry – Smoked out – Rolling up under-the-counter trading in an emblematic product.

69. (2–8 July) – Zimbabwe and its diamonds – Forever dirty – Robert Mugabe is being favoured once again, to the detriment of his people.

70. (25 June–1 July 2011) – Domestic workers – Free the maids – A new treaty aims to stop abuse.

71. (18–24 June 2011) – Corruption in Argentina – The mother of all scandals? A once-revered human-rights group runs into a controversy.

72. (28 May–3 June 2011) – Turkish sex scandals – Feeling blue – Another opposition party is laid low by clandestine videos.

73. (28 May–3 June 2011) – Russian justice – No surprises – Khodorkovsky loses his appeal; Russia loses a chance to modernize.

74. (20–26 August 2011) – Chinese financial scandals – When it matters – Markets in China are barely fazed by scandal, unless the state is involved.

75. (9–16 July 2011) – Carson Block – Red-flag raises – The man behind Muddy Waters, a scourge of listed Chinese companies.

76. (11–17 June 2011) – Listed Chinese companies – Red alert – Scepticism about the accounts of Chinese companies spreads.

77. (26 February–4 March 2011) – An online scandal in China – Alibaba and the 2,236 thieves – China's top e-commerce firm fights to win back customers' trust.

78. (18–24 June 2011) – A bank scandal rocks Afghanistan – Black holes – The political fallout of the bust Kabul Bank.

79. (16–22 July 2011) – China's film industry – Kung fu propaganda – There's a ton of easy money in praising the party.

80. (20–26 August 2011) – Politics in Brazil – Dilma tries to drain the swamp – As another minister goes, Brazil's president may find that the price of trying to clean up politics involves forgoing reforms the country needs.

81. (3–9 April 2010) – South Africa – Black empowerment – Instead of redistributing wealth and positions to the black majority, only a few individuals have benefited.

82. (13–19 August 2011) – China International Fund – The Queensway syndicate and the African trade – China's oil trade with Africa is dominated by an opaque syndicate. Ordinary Africans appear to do badly out of its hugely lucrative deals.

83. (28 May–3 June 2011) – China in Laos – Busted flush – How a Sino-Lao special economic zone hit the skids.

84. (23–29 April 2011) – Leaders – Africa and China – Rumble in the jungle – Why the Beijing regime needs to act to avert a backlash against Chinese investors in poor countries.

85. (23–29 April 2011) – The Chinese in Africa – Trying to pull together – Africans are asking whether China is making their lunch or eating it.

86. (9–15 April 2011) – Corporate governance – The shareholder awakens – Companies' owners are slowly beginning to hold bosses to account, starting with closer scrutiny of their pay.

87. (20–26 August 2011) – The world this week – Business – CCTV, China's main state broadcaster.

88. (19–25 March 2011) – Mexico's communications monopolies – Amigos no longer.

89. (12–18 March 2011) – Reputation management – Glitzkrieg – Respectability is for sale. Here is a buyer's guide. Names are omitted to protect the guilty from blushes and us from lawsuits.

90. (19–25 February 2011) – Australia and Indonesia – A row over cows – Indonesia curbs beef imports.

91. (2–8 April 2011) – BP's Russian troubles – Dudley do-wrong – Bob Dudley, BP's boss, has got the oil giant into a mess over its Russian deals.

92. (3–9 September 2011) – Oil in Russia – Exxonerated – Where BP failed, Exxon succeeds.

93. (16–22 July 2011) – Off its trolley – Carrefours.
94. (25 June–1 July 2011) – Foreign law firms in Brazil – Keep out – Brazilian lawyers don't want pesky foreigners poaching their clients.
95. (10–16 September 2011) – The redback abroad – Offshore thing – London wants to become a hub for trading in the yuan.
96. (30 July–5 August 2011) – Germany's Mittelstand – Beating China – German family firms are outdoing their Chinese rivals. Can they keep it up?
97. (19–25 February 2011) – China's luxury boom – The Middle Blingdom – Sales of costly trifles are even better than you think.
98. (19–25 February 2011) Hollywood goes global – Bigger abroad – Forget the Oscars. Films need foreign viewers, not American prizes.
99. (3–9 September 2011) – Liverpool and China – Here comes the yuan – A city's bid to revive its fortunes through the local and the global.
100. (5–11 March 2011) – Diageo's deals – Replenishing the drinks cabinet – Raki with a bourbon chaser?
101. (26 March–1 April 2011) – Cyril Ramaphosa's business empire – Big man, Big Macs – Another giant deal for one of South Africa's biggest tycoons.
102. (2–8 April 2011) The tobacco industry – The last gasp – For Big Tobacco, South-East Asia is the final frontier.
103. (13–19 August 2011) – American manufacturing – Sticking it to China – A factory in rural Georgia helps East Asia eat.
104. (19–25 March 2011) – Online-coupon firms – Groupon anxiety – The online-coupon firm will have to move fast to retain its impressive lead.
105. (2–8 July 2011) – The world this week – Business – Diageo. . . Shui Jing Fang.
106. (19–25 February 2011) – Walmart in South Africa – The beast in the bush – A hungry predator stalks Africa.
107. (10–16 September 2011) – Britain and emerging-market firms – The new special relationship – Amid the economic gloom, Britain is at the leading edge of an important global trend.
108. (10–16 September 2011) – India's industrial output – Tata for now – The country's biggest manufacturer is Indian. What does it seek from and give to Britain?
109. (3–9 September 2011) – Angola and Portugal – Role reversal – An ex-colony may be getting the better, in economic terms, of its old master.
110. (16–22 April) – Gulliver's Travels – HSBC's new boss must save a great firm from mediocrity.
111. (14–20 May 2011) – Multinational manufacturers – Moving back to America – The dwindling allure of building factories offshore.
112. (6–12 August 2011) – Papua New Guinea – Muddy succession – An ousting of the grand chief.

113. (2–8 July 2011) – Leaders – China abroad – Welcome, bienvenue, willkommen – America needs to worry about the contrast between its attitude to China and Europe's.
114. (12–18 March) – Fashion for the Masses – Global stretch – When will Zara hit its limits?
115. (16–22 April 2011) – Retailing in India – End for the supermarketers – Opening up India's chaotic, underdeveloped retailing industry to foreign supermarket chains would bring many benefits.
116. (9–15 April 2011) – The troubles of Saab – A phoenix struggles to fly – Separated from GM, a Swedish carmaker finds the going tough.

Recommended Further Reading

On BRICS and especially Brazil, Russia, India and China

Arestis, P. and de Paula, L.F. (eds) (2008) *Financial Liberalization and Economic Performance in Emerging Countries*, Palgrave.

Bhagwati, J. and Calamiris, C.W. (eds) (2008) *Sustaining India's Growth Miracle*, Columbia Business School.

Bramall, C. (2009) *Chinese Economic Development*, Routledge.

Brandt, L. and Rawski, T.G. (eds) (2008) *China's Great Economic Transformation*, Cambridge University Press.

Cavusgil, S.T., Ghauri, P.N. and Agarwal, M.R. (2002) *Doing Business in Emerging Markets*, Sage Publications.

Chakravorty, S. and Lall, S.V. (2007) *Made in India. The Economic Geography and Political Economy of Industrialisation*, Oxford University Press.

Croll, E. (2006) *China's New Consumers. Social Development and Domestic Demand*, Routledge.

Dicken, P. (2003) *Global Shift*, 4th edn, Sage Publications.

Eichengreen, B., Park, Y.C. and Wyplosz, C. (eds) (2008) *China, Asia and the New World Economy*, Oxford University Press.

Enderwick, P. (2007) *Understanding Emerging Markets: China and India*, Routledge.

Estrin, S. et al. (2009) Entry mode in emerging markets, *Strategic Management Journal*.

Farndon, J. (2008) *China Rises*, Virgin.

Goldman, M.L. (2008) *Petrostate: Putin, Power and the New Russia*, Oxford University Press.

Goldstein, A. (2007) *Multinational Companies from Emerging Markets*, Palgrave Macmillan.

Goodman, D.S.G. (ed.) (2008) *The New Rich in China: Future rulers, present lives*, Routledge.

Gordon, L. (2001) *Brazil's Second Chance. En Route toward the First World*, Brookings.

Hoffman, D.E. (2002) *The Oligarchs: Wealth and Power in the New Russia*, Public Affairs Books.

Hutton, W. (2007) *The Writing on the Wall: China and the West in the 21st Century*, Abacus.

Johnson, C. and Kagerman, D. (2008) Reinventing your business model, *Harvard Business Review*, December issue.

Karnani, A. (2007) The mirage of marketing to the bottom of the pyramid: how the private sector can help alleviate poverty, *California Management Review*, 49(4).

Khanna, T. and Palepu, K.G. (2004) The future of business groups in emerging markets, *Academy of Management Review*, 43(3).

Khanna, T. and Palepu, K.G. (2010) *Winning in Emerging Markets*, Harvard Business Press.

Kvint, V. (2009) *The Global Emerging Markets*, Routledge.

Morduch, J. (1999) The microfinance promise, *Journal of Economic Literature*, 37(4), 1569–1614.

Naughton B. (2004) *The Chinese Economy: Transitions and Growth*, MIT Press.

Navaretti, G.B. and Venables, A.J. (2004) *Multinational Firms in the World Economy*, Princeton University Press.

Pedersen, J.D. (2008) *Globalization, Development and the State. The Performance of India and Brazil since 1990*, Palgrave Macmillan.

Reinert, F.S. (2007) *How Rich Countries Get Rich and Why Poor Countries Stay Poor*, Constable.

Rodrik, D. (ed.) (2003) *In Search of Prosperity: Analytic Narratives on Economic Growth*, Princeton University Press.

Rothermund, D. (2008) *India: The Rise of an Asian Giant*, Yale University Press.

Rudra, N. (2008) *Globalization and the Race to the Bottom in Developing Countries*, Cambridge University Press.

Segel, A., Chu, M. and Herrero, G. (2007) *Patrimonio Hoy: A Financial Perspective*, Harvard Business Case 9-207-059, November.

Sengputa, J.A. (2008) *Nation in Transition: Understanding the Indian Economy*, Academic Foundation.

Smith, D. (2008) *The Dragon and the Elephant: China, India and the New World Order*, Profile.

Wolf, M. (2004) *Why Globalisation Works*, Yale University Press.

Internet sources

Asian Development Bank: http://beta.adb.org/

European Central Bank: http://www.ecb.int/home/html/index.en.html

Financial Times: http://www.ft.com/home/uk

Goldman Sachs Global: http://www.goldmansachs.com/

International Monetary Fund (IMF): http://www.imf.org/external/index
   .htm
OECD: http://www.oecd.org
Transparency International: http://www.transparency.org
World Bank, World Economic Indicators: http://www.worldbank.org/

Journals and newspapers

Asian Development Bank
The Banker
The Economist
European Bank for Reconstruction and Development
The Financial Times
IMF Capital Markets
International Journal of Urban and Regional Research
International Review of Economics and Finance
Oxford Review of Economic Policy
Review of African Political Economy
The Wall Street Journal
World Development
World Economy

Index

Index compiled by Annette Musker